"If Whitley Strieber isn't fibbing in his new book COMMUNION . . . then it must be accounted the most important book of the year. Of the decade. Of the century."
—*The Nation*

"Strieber comes through as both sensible and sincere . . . His book deserves to be taken seriously."
—*Boston Herald*

THE SECRET SCHOOL

"Whitley Strieber has written an inspired, haunting, momentous book. Everyone concerned with the awesome mystery of what we are and what we may become should read THE SECRET SCHOOL."
—Graham Hancock, author of *Fingerprints of the Gods* and *The Message of the Sphinx*

"Incredibly profound. With great eloquence, compassion, and wisdom, Whitley Strieber takes us on a journey beyond time to describe a sacred science of the soul. THE SECRET SCHOOL is a gripping recollection of his (and our) past and future."
—Brian O'Leary, PH.D., former astronaut and author of *Miracle in the Void*

"THE SECRET SCHOOL is Whitley Strieber's courageous journey to childhood in search of the truth. Do not settle your own accounts with reality until you read this."
—Larry Dossey, M.D., author of *Prayer Is Good Medicine* and *Healing Words*

Also by Whitley Strieber

Nonfiction

Communion
Transformation
Breakthrough
The Secret School

Fiction

The Wolfen
The Hunger
Catmagic
Majestic
Billy
The Forbidden Zone

(with James Kunetka):

Warday
Nature's End

CONFIRMATION

The Hard Evidence of Aliens Among Us

Whitley Strieber

St. Martin's Paperbacks

Interview with Monsignor Corrado Balducci reprinted with permission of Michael Hesemann, editor, *Magazin 2000*, copyright © 1997. All rights reserved.

Poem #435 from *The Complete Book of Poems of Emily Dickinson* by Thomas H. Johnson is used on page 93 with kind permission from Little, Brown and Company.

CONFIRMATION: THE HARD EVIDENCE OF ALIENS AMONG US

ISBN: 0-312-96704-7

Printed in the United States of America

St. Martin's Press hardcover edition / May 1998
St. Martin's Paperbacks edition / February 1999

10 9 8 7 6 5 4 3 2 1

Dedication

In memory of Dr. Paul Hill
the author of Unconventional Flying Objects,
a thirty-year veteran of NASA and a true hero
of our age.

This book is dedicated to the children of the
close encounter experience. Our generation
will find the answers,
but it is theirs that will gain the heavens.

I have no greater joy than to hear that
my children walk in truth.

3 JOHN 4

Contents

Acknowledgments   xi
Introduction: Something Truly New   1

Part One: Theater in the Sky   7

One: Miracle over Mexico   9
Two: August 6, 1997   26
Three: Alien Shadows   37
Four: An Undiscovered Country   47
Five: Never a Straight Answer   60
Six: Hidden Hardware   73

Part Two: Close Encounter   93

Seven: An Emergency Situation   95
Eight: The Journey Begins   107
Nine: Beyond the Dark   119
Ten: Innocence   132
Eleven: Worlds Beyond   146
Twelve: Yes Or No   158

Part Three: Hard Evidence   175

Thirteen: Early Days   177
Fourteen: The One Within   190

Fifteen: Dr. Roger Leir's Discovery   201
Sixteen: Jesse's Story   219
Seventeen: "Junior"   233
Eighteen: My Implant   245
Nineteen: What Do the Implant Data Mean?   259
Twenty: "A New World, If You Can Take It"   277

Appendix: Interview with Monsignor
Corrado Balducci   293
Afterword   307
Further Reading   309
Index   312

Acknowledgments

I would like to acknowledge the work of my wife, Anne Strieber, without whose brilliant, patient, and insightful support, Confirmation could never have been written.

Monsignor Corrado Balducci, Tim Edwards, Britt and Lee Elders, Karen and Jose Escamilla, Michael Hesemann, Alice Leavy, Dr. Roger Leir, Jesse and John Long, William Mallow, Jaime Maussan, Daniel Munoz, and Richard Strieber all gave generously of their time on behalf of the book.

I would also like to thank Dr. Mark Carlotto, Kim Carlsberg, Colonel Philip Corso, Jim Dilettoso, Dr. Jack Kasher, Tom King, Derrel Sims, Yvonne Smith, and John "Bro" Wilkie. Their contributions to the understanding of the UFO and close encounter experiences were of enormous help to me.

In addition, I would like to thank the witnesses who contributed their stories to this book, as well as the many unnamed scientists, military and medical personnel who gave generously of their time and expertise.

Any errors in this book are my own.

Introduction

Something Truly New

UFOs are nonsense and alien abduction is a fantasy—
so says science and so says the press. But science also
keeps the door open, as it has for the past fifty years,
waiting for some sort of evidence that would make the
subject worthy of study.

Such evidence has been found and will be discussed
in detail in this book.

In an interview with *Nova* in 1996, the late Dr. Carl
Sagan said that for the UFO phenomenon "to be taken
seriously, you need physical evidence that can be examined at leisure by skeptical scientists: a scraping of
the hull of the ship, and the discovery that it contains
isotopic ratios that aren't present on earth, chemical
elements which form the so-called island of stability,
very heavy elements that don't exist on earth, or material of absolutely bizarre properties of many sorts—
electrical conductivity or ductility. There are many
things like that that would instantly give serious credence to an account."

The new evidence deserves just that sort of approach. From the beginning, the scientific community
has, very appropriately, supported a policy of isolating
the UFO phenomenon and everything connected with
it from the mainstream of its efforts because there just
wasn't any way to support the incredibly improbable
idea that there could be anybody here except us. So

the whole phenomenon has been explained as a combination of hallucinations, confused misperceptions of ordinary events, and outright fraud. In any case, what possible tools of science could be used to extract hard evidence from a collection of wild stories?

The evidence exists, and so do the tools. An organized effort can be made in three different major areas that will reap a scientific harvest substantial enough to offer us, no matter its orgins, a rich return of new knowledge. Moreover, this effort may well answer the key questions once and for all: Is somebody here? If so, what are they doing?

In my ten years of experience as a publicly identified close encounter witness, I have met dozens of scientists, political leaders, reporters—all sorts of people who might be concerned with a matter like this—and, with a few exceptions, I have found them open-minded and fascinated but unwilling to change their position of denial until substantial amounts of physical evidence became available. I have agreed completely with this posture, because science should not spend time and money tilting at windmills, and the public should not be seduced by misplaced scientific and official interest into believing that aliens are here if that isn't true.

But many scientists are becoming aware of what is happening, and even as I write this, there is a new level of interest building. On October 10, 1997, a panel of nine scientists released a statement that "some UFO evidence may be worthy of scientific investigation." Before coming to this conclusion, they reviewed evidence provided them by UFO investigators and promised a report in a few months that "makes recommendations for further research."

Among the scientists involved were panelists from

France, Germany, and the United States. France was represented by Jean-Jacques Velasco, who heads the ongoing official investigation of UFO reports being conducted by CNES, the French space agency. Also attending were Thomas Holzer of the High Altitude Observatory, Peter Sturrock of Stanford University, Randy Jokipii and Jay Melosh of the University of Arizona, James Papike of the University of New Mexico, Guenther Reitz from Germany, and Francois Louange and Bernard Veyret also from France. These scientists were not asserting any particular belief about UFOs but only seeking to "play a more active role in helping to unravel this fifty year old mystery."[1]

In addition to scientific support, the religious community is beginning to respond to the growing evidence. I am grateful that Monsignor Corrado Balducci of the Vatican has allowed an interview with him to be added as an appendix to this book in which he states his opinion that the growing body of witness testimony "should not be ignored," and that superstitions about our visitors being demons should be abandoned along with official denial of the reality of the phenomenon. Among other things, Monsignor Balducci is an expert on demonology.

Over the course of this book, I will be suggesting specific directions for research in a number of areas, among them behavioral science, brain science, psychology, atmospheric science, propulsion technology, materials analysis, and, if it becomes apparent that aliens really are present, then a whole new area of cultural anthropology as well.

Ironically, even as it asks the best questions I have

[1]Press release, Society for Scientific Exploration, Oct. 10, 1997.

ever come up with, this book does provide some key answers, and they present an incredible picture indeed. What it all means, science must tell us. But if I am right about what it suggests, what is by far the most extraordinary event in history is unfolding right now.

Gone are the arguments that science has nothing to work with. Behavioral science has not only the witnesses but also physical proof that something unknown has happened to at least some of them, in the form of apparent implants that have been removed from their bodies. Any surgeon can remove these objects, usually in a simple office procedure, and there seem to be thousands of witnesses displaying the signs of their presence, which can easily be confirmed by X ray. This potential harvest of objects also means that materials science can acquire a substantial sample for study. And it doesn't end there. Fantastic advances taking place right now suggest that we may soon actually be able to find out, in an absolutely physical way, exactly what parts of the wild alien abduction stories are true and what are not.

The evidence, if it is properly addressed by science, has the power to change completely the way we deal with this issue, possibly providing us with wonderful new discoveries and information. But there are problems. Not everybody is open-minded. Not everybody is ready to entertain such evidence as may be presented.

Certain important elements of the American press were once much more flexible in the way they approached the phenomenon, but for the past twenty years, the opposite has been true. On January 13, 1979, *The New York Times* published a story entitled "CIA Papers Detail UFO Surveillance," claiming that declassified documents confirmed that the government was deeply concerned about UFOs. Director of Central Intelligence Stansfield Turner was "so upset" about this article[2] that he conducted an internal survey to determine whether the claim was true. Donald Wortman, deputy director for administration, reported to him that there was "no organized Agency effort to do research in connection with UFO phenomena. . . ."

Since this event, the American press has generally closed the door on the UFO phenomenon. Perhaps, though, it now has needed justification to reexamine its position.

Some of the evidence that I will present is extremely provocative, even incendiary, and raises a concern that by denying the reality of the mystery, the press may actually have ended up spreading the very sort of false belief that it has been trying to prevent.

Understand, I don't think that anybody is to blame for this. It happened because the idea of aliens being here was so improbable and the evidence was so equivocal. But as a society, it would seem that we can now take the whole question another step forward and maybe at last start to move toward some satisfactory answers. Taking an interest need not imply a commitment to belief in alien contact, but we must seriously ask who or what is causing the UFO and close encounter phenomena, why it is taking place, and, above all, what its significance may be.

It is also necessary to face the fact that the existence of the evidence means that there really may be aliens here—aliens who are creating an extraordinary theater in the sky while at the same time entering the personal

[2]*Studies in Intelligence*, semiannual unclassified edition, #1, 1997, p. 78.

lives of many people in extremely bizarre and secretive ways. Unless we deal in an organized and effective manner with the hard evidence that has come to light, we are going to remain passive to what could be not only a valuable knowledge resource but also an intrusion into our world that may or may not be in our best interest. Given its intimacy and the incredibly provocative nature of many contact reports, that does not seem wise.

Part One
THEATER IN THE SKY

The heavens declare the glory of God;
and the firmament showeth his handiwork.

—Psalms 19:1

1:

Miracle over Mexico

So, what is all this evidence? Alien bodies, perhaps, or faster-than-light communications equipment? This is not a book of proof of alien presence but of evidence that confirms that an unknown phenomenon is unfolding among us. This phenomenon emerges in three distinct areas: the first is a dramatic growth in amateur video recording of strange things in the sky; the second is the unexpectedly huge body of close encounter testimony that is far, far different from anything that has thus far appeared in print; the third is the unexplained objects that have been surgically removed from some close encounter witnesses, myself included, who claim to have been implanted with them during their encounters.

All three of these areas present provocative evidence, but it would seem appropriate to begin with unidentified flying objects: what we see in the skies. To do this, the first place to go must be Mexico, which has, since 1991, enjoyed the most incredible and best documented series of UFO sightings in history. In this book, incidentally, the term "UFO" means only that an object is unknown. It is not an assertion that the object is an alien spacecraft.

On July 11, 1991, people all over Mexico City were watching the sky. But the weather was cloudy, and that made their anticipation uneasy. Still, there were people on the roofs, on every street corner, in the parks. By 1:15, everybody was looking upward. But would the clouds part?

Slowly, it got darker, and as it did, the clouds did indeed open. There was the sun, a corner eaten by shadow, then a half, then more. Then the moment came: a total eclipse. Video cameras were trained at the heavens as an estimated ten million people observed one of nature's greatest wonders.

But they saw considerably more than an eclipse. They also observed an object immediately below the blacked-out disk of the sun, and to some people this object looked very much like a UFO.

At six minutes and fifty-four seconds, this was an eclipse of unusually long duration, so a considerable amount of video was made of the object. The eclipse was doubly important to the Mexican people, because it also marked the beginning of a new age in the calendars of many ancient Mexican tribes[1], including that of the Aztecs, who founded Mexico City and still form a large part of its population. The Aztecs saw this eclipse as the moment of passage from the Fifth Sun to the Sixth. The earliest known Mesoamerican eclipse predictions, and the first one mentioning this event, come from the Dresden Codex, one of the remaining Mayan calendrical texts.[2] Both the Mayas and the Aztecs consider this eclipse to be a fundamental change of age.

Even though the object seen beside the sun created a local sensation, the only report of it that reached

[1] Fernando Diaz Infante, *La Estela de los Soles o Calendario Azteca* (Mexico City: Panorama Editorial, 1986).

[2] Adrian Gilbert and Maurice Cotterell, *The Mayan Prophecies* (Shaftesbury Element: 1995) pp. 38–39.

most people in the United States was a statement that it was a misperception of the planet Venus. UFO researchers in the States have claimed that videotapes of Venus can be made that appear similar to the Mexican video, specifically, to the ones that show what appears to be a structured metallic object with a shadowed base and currents of disturbed air swirling around it. In an effort to substantiate these claims and explain the Mexican videos, I and others have made our own videos of Venus. But, no matter whether in lighting conditions similar to that of the eclipse or not, this has proved to be impossible. Venus doesn't look a thing like the Mexican videos, in fact. In general, it seems that when claims like these are made, the claimants must duplicate their work in public. Moreover, Venus was not below the sun during the eclipse, which is where the unusual object was located.

Given that a number of stars became visible during the eclipse and appeared on amateur video as early as 1:04 P.M., it has been easy to dismiss all of the recordings as simple mistakes. But some of these videos almost certainly are not of celestial objects, as will be seen.

Perhaps because of the fact that the place and time of the object's appearance fit one of their own important mythologies, the Mexican people were not so ready to dismiss it. One man who was particularly interested was Jaime Maussan, the anchor of Mexico's version of *60 Minutes* and one of the country's most popular television personalities. On the air one night after the eclipse, he made what was to prove to be a historic request. Responding to the high level of public interest, he asked, as a guest on the program *What Is Your Opinion?*, for viewer reaction to the reports. The call-in program, which normally went off the air when

interest faded around midnight, continued until 10:30
the next morning.

Maussan, who had asked people to send in their
videos, was deluged with tapes, a process that has now
continued for seven years. The objects—or whatever
controls them—seem almost to respond to all the attention. Although this massive wave of sightings has
not been commented on outside of the UFO press and
a few paranormal-themed television programs in the
United States, it stands as the largest-scale and longest
such wave in history.[3] It is impossible that some of the
videos were hoaxed by their makers, because they
were made in public while hundreds, thousands, and
sometimes even millions of people were observing the
objects. Some of these same videos, such as one of a
metallic cylinder hanging motionless in the sky in
broad daylight, were made as crowds visibly reacted.

Few places could have been found that were better
suited than Mexico to what happened there: Generally
open-minded people had access to excellent technology that could make a visual record of anything they
wanted, and do so easily and inexpensively. So as the
eclipse of July 11, 1991, reached totality, millions of
eyes—and many camcorders—pointed upward. Later,
hundreds of people would submit copies of the videos
they made that day to Jaime Maussan. Many of these
were indeed of stars, but his investigation would disclose that seventeen of them appeared to be of unexplained objects.

Still, none of the seventeen anomalous videos in
Maussan's possession was gathered by atmospheric

[3]Jaimie Maussan has a file of more than 170 hours of video collected
from around Mexico, with the first tapes being deposited in July of
1991 and the most recent, as of this writing, in August of 1997.

scientists or astronomers. They are not perfect. The people making them were not generally thinking of things like triangulation. Often only the object and surrounding sky are visible, so the relative location of the object cannot be determined.

However, there exists one image that completely defies explanation. It was taken by a Mr. Fuentes at 1:23 P.M. and shows the object leaping across the sky. Because the height of the object is unknown, the distance of the movement also cannot be determined. It appears to be a substantial motion, and if the object is far away, then it could be many miles. Since the object moves only once and does not return to its point of origin, this cannot be explained by the sort of shimmering, bouncing, or momentary defocusing that might result from atmospheric disturbances. The object makes a sudden, arrow-straight motion from one stationary position to another and does not shimmer or bounce either before, during, or after the motion. Admittedly, the speed of the motion (just at a second in duration) suggests the possibility that it may be the result of some sort of transient atmospheric effect on a star, but the fact that it does not return to its original position also rules out that possibility. In fact, the object remains motionless in the second position.

A television executive, Guillermo Arreguin of Televisa, was observing an object as well and made a professional quality recording of it on his personal equipment. This video reveals an object with a definite elongated shape, inward sloping sides, and flat upper and lower surfaces. It is shadowed on the bottom and appears to be disturbing the air around it and emitting a faint violet light from the shadowed area. Seen by the naked eye, it was reported that this object looked nothing like a star.

So if it was not a star, could it have been a secret aircraft hovering over Mexico at high altitude? If so, then it was an extraordinary plane, because at approximately the same time, eighty-five miles southeast of Mexico City in Puebla, Efrain Breton and his family were observing the eclipse with, among other things, a video camera. According to their time-stamp, they were recording the object at 1:22 P.M., but there is no indication that they noticed the movement that was recorded by Fuentes. Given that these were not professional recordings, it's easily possible that the times on the tapes were not exact.

In the Puebla video as well as some of those taken in Mexico City, a faint star can be observed in the same position above the object. This leads to the conclusion that the videos are of the same object, which must be extremely high. In fact, to be visible in two different places that far apart, the object would need to be at an altitude of more than fifty thousand feet, giving it a probable diameter of at least a quarter of a mile.

Both the Breton and Arreguin videos reveal the same lower-surface shadowing and atmospheric effects, an additional strong suggestion that it is, in fact, the same object. If it is, then its size and height suggest that it lies well outside the envelope of functionality even of the most extremely advanced aircraft. If it was Venus, then the combination of rapid atmospheric cooling and the brightness of the planet at that particular time must have been what caused the shimmering air that is visible on the images beneath the object. It is hard to see how Venus could be this radically distorted, however, when a star visible nearby in the same frame is perfectly normal. This probably defeats the claim that the object was Venus.

Unfortunately, the Fuentes video, which shows the object in sudden movement, does not also show it in relation to the star that appears in the Breton and Arreguin videos. So it cannot be concluded that the object that made the impossible motion and the one that was seen in Puebla and Mexico City to have a shadowed base are the same thing.

The likelihood that the objects are manmade is diminished by another video, this one made at approximately the same time by Luis Rodolfo Lara in the town of Tepeji Del Rio. In this video, the object is seen to be maneuvering in relation to two other smaller objects, also moving, that appear above it. In this video as well, a faint pinkish colored area appears beneath the object, accompanied by apparent atmospheric distortion.

Could this be, then, a rigid device held aloft by the same mechanism that powers a hot-air balloon? It is clear that there is something glowing and distorting the atmosphere underneath the object in some of the videos, but there is no point of origin visible, which would be the case if this was heat being produced by a kerosene burner. The problem with this theory is that the object recorded in Puebla and Mexico City must be the same, and therefore the balloon would have to have been gigantic and operating at the upper edge of the atmosphere, almost in outer space. This would have been well outside of the capability of a hot-air balloon no matter how large.

So it is not unreasonable to entertain the notion that this object, contrary to all the assertions that it was Venus, was not a known object at all. If it was Venus, then another video should be produced showing the planet distorting in a similar manner while stars visible in the same frame remain unaffected. Using an analog

VHS camera of the type generally available in 1991 and in use during the eclipse, I have not personally been able to achieve this effect, although I did see some slight distortion of Venus and other stars shot on the twilight horizon on the evening of October 17, 1997.

In the United States, the stories coming out of Mexico were ghettoized, in the sense that reports were more or less confined to media that cover the paranormal and thus isolated from the general public. Astronomers, meteorologists, and atmospheric scientists all ignored the phenomenon. Among the few serious investigators are Britt and Lee Elders, who have produced a series of excellent video digests of the material after engaging in years of on-site investigation, meeting witnesses, following up stories, and having the video examined by professionals. Their fascinating digests cull the material and concentrate on what is provably strange.

Like the Elders, I have found Maussan and his associate Daniel Munoz to be extremely competent and thorough investigators who are more than willing to share data and to assist outside investigators.

After July 11, 1991, there developed in Mexico a heated debate about the videos. In general, though, the Mexican people came to agree that the object was an unknown. Many millions had seen it and had observed with the naked eye considerably more structural detail than was transmitted by video. So word of mouth supported the idea that it wasn't Venus or a star. The parts of the Mexican scientific and astronomical communities that supported the American contention that the object was Venus offered no evidence. Nobody did the obvious, which was to create, in public, sample videos of the planet or a star showing the same effect.

If the Mexico sightings had begun and ended on

July 11, the vast number of witnesses still would have made them one of the most remarkable cases ever recorded. However, this is not what happened. In fact, July 11 was the beginning of an extended period of sightings that, very simply, ranks as the best-recorded series of unknown events in history, and which, as of August 1997, involves what could well be the clearest daylight video image of a UFO ever made.

After the July 1991 eclipse, the state of Puebla had so many sightings that viewing them became a nightly ritual. These objects were, for the most part, lights in the night sky. There was no detail to distinguish them from stars, except for their slow movement. They appeared to concentrate in the area of Mt. Popocatepetl, the volcano that dominates the area.

However, the proliferation of genuine sightings and all the excitement also caused the appearance of probable hoaxes. In September of 1991, during a television discussion about the phenomenon being broadcast by Super Channel 3 in Puebla, there was a major sighting in the area—as the panel discussed UFOs, one hovered in the sky above the city. This object was flashing a strobe light on an irregular interval and might have been an airplane except that it remained almost motionless for twenty-six minutes.

Over the village of Metepec near Puebla, the same phenomenon was repeated the next night. Meanwhile, in Puebla, an object hovered over Super Channel 3's transmission tower. This object glowed with internal light, but did not strobe. It first hovered, then moved, meaning that it was not a celestial object.

However, none of these objects ever did anything that suggested that it wasn't a balloon. There were none of the characteristic dramatic maneuvers that would have proved that they were real UFOs.

The next extraordinary event that happened in Mexico was the beginning of one of the most astonishing sequences of UFO videos ever made, and in this case there was no question of authenticity.

The first event in the sequence took place on September 16, 1991, at the National Independence Day parade. There were flybys of aircraft during this parade, including flights of jets and helicopters. Vincente Sanchez Guerrero, a member of Maussan's crew, was there obtaining footage for news coverage of the event. There was no expectation that anything unusual would happen.

An unknown object was recorded by Sanchez hovering beneath a flight of jets. The object, clearly visible in front of a heavy cloud cover, oscillates light and dark surfaces in a pattern of vertical movement. After the planes pass, it begins to ascend, gathering speed until it moves above the upper edge of the background of cloud cover and becomes visible against the open sky.

Adding to this already amazing display was the completely incredible fact that it was repeated at the next two annual parades as well. The result was that UFOs were recorded maneuvering among the aircraft at three successive air shows, on September 16, 1991, 1992, and 1993.

The 1992 event was recorded by Demetrio Feria, a professional videographer who was taping the parade. Immediately after a flight of jets passed, a small object was observed moving just below a thin cloud cover, almost directly overhead. This object displayed a dark surface, but there was insufficient detail to determine anything other than its slightly elongated disk shape and the fact that half of it was darkly shadowed, the other half reflecting sunlight.

The next year, one of the most profoundly inexplicable of all UFO videos was made at this air show. Filmed by Alejandro Leal, who was taping a flight of helicopters, the object appears as a small, shiny ball that proceeds to maneuver *among* the helicopters, displaying an ability to avoid them and not be affected by their rotor wash as it passes beneath and beside them.

The object can be estimated to be between eighteen inches and three feet in diameter. It can't be a balloon because it moves upward of seventy miles an hour and engages in a broadly curving and obviously organized maneuver. It passes through the flight of helicopters but does not get blown away or even disturbed, not even slightly, as would happen to anything that was dependent on the air for its lift. Instead, this object makes an easy, assured movement that no design dependent on the air for lift could accomplish. The object isn't an aircraft of any kind, because it isn't flying. Instead, it is vectoring inside the air mass, its lift being accomplished by some means that is independent of the air.

It seems possible, then, that the amount of notice afforded them at the first air show brought the objects back for a second and third time. This evidence of intelligent planning mirrors what was happening in the Puebla area but with the difference that the daytime video record provides far more convincing evidence that the UFOs were genuine.

It would be worth considering the possibility that whatever is behind the appearance of these objects may actually be seeking notice and is well aware of the conditions under which it may be obtained.

That the objects sometimes seek notice and react to observers is further made evident by a video recorded by Felipe Gonzalez on July 25, 1992. In this case, the object first appeared near a billow of cumulus cloud on a fine day. While both the object and the cloud are clearly visible, it is not possible to determine the size of the object because there is no way to tell how far away from the cloud it is.

The video is quite clear, and as this is broad daylight, the object cannot be a star. Also, it has an angular shape, tapering to a sharp end. It cannot be a balloon, because of this sharp point.

So maybe it is a model airplane, or even a real one that has had its appearance distorted by some atmospheric phenomenon.

Again, this would seem to be impossible because of the absolutely remarkable flight characteristics displayed by the object. This one moves slowly toward the cloud, slows down, speeds up, briefly stops, then slips behind the cloud. A moment later it appears in a small cleft in the clouds, darts across the clear space between them, then seems to hide with just an edge peeking out from behind the cloud—almost as if it is aware of the observer.

The object then disappears behind the cloud again. A moment later, it reappears in a broader cleft. It crosses this cleft, pausing for a moment in the center, then slips behind the cloud on the far side. Incredibly, it stops there completely for a moment, then disappears and reappears, "peeking out" from behind the cloud. It looks exactly as if it was playing with the observer, then finally is gone behind the cloud. Whether it was playing games or not, the motion displayed cannot be attributed to any known form of aircraft or aerial device at all.

Could it then be a computer simulation? This would be quite possible in 1997, but in 1992 it would have taken a considerable amount of computer power to accomplish. In either situation, there would be a characteristic signature of digital enhancement from the use of such programs. Because information is being added to the existing image, there are slight distortions in the surrounding pixels that can be detected on a computer. But this image, when examined, shows no evidence of such distortions. Not only that, in a pixel-by-pixel examination, the sky color is seen to be blurred across the object, the opposite of what would happen if it was a digital inclusion. A similar effect could be created, but on a detailed examination the evidence of this work would be detectable.

Also in 1992, on June 25, Demetrio Feria had taped an object racing across the sky beneath cloud cover at 5:30 in the afternoon in the Federal District of Mexico which, once again, could not have been a star, a balloon, or a plane. As it moves, apparently at a very high speed, it oscillates slightly, turning a darker area toward and then away from the observer. This appears to be a solid, coherently structured object. The daylight image is plain to see.

This same pattern of oscillating movement was recorded by Tim Edwards in Salida, Colorado, during a period in 1995 when he taped a remarkably strange video sequence, footage that takes the UFO phenomenon to the same level of strangeness that the witness testimony has taken the close encounter reports.

To begin this journey into high-level strangeness, we must go first to June 6, 1994, to a tape made at 6:16 P.M. by Juan Flores Arroyo in Mexico City. The Arroyo family were outside with their video camera when they noticed a bright object in the still blue sky. This was precisely the sort of UFO that the skeptics generally dismiss as an unusually bright star. In this case, however, video evidence exists that clearly shows this not to be the case.

What it *does* show would appear at first glance, to be impossible. The object remains stationary for a short time, glowing brightly. It then becomes somewhat more dim and proceeds to eject a slightly less clear version of itself, which slowly moves away and disappears.

The famous "Doctor X" case reported from France in 1957 contains a version of this observation. The doctor, who along with his son had a legendary close encounter, saw a UFO double as it approached him.

It is one thing for testimony about such a phenomenon to be offered, another one entirely for it to be recorded by a video camera.

What might something like this mean? It could be, simply, that the object ejected some sort of waste material that then floated away and dissipated. It could also be that it created a projection of itself akin to the holographic projections of personnel and equipment that have been theorized by nonlethal weapons researchers for military applications.

No matter the weather conditions, stars never appear to double in the sky, with the secondary image slowly floating off like a puff of smoke. It could not be a flare, because the object was not bright enough, and there was no slow descent. It could not be a firework, because its duration in the sky is much too long. There is a video of something similar from the United States that is connected to one of the strongest and most disturbing of all close encounter cases, which involves not only video and still photography of a UFO but also an apparent implant found in the witness and surgically removed.

There is a great deal of video from Mexico that

really cannot be explained. There is also a great deal showing stars and other commonplace phenomena that have been misinterpreted by witnesses. But there are other cases where the matter is not clear cut, and some of these are quite interesting.

On May 3, 1994, in the border city of Juarez, Francisco Javier recorded something that has the appearance of an open clam with some sort of material lodged between its two halves. This object was strobing blue-white flashes from a faintly visible structure on its bottom as it moved slowly through the night sky. It offered no maneuver that could not be accomplished by a balloon or slow-moving aircraft.

On May 5 in the same city, Rosi Uribe recorded an object like an elongated plate with a glowing domed superstructure moving slowly along and strobing in the same manner. This object was recorded for some minutes and was close enough to reveal a certain amount of detail in the video image. The platelike surface was lit by what appeared to be a glow being emitted from the roof of the superstructure, which has a number of dark areas along its face.

Although it is not possible to gain an exact measurement of the size of the object, because its distance from the camera is unknown, the video includes a view of the city the object is traveling over, and it can be estimated that it is at an altitude of approximately fifteen hundred feet. The amount of detail visible suggests that the object is fairly large, although not huge.

Video was made of a similar structure over Stuttgart, Germany on May 29, 1993. Although it wasn't strobing, it appeared identical in shape to the enlongated plate recorded by Uribe. Taken at 10:00 P.M., this video also shows the object moving slowly and at very low altitude. This time, though, the entire surface is glowing bright red-orange. The object is quite low, and its movement against the foreground of hills, trees, and flat, unlit landscape suggests that it is traveling at slow speed. There is something eerie about this video, because the object is so low and moving so slowly that it seems as if it ought to fall out of the sky.

That something so bizarre would be seen in two such widely separated parts of the world is interesting. But it also appeared again, this time in 1995 over Miami, Florida. The Miami tape offers enough detail to determine that the object could easily be precisely the same thing recorded over Juarez. This tape also shows an airliner near the unknown object, and so it is difficult to conclude that some sort of bizarre atmospheric effect transformed an ordinary plane into what appeared to the video camera to be a UFO.

But the object never, in any of the videos, does anything that a dirigible or blimp couldn't do. So could it then be some sort of hoax, constructed for the purpose of attracting attention and spreading false belief in UFOs? Possibly, but it is hard to imagine the hoaxer transporting his "flying saucer" from city to city in the hope that it will get the desired notice. Some UFO investigators have suggested that videos like this could be blimps, and a German television station has claimed that the Stuttgart video is an advertising blimp. No reason was given for this by the station beyond the fact that there appears to be no other way to explain the object.

In general, for amateur video to be definitively ruled an unknown, it would seem essential that, among other things, some maneuver be recorded that cannot be accomplished by any known aircraft. But given that there is so much amateur video that fulfills this criterion, has not been digitally enhanced, and was taken under conditions so public that a simple hoax must be ruled out, a dedicated scientific effort would almost certainly result in high-quality professional recordings. This could lead to valuable insights into, among other things, what keeps the objects aloft. As we desperately need some form of engine that can efficiently transport large numbers of people, supplies, and equipment into space, this would seem to be a valuable area of research. But the present emotional climate within the scientific community still makes such research difficult.

Throughout the 1990s, UFOs have continued to appear in Mexican skies. For example, on January 28, 1996, an enormous light entered Mexico from the north, proceeded to the center of the country, then turned east and crossed Yucatán, disappearing over the Gulf of Mexico. While Americans watched the Super Bowl, this awesome display was seen by millions. It appeared to involve something breaking up at high altitude, and for the first part of its flight followed a ballistic trajectory typical of a descending meteor. However, the turn it made is hard to explain. It would be highly unusual for all the fragments of a large meteor to leave a ballistic trajectory at the same time and turn in the same direction.

On August 6, 1997, what is perhaps the clearest video of a UFO ever made was recorded over a wealthy suburb of Mexico City. As of October 15, there were, in addition to the video, twenty-four eyewitnesses, including two who have been added to the small but disturbing number of witnesses who have suffered unusual injuries.

2:

August 6, 1997

In the southwestern quadrant of the huge Federal District of Mexico lies the wealthy suburb of Bosques de las Lomas. It is the richest suburb of Mexico City and so far had not been an area of UFO sightings. But on August 6, 1997, that changed.

On that day, a group of young men in an office observed a strange object in the air beside a nearby building. This object caught their eye because it was in motion; it was rotating and oscillating at the same time. They pointed their digital video camera at it and took approximately ninety seconds of what may be the clearest imagery of a UFO yet made.

This video came to the attention of Jaime Maussan in September of 1997. In this case, the witness who filmed it wanted to remain anonymous, but a search of the area has uncovered twenty-four other people who saw the object, including one who apparently suffered physical side effects from standing approximately fifty feet below the object for a few minutes and another who may have experienced more serious injuries.

The video was taken from a window approximately three hundred feet from the object, which has a diameter between forty and sixty feet. The object is gray and smooth-sided, a familiar top-shaped UFO with a domed upper surface that flares out to curling edges that surround a relatively flat bottom, which is pale in color but surrounded by a darker ring. The two ends of the object appear to be slightly darkened and remain motionless. Somehow, the rest of the object seems to be rotating, or some sort of film on the surface is being agitated by regular waves of motion that create this appearance.

The setting in which the object appears, at an initial altitude of about a hundred feet, is a cityscape, with the object hovering over an area of low buildings. There is a high-rise apartment building in the right foreground. No people are visible in the video at any time. The object hovers for about ten seconds, rotating and oscillating in a clumsy-looking manner. Continuing with these same motions, it then accelerates toward the apartment building, moving at slow speed, probably no more than ten or fifteen miles an hour. It also ascends approximately another hundred feet and can then be seen moving along just above the roof of the apartment building and some distance beyond it.

It finally moves behind another building and never re-emerges. Neither a moment of appearance nor of disappearance is recorded on the video, and the object never moves at a speed that would rule out hoax, although the clarity of the image and the strangeness of the object are enough to make this video worth examination.

On August 3, 1997, three days before the object was recorded on video, it was reportedly observed by a number of witnesses, including one who, as of this writing in October of 1997, is hospitalized with unexplained and uncontrolled normal pressure hydrocephalus (NPH), the first symptoms of which occurred after he had watched the object at low altitude overhead for half an hour.

This man is in this thirties, but NPH is a disease of the elderly. It is usually attributed to surface inflammation of the brain due to subarachnoid hemorrhage or diffuse meningitis.[1] But this syndrome is so rare that there is little information about it, and often there is no evidence of what may be causing it in a given case. It should be noted that the witness showed evidence of drunkenness on admission to the hospital.

A few days after watching it, he began to experience problems with movement and was diagnosed at that time. Whether his proximity to the object was a causative factor remains unknown, but since this disease is associated with inflammation of the surface of the brain, and the witness was standing under the object for so long, the possibility must be considered, especially in view of the injuries to another witness.

This witness, who happened to be standing immediately beneath the object as it was being videotaped, also experienced physical side effects. In her case, these took the form of burns to her face and arms. She could feel a weight from above, as if some invisible force was making her body feel heavier. In addition, she felt as if she was experiencing a static charge over her whole body. The day after the sighting, she developed a sunburn on her face and arms, the areas of her body that had been exposed to the object. This sunburn persisted until early September, when it finally faded, with—so far—no lasting effects. An ordinary sunburn that persists for three weeks is unusual, and the long duration of this burn suggests that there was energy present beyond the infrared, which is the component of sunlight that causes burns. The possibility exists that these wit-

[1] *The Merck Manual*, 16th ed. (Rahway, NJ: Merck & Co., 1992), pp. 2542–43.

nesses were exposed to ultraviolet, radio, microwaves, radar, X rays, or an unknown form of energy.

So, were these people injured by this object, and was it a genuine UFO? Among the other witnesses was one who saw it just before it disappeared, and her testimony is useful. As it went out of view of the group with the video camera, it came into her line of sight. A fashion photographer, she rushed to get her camera. Unfortunately, when she returned, she saw only a violet haze in the air, which rapidly dissipated. This violet haze is a known aspect of the UFO phenomenon, and scientists have already theorized about its possible significance. (It will be discussed in more detail in Chapter Four.) Another convincing detail is the fact that Maussan, who received the video on September 26, went to the area to interview people at random in order to find out if anybody could remember seeing it. The first such person he found was the twelve-year-old daughter of a street vender, who was able to describe it in detail before seeing the video.

Maussan provided both me and Jim Dilettoso of Village Labs in Tempe, Arizona, and Britt and Lee Elders, with copies of the tape for analysis. Mr. Dilettoso sought to determine whether the object might be suspended from a helicopter above it and outside of the frame of the camera, or, if it was a balloon, then tethered to a cable underneath. To accomplish this analysis, he located the axis of the object by finding the point around which it was oscillating. He then drew a straight line through this point and followed the movements of this line frame by frame to see if it intersected at an apex above the object. He found that this line of axis remained unbroken for as many as ten frames at a time, but then it "jumped," meaning that any cable would have broken. So the object cannot be dangling from a wire or affixed to a tether. The tether possibility is made even less likely by the fact that the center of the undersurface is completely free of any markings or variations that would indicate the presence of a hook, and the rotation would seem to preclude tethering to the outside edges. Dilettoso also estimated the diameter of the object as between forty and sixty feet, meaning that it is, at its thickest point, approximately twelve to sixteen feet thick.

The fact that there is considerable motion caused by handholding the camera reduces the likelihood that the image of the UFO has been digitally added to the tape. To do this would require a massive effort because no two frames are ever in the same place. At best, an illusion of motion could be created this way, that would be obvious on frame-by-frame analysis of the video. Mr. Dilettoso also ascertained that, although the video had been made with a digital camera, it had not had digital information added to it later, which makes it less likely that this video is a special effect. However, it should also be noted that, if it was made digitally and then the digital tape was shot from a screen, no digital signature would appear on the new tape, effectively covering the digital track. To determine whether there might have been any tampering concealed in this way, I transferred the segments of the image where the object passed behind building walls into digital format and, using Adobe Photoshop 4.0, examined the pixels of the moving object to see whether any of them were in the wrong place. If the object was a digital image, it would be extremely unlikely that this part of its motion across the field could be accomplished without some pixels falling out of place and appearing in front of the building. But the image was clean.

So the object was almost certainly physical, either a radio-controlled model of a UFO or the real thing. If radio controlled, then it was probably held aloft by helium or hydrogen, because there appear to be no air vents that would enable a column of air to be emitted from a concealed propeller. If it was an untethered balloon, then it was probably controlled by jetting air through a duct that would account for the darkened areas at the two ends of the object parallel to the camera. The "rotation" then would be something like a loose Mylar covering blowing in the wind.

The one remaining question became whether or not the object was flying or moving by some other means. If flying, then it can be concluded that it was a model. But if it wasn't, then it was a genuine UFO. An object that is flying, such as a balloon or a plane, is held aloft by air. In fact, everything that we make that moves through the air is either flying or, like a bullet or a rocket, on a propelled ballistic trajectory. This UFO was certainly not on a trajectory of any kind, since it hovered and maneuvered in an entirely independent manner. So the crucial question became, was it vectoring—that is to say, being held aloft by some means that was independent of the air?

If flying, then the object would exhibit a reaction to the air around it as it accelerated. Also, since it was oscillating, its center of gravity was off its axis, or there was a tilted gyroscope inside the object. In either case, some of the oscillation would be transferred into any lateral motion, causing the object to describe a series of partial curves as it moved across the sky. Also, as it nears the building, it ascends. Then it stops at a certain altitude and rises no farther. As this is a very difficult maneuver for a lighter-than-air craft to accomplish without complex and sensitive controls, it seemed impossible that there would be no wobbling at the top of the ascent, especially as the volume of gas that could be contained inside this object would be too small to sustain the weight of a pilot, meaning that the object had to be radio controlled. If this was a lighter-than-air craft, the ascent had to be accomplished by airflow, as nothing was dropped from it before it rose to lessen its weight. In any case, regaining control over this type of ascent by use of airflow from an upward-directed fan or propeller would not be possible without some sort of bouncing or wobble.

Working at Bauhaus Media in San Antonio, I examined the tape to see if actual motions could be determined. We examined the image at various levels to see if we could detect any signs of downdraft below the craft. There were some possible indications of air movement, but they were not persistent and were probably due to the smog and debris in the air at the time. We then stabilized the critical first section of the recording, removing all camera shake from the image of the object itself. We did this from a few seconds before the object begins its acceleration to where it completes its ascent. To accomplish this, we used Avid Illusion software on a Silicon Graphics O2 computer. To get the cleanest possible image off the VHS tape, we utilized an uncompressed serial digital interface straight from the copy in our possession.

This process had the effect of transferring all camera movement out of the object, so that only the motions that it had itself made in relation to a fixed surface nearby (the corner of a building) remained.

We observed a slight upward tilt in the direction of motion at the moment of acceleration. However, this same angle comes and goes even when the object is hovering and appears to be a side effect of its oscillation. There was no additional "buck" resulting from acceleration. In addition, the ascent appeared smooth. It was not affected at all by the oscillations. When the object completed its ascent, it did so without the slightest wobble or adjustment. The end of the ascent is as clean and abrupt as the beginning.

So the probability exists that this object was not air-dependent. Even saying this, though, hoaxers can be extremely clever, and in the absence of absolutely impossible maneuvers, such as disappearing on camera or accelerating so quickly that the movement cannot be explained, fraud cannot be completely ruled out.

If I was hoaxing something like this, I might very well choose to make my balloon oscillate in order to disguise the fact that it was air-dependent. Still, it seems impossible to do this while also accomplishing straight trajectories and a perfectly clean ascent. Given all the witnesses, the physical injuries reported, and the fact that the object also displays the "walking" effect of a tilt-to-control device as it moves above the top of the building, there is every reason to accept the video as worthy of consideration as possibly genuine. Tilt-to-control involves moving forward by slipping off a supporting column of air or energy, then raising the leading edge to bring the column directly under the craft again. Platforms designed by long-time NASA aeronautical engineer Paul Hill using air for tilt-to-control support were tested in the 1950s. (His assertion that he based his designs on observations of UFOs will be discussed in Chapter Six.) But the Mexican craft was probably not using air for support, because of the precision of movement observed.

If it is a genuine unknown, then it should be of interest to scientists working on propulsion technologies. This leading-edge research is beginning to be carried out in numerous labs, due to the fact that current engines, based on heat energy, have already outlived their usefulness.

At the present time, the idea of colonizing the solar system with millions and then billions of people seems far-fetched, but within a very few years it will be seen as a necessity if humanity is to continue to maintain a growth-based economy and to thrive. In addition, we must find a way to relieve Earth of its growing burden of radioactive and other pollutants, and the ability to get them into space inexpensively and incinerate them in the sun would be a practical alternative if we could leave Earth's gravity cheaply and efficiently, instead of relying on rockets with all their expense and pollution.

The combination of the way the object maneuvered, the nature of the sensations and injuries experienced by the witness who stood under it, and the violet haze that persisted after its sudden disappearance might combine to give somebody who is aware of the various new propulsion technologies now under discussion some valuable information.

With this in mind, I took the video to some scientists who had attended NASA's Breakthrough Propulsion Physics Workshop that was held August 12–14, 1997, at the Lewis Research Center in Cleveland. Papers were presented at this workshop, which, among other things, discussed leading-edge ideas such as whether the vacuum of space can be engineered to extract energy from it.[2]

The idea of "engineering the vacuum" was first proposed by Nobel prize winner Dr. T. D. Lee in his book

[2]H.E. Puthoff, "Can the Vacuum Be Engineered for Spaceflight Applications? Overview of Theory and Experiments," NASA Breakthrough Propulsion Physics Workshop, Lewis Research Center, 1997.

Particle Physics and Introduction to Field Theory.[3]
The theory is based on the fact that "empty" space isn't empty at all. In fact, it contains many different energetic processes, some of which may be exploitable for a whole new type of power.

Interestingly enough, a system that drew its energy from the vacuum would work as well in an air envelope, because the subatomic source of its energy is present everywhere. Dr. Robert Forward of the Hughes Research Laboratory has already demonstrated that the vacuum can be exploited for energy.[4]

The physicist who looked at the tape was intrigued and disappointed at the same time. He was intrigued for the same reason that I was: There is a reasonable likelihood that the tape is authentic, and if it is, then it is the clearest image of a UFO in operation that has ever been made. The disappointment came from the fact that there is no "clincher" in the tape. The object performs no maneuver that would be completely impossible for a radio-controlled model. However, the way that it functioned was fascinating to him. It is quite possible that something that relied on a column of energy to hold it up might make slow speed maneuvers very much like those that appear on the tape.

Unfortunately, the video did not reveal any of the signs of excited air around the object, such as that seen in some of the earlier Mexican video, that might have helped in making some guesses about the nature of the supporting field. The image is not quite enough to en-

[3]T.D. Lee, *Particle Physics: An Introduction to Field Theory*, (London: Harwood Academic, 1988).

[4]R.L. Forward, "Extracting Electrical Energy from the Vacuum by Cohesion of Charged Foliated Conductors," *Physics Review B* 30, no. 4, (1984): 1700–02.

able us to close the book and say that UFOs are definitively real. To do that, we need an actual UFO in our hands, or a professionally made record that shows enough detail to convince absolutely that the object under observation is a real unknown. Such a record could be obtained with considered scientific effort, and the existing videos and films are, of course, available for examination.

Interestingly enough, such film has not only been made in the past but also has been analyzed by scientists, pilots, and aeronautical engineers (this will be discussed in Chapter Six). But before we turn to that material, it would seem productive to go a little deeper into the Mexican experience. If UFOs are spacecraft, then perhaps they have aliens aboard, and maybe somebody might at some point have made a video of such a creature. Maybe so.

3:

Alien Shadows

Video has appeared on TV around the world that claims to depict aliens. Best known is the "alien autopsy" film aired on television in 1995. However, this film has come under criticism because of authentication problems. Allegedly made from film taken of an autopsy of an alien whose spacecraft crashed in the New Mexico desert in 1947, the video shows a humanlike body with large eyes and six-fingered hands. If it is a real body, it isn't human, because the six fingers are all different, and human beings have genetic information for only five different fingers. In a human being, a sixth finger must always be a repeat of one of the other five. In addition, when the leg is manipulated, the movement of the femur within the hip socket appears to be anatomically correct, a subtlety that would be hard for a special effects artist to duplicate.

The owners of this video have never produced any of the original 16-mm film with image on it for testing. The original film would need to be displayed along with laboratory aging results in order to verify its authenticity. What has been done so far is to display the aging results of some white film leader in the Fox television program that aired in the United States. Because of the lack of verification, this video, as subtly convincing as it is, must remain open to question.

I was asked by a television program to view two

videos of apparent aliens. One had allegedly been smuggled out of the legendary Area 51 and come into the hands of the owner of a small video concern. The other was said to have appeared anonymously in the mailbox of the owner of another small video concern.

I don't spend time and money on anonymous evidence, but I was willing to look at the videos. In the one supposedly from Area 51, there appears a figure with a huge head and black, platelike eyes. It is behind glass, and seated near it is a man who appears to be concentrating. There is no movement at first, but soon the alien's huge head begins to wobble. Its tiny mouth opens, and fluid begins to issue from it. The creature is obviously in distress. As it collapses, two people in white protective clothing appear and begin trying to collect the fluid, as if for examination. In the lower right quadrant of the screen, there is a bright, bouncing green light that appears like a laser.

I saw this video in the company of a number of other close encounter witnesses. Although I was given little reason to believe that it was real, and so stated at the time, the edited version of my statements that appeared publicly included only my emotional reaction to the harsh situation and obvious distress of the creature.

The next video, given to me by the same program, "Strange Universe," involved an alien body being drawn out of a black plastic bag by what I assume is a mortician or coroner. It's very realistic, but there isn't any way to verify it, either. Also, there appears to be some sort of an overlay in the video designed to obscure the image, and the video was made with an old camera, which hardly seems likely if it was really the work of some sort of supersecret government agency.

The one other piece of video of an apparent alien that has been produced does not suffer from anonymous authorship. On the contrary, not only is the author of this image known, but it is part of what is arguably one of the strangest and best-documented series of UFO appearances that have ever been investigated.

On the night of September 12, 1994, a new radar system was being tested at Mexico City's international airport. During the test, a large stationary radar return appeared on observers' screens. This return persisted for five hours, with the object showing little, if any, movement. Then it abruptly disappeared.

Technicians evaluating the radar had concluded that they were seeing a malfunction, but two nights later the object again appeared over Metepec, about forty miles from Mexico City. This time the airport in Toluca also got it under visual observation. People on the streets of Metepec noticed it as well, among them a witness who had a video camera. She was not able to get it to work that night. But the next night, September 15, with the camera now working, she noticed a glow in a cornfield behind her home. When she looked more closely, she observed what appeared to be a living creature of some sort standing near the corn. The creature was clearly visible and for a very disturbing reason: Its head glowed from within.

She described what she saw to Jaime Maussan: "I saw it turn its head and look at me in the window where I was standing. It seemed that it was also surprised. Its eyes were sad. They looked like the eyes of a monkey, very deep, but also sad. It moved in a way that made me think I had caught him by surprise. That's when it turned back and disappeared. That's what happened, not more, not less."

When asked if it could have been fake, she states that it displayed facial movements and "had eyes like ours." She further said, "I want to tell you something straight. I don't know anything about these things." Commenting to Maussan about his work, she continued, "When I see you on TV, I change the channel. Because I do not believe in these things. Not at all. I believe that we are a million light-years behind these people."

An interesting internal contradiction in her statement, obviously. She doesn't believe, and yet she feels that we are far behind "these people." Frankly, if she had not seen an image that she couldn't explain and finds it almost impossible to believe, I doubt that she would have made this contradictory statement. She would have said one or the other. This innocent lapse of logic, as the weirdly impossible memory overlays the long-held beliefs and produces the contradiction, is strong evidence of her sincerity.

The figure observed on the video is glowing in a featureless dark background. It seems to be hunched forward, or the head set into the shoulders in such a way that the chin, which is long and narrow, comes down as far as the center of the chest. The body, which is revealed by the glow that is either emanating from the head or coming down from above, appears to be wrapped in gray-tan material. This material can be seen flowing onto the ground around the figure. As the witness taped the figure, she described it to the friend who was with her but not in the room. "It's horrible," she said, "it's looking at me. It's a dwarf, it's horrible." She stated that it seemed extremely sad, an impression that many close encounter witnesses report.

In addition to its long, narrow chin, the face displays the dark and sunken eyes that the witness describes, as well as two extrusions on the upper part of the forehead. Each is about three inches long and jointed forward at a ninety-degree angle.

The body covering displays folds like a blanket or shroud. There is no visible tailoring. This material conceals whether the creature has feet. As the creature moves away, it seems slow and hunched, as if it is carrying a great weight. Its movement is steady enough but appears laborious as it disappears into the cornfield behind the house.

So, was this a practical joke at her expense, or was it real? The tape is analog, not a digital composite, so if it was a prank, then it was played by constructing a figure, perhaps out of papier mâché and a light, then turning it on, with the operator guiding it from under the blanket. It would be a simple effect to accomplish, and the poor quality of the video makes it impossible to distinguish enough detail to determine this.

The next morning, the cornfield behind her house was found to be trampled down, as if something heavy had wandered through it, crushing a couple of acres of corn.

Even given this strange side effect, if it ended there this story would have to be added to the long list that cannot be resolved due to the lack of professional involvement and investigation while the event was in progress.

But the story does not end there. Maussan followed up the sighting reports with a request for information from the Mexico City airport tower, which is how he learned about the radar observations and the Toluca visual contact. Over the next month, the tower informed him of six more radar contacts around the area with what appeared to be the same object and gave him the coordinates. He followed up by overflying the locations in a helicopter. In each case, there was a field of crushed plants beneath the place where the radar contact had occurred, looking exactly like the cornfield behind the Metepec witness's house. In one of these fields, Maussan found and made a videotape of a bizarre plant that appeared to be a pumpkin vine out of which was growing the leaves of other plants. Unfortunately, as no scientists were involved, this plant was not collected. Little can be gained from the video except to say that it looks strange.

It seems reasonable to think that there might have been some connection between the objects sighted on radar and the crushed fields that appeared below them. Unfortunately, though, there is nothing about the Metepec video that makes it possible to state for certain that the witness was not the victim of a hoax. Still, it is probably the closest thing there is, at present, to a video of a visitor with authenticating support.

Most of the videos from Mexico, and most earlier photographs, film, and videos of UFOs, show what appear to be machines flying around in the sky by wondrous means. But beyond the strange actions and maneuvers of what seem to be structured aerial devices of some sort, and the one alien video, there lies another world of much more problematic videos that suggest that the camera has uncovered skyborne phenomena of ultrahigh-level strangeness. This video record, taken as a whole, is so strange that it is almost beyond conjecture. And yet it is there, readily accessible to whatever analysis can be applied. It leads one to the fascinating conclusion that, if it does not prove accessible to conventional explanation, then our world has not been completely explored, in the sense that it contains a large-scale phenomenon of some kind that we have not yet noticed.

The first of these strange tapes is also the last of the Mexico videos that I will discuss. I consider this a door into the next level of the UFO video. From here on, the path becomes really dark, the way completely unknown.

Carlos Diaz is a photographer. He is also a native Mexican, an Indian of Toltec ancestry. He lives in a small town in northern Mexico and has impressed people such as Maussan and Dr. John Mack with his simplicity and honesty. He has never asked any money for his videos and has been entirely forthcoming in explaining them. According to his explanation, he created them at night near his home, in general by going outside at times that somehow seemed to him to be appointed and awaiting the appearance of the object. In other words, he feels, like so many witnesses, a sense that he is "called" to his meetings.

What Mr. Diaz has produced is a group of videos of a low-hovering object that appears to be a bladder glowing with internal light, or some kind of discrete plasma. It appears and disappears instantaneously, and at times its orange glow varies slightly.

A close examination reveals dots of light that are apparently internal to the object. Mr. Diaz has taken a number of stills of it, which could easily be hoaxed with simple equipment. However, he has also made a video that is much more interesting because it is not as easy to dismiss.

This video is approximately thirty-five seconds long and is divided into two shots. It was taken at night. In the first shot, Mr. Diaz's rural house can be observed in the foreground. In the dark sky above the house, there is a bright object. It is luminous but not radiant, with the result that color and shape can be distinguished. The camera is then zoomed, and some detail can be observed as well. At this point, its configuration is somewhat like the glowing object taped near Stuttgart that I referred to in the previous chapter.

The witness is approaching the object, walking with the camera trained on it. It is thus impossible to tell if the apparent small maneuvers are a result of camera movement.

There is then a cut, and the object appears in more detail and at a different angle. The rural sounds—a rooster crowing, crickets chirping—continue across the cut. What has happened is that the witness has moved closer to the object, walking through a field and up onto a hillside with the camera off, then turned it on again. Aside from testimony, there is no way to tell how long the camera was off.

It does appear that a slight oscillating maneuver that was beginning to occur just as the camera was turned off is just ending as it is turned back on. The object then remains completely motionless. It is visible against a featureless black background.

Carlos Diaz has struck investigators who have met him as a very honest man. There is not the least indication that these tapes are hoaxed. But the only way it is possible to tell that the camera is still outside, or that it is the same night, is Mr. Diaz's testimony. The object remains visible for about ten seconds and then disappears, as if a switch has been thrown on its light source.

Some might argue that the video could have been created in any number of simple ways. It could involve, for example, an object with a light inside suspended from a wire or lying on a tabletop. There is no way to evaluate this piece of video except to confirm that the form was not added digitally. But given how many other simpler, cheaper, and more undetectable analog methods could have been used, this isn't proof of anything.

The first part of the video would have been harder to fake. The zoom from the first frame containing background detail to the final one containing only the object against a black background is continuous. It could be possible to do a double exposure, first exposing the background, then repeating the zoom against a black surface with the lighted object suspended in front of it. If this was the case, though, the camera motion that occurs when the witness begins to walk would be a major problem to adjust perfectly so that the object's movements were consistent with it.

Diaz has impressed researchers who have met him and does not appear motivated to exploit his video beyond a natural desire that it receive the notice he feels that it deserves. In other words, he is like most legitimate witnesses with hard evidence—neither hungry for publicity nor unwilling to stand up, if asked, for what he has seen. So if we grant that his video may be genuine, then what is it and how does it differ from other videos of unknown objects?

Mr. Diaz has claimed a certain level of communication with the object and regards it as a plasma that is, itself, a living creature. If seeming plasmic structures like this one and the fiercely glowing object that was taped near Stuttgart are real, then what would they be? Creatures? Natural formations? Technological objects?

If they are creatures, then they are so different from anything that we identify as a living organism that we would have to redefine our concept of life in order to include them. It is easy to say a phrase like "plasmic being," but what would that actually mean? A living gas? Electrons that think?

These are not questions that can be answered, not yet. We can, however, explore the whole area further. Come with me into the realm of the *really* strange.

4:

An Undiscovered Country

In March of 1994 in the town of Midway, New Mexico, video producers Jose Escamilla and his brother, Manuel, saw something that they did not understand on a video they had made. The recording was made on a clear day and shows a rod-shaped shadow racing across the sky. At first, the Escamillas assumed that the shadow was an insect or bird passing near the lens of the camera. But they remained curious about it, and over the course of the next few months they began experimenting.

Along with the shadows that they continued to capture on camera, which Jose's wife, Karen Escamilla, named "rods," they shot birds and insects at two-thousand frames per second. They found that even the flapping wings of insects could be seen at this very high shutter speed, but the rods appeared the same, revealing no more detail than they had at lower shutter speeds.

Now quite intrigued, the Escamillas began filming the skies over Midway more extensively. The rods are not readily visible with the naked eye; they move at such a high speed that they can hardly be registered. But a video camera is different. Unlike an eye, it does not need to follow an object in order for it to be noticed. It simply records everything that passes its lens and emits light in the sensitivity range of its receptor system. To record their images, the Escamillas used a simple procedure: They set up a camera, aiming it at a fixed point in the sky, and let it run. They then examined the video and sometimes found some of these rod-shaped objects.

The rods they filmed appeared to them to be between fifty and a hundred feet long, but there was no certain way to tell. In one of the most spectacular videos taken by Jose Escamilla, the objects are seen speeding just above the peaks of a mountain range. One of them hits a mountain and, slightly bent and foreshortened, moves off more slowly in another direction. Because these objects were obviously moving just above this mountain range, their size has been determined to be five hundred feet in length. Another video shows the rods plunging into the ground and disappearing, which seems to contradict what happened when they hit the mountain, almost as if parts of the earth were solid to them and others were not.

Of course, most of the objects that appear when a video camera is set up and allowed to record the sky undisturbed are birds, bits of dust or seedpods, insects, and other normal airborne debris. I have proved this to my own satisfaction by experiment. What's more, the closer the object and the faster it moves, the stranger it looks. A fly, for example, can turn out looking like some kind of otherworldly flying centipede if it is a few feet from a lens that is correctly focused. But the images discussed in this chapter, the Escamillas' included, were made with focus set on infinity. At this focus, little or nothing is recorded of objects passing at close enough range to induce this type of distortion. Moreover, this sort of shadow doesn't strike and bounce off a mountainside, or dive into the ground.

Lest it be assumed the Escamillas somehow faked the first Midway video, or that they have mistaken an artifact for something real, it should be noted that the rods have been photographed in other places, at other times. In 1976, Trevor James Constable published *The Cosmic Pulse of Life*.[1] In this book, he maintains that there are living creatures of unknown species and genus who inhabit the sky much in the same way that fish inhabit the sea. He published a number of pictures in the book made on infrared film.[2] They bear a striking resemblance to video being made by the Escamillas and others.

Some of the most arresting video was made near Monterrey, Mexico, by Santiago Yturria. Escamilla and Yturria taped the objects extensively around Monterrey, and on one of the tapes a rod actually passes between Mexican investigator Jeronimo Flores and the camera that is recording an image of him. As the shot was being made at an extremely high shutter speed (one ten thousandth of a second), any bird, insect, or piece of ordinary debris would almost certainly have been visible, or at least more clear, in still frame. But what happened was similar to the other rod footage. The object remained as indistinct in still frame as it was in the moving video. Even at that high a shutter speed, no new information appeared.

In December of 1995, Escamilla recorded the rods moving over a building in Roswell, New Mexico. The camera was a little less than half a mile from the building. Two rods were recorded moving above it. Unfortunately, it was not possible from this video to determine if they had been behind the building or be-

[1]Trevor James Constable, *The Cosmic Pulse of Life* (Tustin, CA: Merlin Press, 1976); reprint Garberville, CA: Borderland Sciences Research Foundation, 1990.

[2]Ibid., Borderland ed., p. 403.

tween the building and the camera. In any case, they were certainly behind a group of telephone wires which enabled him to estimate that the objects were ten to a hundred feet in length. By observation, it is clear that they were moving at very high speed. No matter what they were, they were at least two hundred feet from the camera and must thus have been moving at a far higher velocity than any bird or insect.

Although their range is unknown, the rodlike shadows seem accessible to being recorded in any number of different places. As of October 1997, Escamilla reports that rods have been filmed in twenty-three states of the United States and in Mexico. These videos continue to be made. On June 15, 1997, a rod was filmed speeding past the Empire State Building in New York City.

Although some scientists who have seen the video agree that it is mysterious, there has been no organized study of the objects, largely because of a lack of publicity and no professionally gathered evidence entering the scientific data stream. This would appear to be an interesting opportunity for the atmospheric sciences.

Interestingly enough, there was some comment about skyborne life forms even before Constable's book was published. I believe that the first mention of this concept was made by Sir Arthur Conan Doyle, in his short story "The Horror of the Heights," which concerns an early ascent to the then-appalling altitude of forty thousand feet. When he reaches this level, the narrator makes the following comment: "But soon my attention was drawn to a new phenomenon—the serpents of the outer air. These were long, thin, fantastic coils of vapour-like material, which turned and twisted with great speed, flying round and round at such a pace that the eyes could hardly follow them." Will fact turn out to mirror fiction? We shall see.

Three other videographers, Tom King of Phoenix, John Bro Wilkie of Los Angeles, and Tim Edwards of Salida, Colorado, have all taped an equally strange phenomenon that may be related in some way to what the Escamillas have found.

The method they use was evolved independently by Wilkie and Edwards, then utilized successfully by King as well. This discovery began with the observation that objects become much more visible in the high light levels that occur near the disk of the sun. If the disk itself is blocked out, the video camera can record detail from this area that cannot be observed with the naked eye for any length of time. I must add that doing this also challenges the ability of a video system to make accurate recordings, and many bizarre images of ordinary objects can be obtained this way. But the images I will discuss here have, frankly, surprised me. I believe that I am, so far, the only person to have extracted this particular material from these videos, so it's perfectly possible that somebody else will be able to demonstrate that they bear some relation to the ordinary world. If not, then the tapes that have been made by these men, especially some made by Edwards in the fall of 1995, are quite simply the strangest video recordings ever made.

On an August afternoon in 1995, Edwards, a Salida, Colorado, restaurateur, had gone outside with his six-year-old daughter to talk to two men who were working on his roof. As he talked to the workers, his daughter kept trying to draw his attention to something in the sky. Finally, he looked up and saw something quite unusual.

Fortunately, he thought to go inside and get his

video camera. What he filmed was a glowing strip in the sky that had rectangular areas of light flowing along its surface. Although to the naked eye it appeared to be a structured object like some sort of gigantic cylinder or platform, on the video recording it presents an almost organic appearance. Jim Dilettoso of Village Labs was able to estimate its altitude at seventy-five thousand feet and its length at approximately one mile.

Less conclusive were the efforts to determine what it was. Some researchers concluded after a look at the tape that it was sunlight reflecting on a kite string. But the object was reportedly seen by observers as far away as California, and seventeen witnesses have been documented throughout Colorado. Additionally, a precisely similar phenomenon was taped on November 8, 1990, in Krasnodar, Russia. For these reasons, the kite string theory is probably not worth pursuing unless its proponents can duplicate the phenomenon using this medium.

If this is something that can be explained, then practically the only thing it could be might be a bizarre exhaust trail left by a high-flying secret aircraft. It is difficult to explain the pulsations of light passing down the object in terms of condensation from a known aircraft's exhaust system. There is alleged to exist a type of engine that emits detonations in series that would produce a contrail looking like a string of pearls, but, as with any contrail, this would extend if it was still being ejected. This object does not extend. Instead, it remains at a discreet length as it moves across the sky.

Then perhaps it is a cloud formed by such an engine during a power maneuver, something like the thick contrail that results when a fighter briefly engages its afterburner at high altitude, leaving an isolated segment floating in the sky.

But the only thing moving in connection with this material is the pulsating light. If this is an isolated segment of contrail, then where is the flow of energy coming from that is causing this movement? As it is not getting longer, it is not still being produced by the aircraft that generated it. Thus there can no motive power to transmit the pulses along its surface.

In addition, each pulse moves down its length in less than a second, meaning that the pulses are traveling at a very high rate of speed. It is hard to see how they could represent emission from any sort of engine, given that the forward velocity of the plane or rocket producing them would also have to be exceedingly high. So the greater likelihood is that the object is unknown and the lights are some sort of sequential flashing process.

Almost as if it was a kind of beacon, it got Edwards to begin searching the skies. After the object was shown on television, he was contacted by Tom King, who also began using the method of taping into sunglow. Along with Wilkie, these men have taped for many hours and produced much anomalous material. After their efforts came to my attention, I contacted them, and they kindly consented to give me copies of their tapes. On a first look, these appeared to me to be tapes of commonplace objects that had been distorted by speed and extreme lighting conditions. Nevertheless, I watched carefully. What I hoped to do was to identify the seedpods, insects, birds, and dust particles that I thought I was seeing, so that I could explain the phenomenon.

The material that I was viewing on Edwards' tapes appeared to be in essentially three areas of sky. There was very close material, which moved at quite high speed. This took the form of white, blurry objects that raced around in the sort of tight trajectories that might be associated with blown material like seedpods. Farther out, there were racing balls of light; these, I thought, might be insects or birds distorted by speed and high light levels. There were, at this level, also shadowy objects racing past and flares of material that appeared to be blowing spiderweb.

Initially, the objects that most arrested my curiosity were higher than any of these. These were cylinders that seemed, because of their distance from the camera, to be moving slowly across the sky, as if with the wind. They were not drifting, though, but always moved in a straight line and always in the same direction.

I accidentally hit the wrong button on the VCR and made a surprising discovery. The frozen frame presented a radically different and unexpected picture. The flying bits of fluff had a very unusual structure to them. As I began moving through the tape frame by frame, I realized that I was looking at something far more interesting than I had assumed. First, the cylindrical objects that I had thought were birds or planes now revealed some surprising features. As I advanced the frames, I saw that dark surfaces were rotating into visibility, then disappearing again as the objects moved. These surfaces displayed blocky designs of dark and light. Both the objects and their motion appeared to be similar to the video made by Demetrio Feria at the Mexican national air show in 1992.

Then I observed one of the closer objects. I had assumed that it was a bit of dust flying past near the lens of the camera. What I saw was astonishing: a segmented object looking like some sort of flying rope with a series of elongated domes on top. The rearmost segment had an opening at its end that appeared to be ejecting violet material that looked something like the emission recorded underneath the object sighted over Mexico City and Puebla in July of 1991.

I could hardly believe what I was seeing. I am not easily able to accept strange things like this at face value, and my first thought was that I might be looking at an image of a flying insect that had been severely distorted. When I showed this to San Antonio video producer Leonard Buchanan, his impression also was that the segmented appearance was caused by the object moving so rapidly that more than one image of it appeared on the same frame. This is not an uncommon phenomenon in video.

The trouble was for me that insects and birds on the tapes were clearly visible. In still frame, enough detail could sometimes be seen to identify species. So what species was this? Even assuming that there was only one segment actually present, what was it—a seedpod? It seemed to be moving extremely fast, but without knowing exactly how far it was from the camera, speed could not be determined. It could not have been fewer than fifteen feet away, because the lens was set to focus at infinity. Any closer, and it would have been out of focus.

The tapes were made by aiming the camera just above the edge of a roof, which was used to block out the disk of the sun. The angle of the shot was so low that the roofline is visible in the bottom of the frame as a dark, straight line.

Lip compression is a phenomenon that causes wind to speed up as it passes an edge. This is why eaves howl during a windstorm. Could the objects have been subject to winds that were sped up by lip compression?

Certainly they could, and maybe that was the cause of the rapid motion.

The problem with this is that the objects move in many different directions, often making U-turns in the air. They do not circulate like clouds of dust or flocks of midges and mayflies caught in small vortices. In fact, they do not move as if they are being blown by wind.

They take a number of forms. The most common does not appear to be a segmented shape that is repeated, but rather a pair of twined cords. Though some of them appear to be emitting violet material, most of them show no evidence of motive power. They have no wings and do not function like any sort of flying craft that we might be familiar with, including conventional UFOs. Like the Escamillas' rods, they seem more like some sort of unknown life-form than any conceivable air or space craft.

The last form that I observed was by far the most bizarre. My best efforts at explanation did not offer even a suggestion of a conventional alternative. This phenomenon appears to occur in the middle to far distance. There are two observations. The first is a cylindrical object that transforms just as it leaves the live area of the tape into something with two appendages and a blunt triangular wing. The transformation takes place over only three frames. The object then leaves the live area of the tape, and no more information is thus available.

A second object appears in the lower right corner of the screen, moves upward toward the center of the live area, then takes a curving dive and disappears. At first this object looks like a tiny flying man. On closer observation, it appears to have four equilateral oblong appendages, squared and possibly segmented. They are slightly darker on the flat ends, suggesting the possibility of shadow visible in a hollow interior. There is nothing to indicate the presence of a head.

The object flexes in its dive, as if it is pliant and under some sort of muscular or other tensioning control. It then leaves the live area, and there is no more information to be gained. At normal speed, these objects are mere blurs. Only by looking at them frame by frame can the detail be seen.

Another amazing object has been taped by John Wilkie over a house in Los Angeles. It is visible only in one frame of the tape. It appears over the roof of a house and consists of three visible segments that look something like streamlined crab shells. Their curving rear areas appear to be open, and they are connected together by a black, ribbonlike spine.

What is it, and what are the other forms that have been recorded? UFO researchers describe them in terms of aliens and spacecraft, but that is only one theory. They are not visible to the naked eye and so might be a newly discovered phenomenon that has been present for a long time. If this is the case, then its presence offers a rich new source of information and insight into life and the world.

Because the evidence has been presented by amateurs in the context of the UFO debate, it has never been seriously examined by science. But the phenomenon appears to be quite real, and therefore any culturally induced hesitancy of this kind would seem to be inappropriate and irrelevant. The fact that the objects are observed in so many places and do not appear hard to tape suggests that they are rather common. Obviously, something like this is readily accessible to scientific study.

It is possible to speculate that something as complex

as our atmosphere might harbor undiscovered life-
forms, especially if they leave no spoor or other signs
of their presence and are not visible to the naked eye,
as would seem to be the case here.

It is not enough, though, to concentrate on only one
level of the phenomenon. To identify what it is, it
would seem that the whole array must be included,
from the high-altitude cylinders to the weblike arrays
to the middle- and low-level material.

If it is a single phenomenon, though, then what
might it be? Surely no single creature would appear in
so many different forms at the same time. There are,
of course, plants with radically different male and female components and colony insects with many different forms. But there is something about this whole
phenomenon that seems to fight the conclusion that it
is, in any expected sense, a simple life-form of some
kind.

It is not to be expected that alien life will be easily
accessible to understanding. It may operate according
to principles that are unknown to us and function according to logic that is difficult for us to see or antic-
ipate.

We have enormous problems communicating even
with terrestrial animals on their own terms. We understand only rudiments of the language of dogs and
know little about how the world appears to them. Animals with complex languages, such as dolphins, offer
us almost no access to their minds. Even more complex aliens may be expected to be correspondingly
harder to understand.

Could we, then, be looking directly into the eyes of
aliens when we look at this array of phenomena? On
August 31, 1997, John Walker published a fascinating
series of speculations about this subject on the Inter-

net.[3] He hypothesizes that people report the bewildering variety of objects that they do "because they're living, space-dwelling creatures." He goes on to suggest that they might have originated as planetary organisms and thus congregate near planets and on them to carry out mating and reproduction, much as migratory turtles do on certain shorelines and islands. "Having evolved from originally planet-bound life, they need the environment of Earth (matter/gravitational field/etc.) to reproduce, just as toads and other amphibians must return to the water to bear their young." He further suggests that the possible presence of aliens might be due to the fact that they are "passengers on rather than builders of the craft," in the same sense that we use horses, and therefore that the aliens themselves may have no more idea of how their "craft" work than the average horseman does of the life that animates his mount.

Although these are only speculations, they do illustrate the wonderfully imaginative thinking that would potentially sweep science and society as we attempted to come to terms with the true weirdness of the UFO and close encounter phenomena.

But before we jump to conclusions about such matters, it would seem sensible to descend a little deeper into the labyrinth of UFOs—whether they exist, what powers them, and what sort of response humanity may already have mounted to their presence. To do this, we must go to the only part of space that we have even begun to colonize, the near-Earth orbital environment. There we will find one of the most interesting, controversial, and ignored mysteries of modern times.

[3]John Walker, "Flying Saucers Explained" (www.fourmilelab.ch/goldberg/saucers.html), August 31, 1997.

5:

Never a Straight Answer

On September 15, 1991, just as the Mexican phenomenon was beginning, an array of unusual objects appeared on a videotape made aboard the space shuttle *Discovery* during mission STS-48. This video was recorded off the live public feed being broadcast from the shuttle by NASA Select TV by Donald Ratch on an ordinary VHS video recorder.

The videotape was made from output from a camera in the shuttle's payload bay between 20:30 and 20:45 GMT near the west coast of Australia. It shows approximately a dozen objects moving in different directions in the area of the orbiter. One of these objects, which has come to be called the "target," appears near the air horizon and is first observed moving in a path that follows the horizon. The objects suddenly stop, then an instant later there is a flash. Immediately, the objects move off at high speed on different trajectories. Two seconds later two streaks come up from below, moving through the area previously occupied by the "target." It has been hypothesized that the two streaks are pulses of energy from some sort of a beam weapon.[1] Previously, that was only a hypothesis, but as will be seen, it has recently gained some surprising

---

[1]R.C. Hoagland, *The Discovery Space Shuttle Video*, (New York: B.C. Video, 1992).

support. Shortly after the event, the shuttle camera pitches down, revealing that there are several more objects, one triangular in shape, moving below the orbiter.

There was considerable controversy about this tape. It was shown on national television and has appeared in UFO documentaries. Responding to congressional inquiries, NASA stated that "the objects seen are orbiter generated debris illuminated by the sun. The flicker of light is the result of firing of the attitude thrusters on the orbiter, and the abrupt motions of the particles result from the impact of gas jets from the thrusters."[2]

Because this explanation was so easy to believe and the alternatives are so incredible, Kress's statement was accepted without question by the press and received little scientific criticism. The controversy was effectively ended. But, in fact, NASA's explanation does not appear to have been a correct one, and scientists who did not agree with it have presented a powerful case that it was wrong.

Professional analysis of this tape has come from two scientists, one a physicist, Dr. Jack Kasher,[3] and the other an imaging specialist, Dr. Mark J. Carlotto of TASC, an advanced photo analysis group in Reading, Massachusetts.[4] Dr. Kasher was a NASA consultant in 1991, and worked on the Strategic Defense Initiative

---

[2]Martin P. Kress, assistant administrator for legislative affairs, NASA, letter to Rep. Helen Delich Bentley, November 22, 1991.

[3]J. Kasher, "A Scientific Analysis of the Videotape Taken by Space Shuttle Discovery on Shuttle Flight STS–48 Showing Sharply Accelerating Objects," Fund for UFO Research, Mt. Ranier, Maryland, 1992.

[4]M.J. Carlotto, "Digital Video Analysis of Anomalous Space Objects," Journal of Scientific Exploration, Vol. 9, #1, p. 45.

(Star Wars) from 1972 until 1992 at the Lawrence Livermore National Laboratory.

Mr. Kress stated that the flash of light was the result of the firing of attitude adjustment jets on the shuttle. (The Orbital Maneuvering System/Reaction Control System [RCS] provides thrust for changes in the speed and attitude of the shuttle.) The orbiter has three groups of these thrusters—one group each in pods located on the left and right sides of the aft fuselage and another group in the nose—but at the time of the event, no such thruster firing was ordered by mission control. About two minutes after the event, however, mission control did order such a firing, to initiate a movement preparatory to a supply water dump.[5] This maneuver took place fifteen minutes after the event.

According to NASA, the movement involved was six degrees, a change of angle that would have been easily observable on the tape, as the air horizon (the top of the canopy of Earth's air) and the ground horizon are both clearly visible, and so is a star. And yet there is not the slightest change in the shuttle's attitude in relation to the horizons or the star after the flash. Carlotto observes that, following the claimed thruster firing, "There is no significant change in the direction of M2" (his designation for the star). He continues, "Yet the apparent motion of all objects including the star must change if the attitude of the spacecraft was altered by the thruster." He concludes, "The lack of any change in attitude following the flash implies that the flash was not due to a thruster firing."[6]

Given that mission control did not order such a ma-

---

[5]Rep. Helen Delich Bentley, letter to Pat Newcomer, Office of Legal Affairs, NASA, January 3, 1991.

[6]Carlotto, "Analysis of Anomalous Space Objects," p.6.

neuver, and the shuttle's position did not change, it seems impossible to dispute the contention that the flash was not caused by the firing of attitude adjustment jets. So that part of NASA's explanation is incorrect.

Speaking for NASA, Mr. Kress further claims that the change in the trajectories of the objects takes place because they are hit by gases from the thrusters. If this was the case, the "target" would have moved in an entirely different manner. For example, the firing of a thruster could not have caused the object to stop at all, let alone half a second *before* the flash that represented the supposed firing. Carlotto's analysis of the tape agrees with my own observation. He states, "Prior to the flash . . . the object slows and seems to stop."

NASA also claims that the objects were "ice particles," which were small and close to the shuttle. But the aft bulkhead camera that took the pictures was focused on infinity when they were made. This is conclusively proved by the fact that the camera pans down to include a view of the shuttle's open cargo bay door immediately after the sequence of events under discussion. At no time is there a break in recording, so the camera was not turned off and then returned to service at another focal setting. What happens as the camera pans down is that its focal system detects the nearby cargo bay door, and the focus is then seen to move off infinity to a closer setting, causing the cargo bay door to come into focus.

In addition, it appears from Dr. Carlotto's analysis that the "target" object first appears and moves below the air horizon—in other words, it was coming up out of the air canopy, not moving on a trajectory near the orbiter as it must have been doing if it was an ice particle ejected from the shuttle itself. "A slight tail at the beginning of the track [of the "target"] suggests that the object may be moving up and out of the atmosphere. . . . Instead of changing abruptly as one would expect of a particle suddenly coming into sunlight, the brightness increases gradually over a one second period."[7] He contends that this is more consistent with a bright object coming out of a cloud layer within the atmosphere, or possibly a very large and distant object moving from shadow into daylight. However, Carlotto states in his paper that he cannot "speculate on what they might be."[8]

The combination of these observations and the fact that the camera was set on infinity when the "ice particles" were recorded suggests in the strongest terms that this part of NASA's explanation is also wrong. In addition, Carlotto analyzed the appearance of ice particles that were released in the separation of the Apollo Command Module from the LEM/Saturn V third stage in an earlier Apollo mission. He found that all of these particles moved in the same trajectories, and that their light levels changed at a rate of seven cycles per second as they tumbled, in contrast to the half-a-cycle-per-second rate of the objects in the mission STS-48 video.

After his analysis, Dr. Kasher concluded, "Once the idea of ice particles has been discarded, there aren't many options left."

Let's examine the sequence *as if* these objects are not ice particles but some unknown form of material. Here is the sequence of events: The dots of light are moving in various different directions. They stop. A

[7] Ibid., p. 8.
[8] Ibid., p. 17.

moment later, a flash occurs. After a further half-second pause, they begin to accelerate in directions that are different from the routes they were taking before the flash. The main object proceeds away from the area, accelerating at very high velocity. Then a fascinating, indeed disturbing, phenomenon becomes visible, when the two streaks of light come up from below, moving through the frame in approximately the same area just previously occupied by the most prominent piece of material.

Dr. Kasher says, "One possible explanation is that we were firing at them."

Could such a thing be true? If so, then it could mean that part of the defense system possesses technology far in advance of what is publicly known and is actively engaged in hostilities against whatever those dots of light represent. Conceivably, it might also mean, then, that the horrifying video referred to in Chapter Three of the alien apparently dying while under interrogation is real. If so, it would certainly be clear why the intelligence community and the military would be protecting this secret so obsessively.

If it is not a video of ice particles, then the following narrative would appear to explain it: A group of unknown objects are approaching the orbiter. They are targeted. But they detect the targeting process. They stop, presumably in order to determine the intended trajectory of some sort of incoming fire. A flash of light takes place, which must have revealed this information, because they then move off at high speed on new trajectories of their own. All of this takes place in less than two seconds. A second later, two pulses of light come up from below, moving through the area where the "target" object was previously maneuvering.

If this is a correct analysis of this tape, then it suggests that an attempt was made to destroy the target object or to warn it away from the shuttle by parties in possession of a sophisticated weapons system that has the ability to locate and fire at targets in near space.

Could such a weapon be possessed by the United States and actually have been in the area that the shuttle was passing through at the time this event took place?

The shuttle was on a course north of Australia and near its west coast. There is a large American installation at Pine Gap near Alice Springs in central Australia that the Australian government has told its citizens is a "research facility." When the incident took place, the shuttle was between twelve hundred and fifty and fifteen hundred miles northwest of Pine Gap.

The facility is managed by the supersecret U.S. National Reconnaissance Office, ostensibly a signals-acquisition organization loosely connected to the Air Force but reporting to the CIA. The installation is as well-known locally as Area 51 is in the United States, as the source of numerous strange flashes of light and UFO sightings. Some of this activity was videotaped at Alice Springs on November 26, 1996, and shows lights maneuvering in a manner inconsistent with aircraft.

Unfortunately, video of moving lights is hardly proof of anything, and the fact that they were taken near Pine Gap does not mean that they had anything to do with that facility. Rumors about Pine Gap are no more conclusive than rumors about Area 51.

However, Pine Gap is most certainly not a research facility. It is, in fact, America's largest satellite intelligence-gathering facility and is one of the largest ground satellite stations in the world. It collects data from a group of satellites manufactured by TRW Space Systems. Visible on the surface at Pine Gap are eight large radomes and about twenty other buildings. The guidance section, housed in a fifty-six-hundred-square-meter facility, is divided into a Station Keeping Section that controls satellites on geostationary orbit, a Signals Processing Section, and an Analysis Section.

The base is serviced by the U.S. Military Airlift Command, which schedules two C-141 Starlifter flights a week, transporting parts and supplies to the facility and probably hard data in the form of tapes or other media back to the United States. The facility is provided with high-frequency communications operating under the International call sign VL5TY and transmitting encrypted communications to Clark Field in the Philippines. KW-7 and KW-13 cryptographic machines are used for teletype and voice encryption to TRW facilities in Redondo Beach, California, reaching the Communications Vault in Building M-4. About half of the daily Pine Gap signals traffic is directed to CIA HQ in Langley, Virginia. The rest goes to the National Security Agency, the National Reconnaissance Office, and the Pentagon.

Whether Pine Gap was involved in the events that took place during shuttle mission STS-48 is unknown. The available hard evidence is on the shuttle videotape.

If the events depicted on that tape involve military action, then a targeting effort began to be made from the ground station sometime after the "target" moved above the horizon and began to approach the shuttle. This targeting process would have relied on a high-intensity return from the target to enable final acquisition and aiming of the weapon. The pulse of light observed would thus have been designed to reflect against the objects, providing the ground-based targeting system with an accurate fix during the instant of reflection.

This would mean that the targeting system probably would be optically based, in other words, a telescopic system. So does a laser weapon targeted by an optical telescope exist in the American weapons inventory?

Actually, one does.

The Mid-Infrared Advanced Chemical Laser (MIRACL) is an antisatellite and antimissile laser defense system currently under test at the army's High Energy Laser Systems Test Facility at White Sands, New Mexico. This is a ground-based laser designed to emit pulses of light energy sufficiently powerful to destroy an incoming missile warhead or an orbiting satellite.

It is intended to be targeted by a telescopic system also under test called the SEALITE Beam Director. This consists of a large-aperture (1.8-meter) gimballed telescope and optics that are designed to point the MIRACL or other laser beam weapons onto a target. It works by optically locating its targets and then feeding their coordinates into the laser beam guidance system.

Colonel Philip Corso, a retired United States Army intelligence officer, in his controversial book *The Day After Roswell*, suggests that such a weapons system has been functional since 1974. He claims that a high-energy laser based system has been developed that can shoot down alien spacecraft.[9]

On August 28, 1997, it was announced that the army was exploring the idea of testing MIRACL

---

[9]Corso, *The Day After Roswell*, (New York: Simon & Schuster, 1997), pp. 267–68.

against a sixty-million-dollar air force satellite. An article that appeared in *The New York Times* on September 1 discussed the various political issues that have arisen connected with such a test, primarily whether it might trigger a continuation of the arms race, as other countries struggle to match America's growing ability to engage in near-space military action.[10] On October 23, 1997, news reports suggested that the laser had malfunctioned and not blown up the satellite.[11] Given the project's political sensitivity, however, and the level of security involved, there is no way to tell if this is true, or whether this is the only weapon we possess with these capabilities. The *Times* article also said, "The United States has no demonstrated way of shooting down satellites, though experts speculate that it may have secret ways that could work in an emergency."

Colonel Corso claims in his book that alien craft tried to disrupt our space program for years. "They had buzzed our capsules traveling through space, interfered with our transmissions, and pulsed us with EMP bursts."[12] Electromagnetic pulses are bursts of energy that can short out electronic components such as computer chips and guidance systems and would definitely be a serious threat to our spacecraft and satellites.

If this sort of hostility has actually been taking place, then the events recorded by the shuttle's camera may make a very different sort of sense. It could be

[10]"Military Is Hoping To Test Fire Laser Against Satellite," *The New York Times*, September 1, 1997, p. 1A.

[11]*San Antonio Express-News*, October 23, 1997, p. 13A.

[12]Corso, *The Day After Roswell*, p. 268.

that the objects were positioning themselves to act against the shuttle or to threaten it in some way.

If so, then what the onboard camera recorded was the targeting, acquisition, and firing of a high-speed weapons system that, although it did not hit anything, did cause the objects to leave the area.

Unfortunately, there is no single piece of evidence that overwhelmingly confirms that we have a record, in this videotape, of a military action that was triggered when these objects came too close to the *Discovery*. And even if that is the case, a substantial amount of further evidence would be necessary before we could be certain that the action involved our own military. If one alien force is here, why not another that is hostile to it?

If the objects had been identifiable as satellites, missiles, or spacecraft owned by a hostile human power, there would be no question but that this is a record of military action against them.

Beyond the bare facts, though, there is nothing more that can be concluded, except that NASA has come through this particular test with its usual flying colors: Never A Straight Answer has once again lived up to its nickname.

What if there is a secret war being fought against an alien presence? One thing is certain: It has to be the least visible war in history and the least dangerous to civilians. We certainly aren't getting blown up, and no *Independence Day*–style invasion seems to be happening.

Not only that, the aliens display remarkable strategic innocence, even stupidity. The reason is that they must have sat passively by for at least fifty years while we painstakingly struggled toward a level of technology with which we could successfully oppose them. It is as if human armies were in the habit of waiting to attack until they were sure that their enemies could defend themselves.

If we are fighting, then the mere fact that we *can* fight means that the aliens are not hostile. If they were, they would have obviously attacked us and won at least a generation ago. There aren't any reasons why hostile aliens would wait for us to catch up technologically before engaging in battle. But there are many that might motivate friendly but misunderstood ones to act in just this manner.

I would be astonished if the United States had gotten itself tangled up in some sort of a secret war with aliens. Even given the effectiveness of the national system of secrecy, it is hard to see how a multibillion-dollar effort like this could be completely concealed for generations.

But if aliens appeared during the early years of the Cold War, I wouldn't be at all surprised to find that the United States had greeted them with gunfire and taken an essentially hostile stance, one that included the firing of an occasional warning shot.

Whatever rationale might have evolved to justify such a policy internally might be hard to sell to the public, for the simple reason that it is likely to be wrong. Otherwise, why haven't the "hostile aliens" blown us all to hell already?

If they are not hostile, then they would have three options. One would be to overpower us. Another would be to leave. The third would be to wait until we calmed down, while engaging in a slow program of acclimatization.

The United States, having made one of history's most spectacular mistakes—a mistake great enough to cause the public to demand an end to the whole system

of secrecy behind which the policy was evolved—
would have an overwhelming motive to continue hostilities, especially if they were what was preventing
public interaction with the aliens and, along with it,
the revelation of the mistake.

The visitors, seeing that it was not the people but
the leaders who couldn't handle their presence, might
well take their case directly to the ordinary citizen—
thus showing up in our bedrooms in the middle of the
night, as they appear to have done.

But before we descend too deeply into speculation,
perhaps it makes some sense to take a look at the possible technology of the UFOs and see if their flight
characteristics emerge out of the world of the imagination, or if they make any aeronautical sense. What
are these things flying around in the sky? Can they
really be spacecraft?

Surprisingly enough, these seemingly magical objects have already been carefully observed by scientists
with outstanding credentials, with unexpected results.

6:

Hidden Hardware

The most extraordinary book ever written about UFOs was finished in 1974, but not published until 1995, after its author's death. Paul R. Hill's *Unconventional Flying Objects* takes an aeronautical engineer's look at the UFO, with startling results.[1]

But why was it hidden, even by Dr. Hill himself, for so many years? I was not able to get an answer to this question, but it certainly suggests cover-up, especially because of the overwhelming importance of this book. We owe its publication to his daughter, Julie M. Hill, who found it among his effects. If it had been published in 1955 or 1965 or 1975, it would have caused a massive international sensation. But its publication in 1995, only after the doctor had died and the UFO question has been publicly declared moot, has hardly been noticed.

There is a fascinating book mentioned by Dr. Hill that examines the way science assimilates new and unexplained phenomena, called *The Structure of Scientific Revolutions*, by Dr. Thomas S. Kuhn. Kuhn explains that theories that supersede established beliefs enter science when tools and methodologies are devised that end any controversy about the data that in-

---

[1]Paul R. Hill, *Unconventional Flying Objects* (Charlottesville, VA: Hampton Roads, 1995).

spired them. The scientific establishment resists the new information as long as it can. Often, it rejects the new ideas so completely that the case is closed and the matter is forgotten. But the data, in the end, always prevail. In this sense, the treatment of the UFO phenomenon has been typical of what happens when new data challenge current beliefs. Applying Kuhn's theories, it seems likely that the UFO phenomenon is about to be integrated into science despite what currently appears to be almost total rejection.

The degree to which science will reject knowledge at any given time is dependent on how remote it is from what science already accepts. As this whole field is extremely remote, to say the least, it isn't surprising that the abundant evidence—at least of strange flying objects—that has been accumulating for fifty years continues to be ignored.

On the other hand, even the most improbable evidence will be accepted if it confirms theory. For example, the "omega minus" particle became accepted in physics even though there were only two events in two hundred thousand trials that indicated that it was real. By contrast, experiments, for example, in psychic transfer do not enter the area of accepted knowledge no matter how many successful trials take place.[2]

When Galileo was one of the few people with a telescope, his theory that Earth and the planets orbited the sun was resisted to the point that the church, acting on the advice of some of the most qualified scientists and theologians of that era, almost arranged to have him burned at the stake as a heretic. But as the number of telescopes kept growing and observer after

[2]D. Radin, Ph.D., *The Conscious Universe: The Scientific Truth of Psychic Phenomena* (San Francisco: HarperCollins 1997), p. 49.

observer saw for himself or herself the truth of Galileo's claims, his theories were gradually adopted.

Like Galileo's data and other controversies of science such as the notion that meteors fall from the sky, the theory of gravity, and whether electricity and then radio actually existed, the UFO phenomenon will be recognized as soon as there are instruments deployed that can reliably acquire the relevant data. These instruments do not have to be invented. The video-recording equipment, high-speed cameras, telescopes, and other needed devices already exist. The key is that they be made use of by qualified scientists, so that a data stream can begin.

As compelling as the amateur video is, it is not a scientific data stream. In addition, the unpredictable appearance of UFOs makes it harder, but by no means impossible, for this phenomenon to be captured professionally. This is because UFO appearances seem to run in waves, and the deployment of sufficient resources during these periods would be likely eventually to bring results. In addition, the odd phenomena recorded by the Escamillas, Edwards, King, and Wilkie seem more general and persistent than ordinary UFO appearances and should thus also be more readily accessible to organized sky recording by atmospheric scientists.

Of course, there will be resistance to any effort to engage in data acquisition of this kind, emanating from the same kinds of sources that Kuhn identifies as being centers of resistance in the past: established authorities (whether civil or institutional to science) who have committed themselves to the idea that the phenomenon is nonsense.

People who have made a professional commitment to a certain theory are threatened when that theory is challenged. In the case of this phenomenon, both science and the press have so completely committed themselves to the idea that the whole area of study is without value that they can be expected to continue to resist fiercely, even in the face of overwhelming evidence that a real mystery is present. If the history of science is any indication of what will happen now, there will be continued resistance to the funding of data acquisition, despite the fact that this would now seem to be outrageously irresponsible. If the process of assimilation of these data is being further deranged by some sort of a government cover-up, then the battle will be all the more fierce and difficult.

That such a cover-up exists is suggested by the fact that Hill did not publish his book during his lifetime. It is clear from statements he makes in it that it was always his plan to publish after his retirement. But instead, he seems to have been unable to do this, and the project had to wait until after his death. In his introduction, written in 1974, he commented that "at last, the UFO witness, long the butt of ridicule from all sides, had some of the heavy guns of science on his side for a change." He made this statement because scientists such as atmospheric physicist Dr. James E. McDonald, Professor James Harder, Dr. J. Allen Hynek, and Dr. David Saunders were vociferously disagreeing with the Air Force's then recently published Project Blue Book conclusion that the UFO phenomenon was not worth studying. Clearly, he thought that science was changing its position more than twenty years ago.

But this did not happen. In part, it was probably due to some sort of government action undertaken within the scientific community in defense of the Air Force and its Blue Book conclusions. Possibly, Dr.

Hill's own failure to publish his book came about as
a result of action of this sort. Also, however, the failure of science to respond to the questions raised by
such powerful and well-credentialed professionals as
Dr. McDonald was due to its continued inability to
acquire useful data. Worse, such data as had been acquired were ignored and even suppressed, and the officially sanctioned fictions promoted by Project Blue
Book went unchallenged.

Dr. Hill was employed as an aeronautical scientist
throughout his career, which began in 1936 with a
professorship at the Polytechnic College of Engineering in Oakland. He was then assigned to the Langley
Research Center, first under the National Advisory
Committee on Aeronautics (NACA), and then under
NASA when it was formed. He was there from 1939
until 1970, retiring with an Exceptional Service Medal
for Outstanding Scientific Leadership.

The reason he was interested in unidentified flying
objects was that he had two sightings that suggested
strongly to him that the phenomenon was real and
caused him to set out to understand what he had seen.
On July 16, 1952, his first sighting took place. It was
made during the 1952 UFO flap, arguably one of the
most dramatic theatricals of this type that has ever
occurred. Dr. Hill's sighting is mentioned in Major Edward Ruppelt's *Report on Unidentified Flying Objects*.[3]

The Langley Research Center where Hill worked
was in Hampton, Virginia, in the middle of an area
full of defense installations and "almost surrounded by
water." On July 16, 1952, two Pan Am pilots made

[3] Maj. E. Ruppelt, *The Report on Unidentified Flying Objects* (Garden
City, NY: Doubleday, 1956), pp. 157–58.

local headlines by reporting a sighting from their plane over Hampton Roads. The moment he read the news, Hill was excited. He had already noticed the tendency of UFOs to reappear in a given area during a "flap." He reported that he thought, "This is the night. They may be back." He went to the area where the sighting had been reported in order to attempt an orderly gathering of data, something that cries out to be done today.

At 7:55 in the evening, he and a friend parked their car on the Hampton Roads waterfront and waited. At 8:00 a flight of UFOs came up over the southern horizon. They were moving in parallel, at an estimated speed of five hundred miles an hour "at what was learned later by triangulation to be 15,000 to 18,000 feet altitude." Hill described them as glowing amber and determined that they were spheres thirteen to twenty feet in diameter.

As an aeronautical engineer, he was in a position to make an entirely professional observation, which he proceeded to do. It seemed almost as if the craft were displaying themselves to Dr. Hill, as they came to a stop in the air directly over his head. He observed them to "jitter" slightly, a description that seems reminiscent of the motion observed in the object that was videotaped in Mexico City on August 6, 1997. They then leaped one ahead of the other faster than the eye could follow—something that was also recorded in the Fuentes video in July of 1991. Moving a little off the zenith, they began revolving in a horizontal circle "at a rate of at least once per second," then shifted their revolutions to the vertical.

Hill described himself as being "awe-stricken." As an aeronautical engineer, he knew the extraordinary flight capabilities that he was observing.

Soon a third sphere came from the same direction as the first two and joined them. As they crossed the lower Chesapeake Bay, a fourth sphere appeared, coming down the coast from the direction of Norfolk, Virginia. The objects disappeared to the south.

Dr. Hill followed up this observation by investigating whether anybody else in the local area had observed it. He found that the Norfolk paper had reported the object that he had seen coming from that direction. It had been observed by a bus driver and his single passenger in Norfolk just a few minutes before it appeared at Hampton Roads. In addition, a ferryboat full of passengers waiting to go from Hampton Roads to Washington had seen the whole incident. The story was carried on the morning of July 17 by the *Newport News Daily Press*, with a detailed description from an Air Force captain and fighter pilot.

Dr. Hill investigated why local aircraft spotters had reported nothing. (In those early Cold War days, spotters were still employed all over the United States, as a backup to radar systems, to watch for enemy planes.) He got a list of them and visited them individually in their homes. They had all seen the UFOs. He reports, "The head spotter said that he had been instructed by the Richmond Filter Center, operated by the Air Force, to report aircraft, and no nonsense, and so he had said nothing." It was from them that he obtained the data needed to triangulate the altitude.

He also reported the observation to his boss at NACA, who dismissed his story completely. His report to Air Force Intelligence resulted in a complaint that he should have called Tactical Air Command during the sighting so that they could have tried an intercept.

He then made an interesting comment, especially so in view of what appears to be on the mission STS-48

tape: "At the time, I already had a growing aversion
to the Air Force's attempted intercepts, but why discuss policy at the bottom of the totem pole?" This
seems to indicate that he was aware of an Air Force
intercept policy, with which he disagreed, and suggests
that he had access to policy makers at a higher level
than the local Air Force intelligence office. But he did
not elaborate.

Through the 1950s, he continually updated his da-
tabase of sightings, with the result that he began to be
able to make determinations about the craft and how
they might be powered.

In 1962, he had another sighting over Hampton
Roads. It was a cloudy day, and he was in a car, with
a broad view through the windshield of the southern
part of Chesapeake Bay and the Roads. "Over the
southern end of the Chesapeake Bay, I was surprised
to see a fat aluminum or metallic colored 'fuselage'
nearly the size of a small freighter, but shaped more
like a dirigible, approaching from the rear." It was
about a thousand feet up and moving slowly. "It
looked like a big, pointed-nose dirigible, but had not
even a tail surface as an appendage." It was much
longer than the Goodyear blimp and had no identifying marks. Dirigibles had by then ceased to be operated by the United States military, and the dirigible
hangar at Langley was long since torn down.

Any question of its being a blimp then ended, as it
began to accelerate "very rapidly and at the same time
to emit a straw-yellow, or pale flame-colored wake or
plume, short at first but growing in length as the speed
increased." Its angle of attack also rose to about five
degrees with the horizontal. Hill calculated that its acceleration across the distance of five miles in four seconds, starting at a speed of one hundred miles per

hour, gave it a speed at the point of disappearance into the cloud cover of eighty-nine hundred miles per hour. The g forces involved would have been one hundred times Earth's gravity, easily enough to destroy any manmade device and kill all of its occupants. Despite the plume of energetic material being emitted, there was no sound.

After his 1952 sighting, Dr. Hill was forbidden by the director of NACA to do or say anything that might create an impression that NACA had any belief or interest in UFOs. The result of this was that he collected data unofficially for twenty-five years, becoming NASA's backroom specialist on UFOs. It is interesting to note how early present government policy regarding this matter began. Even as it was officially keeping an open mind in the 1950s, one of the primary professional sources of confirming evidence was silenced.

Dr. Hill became a sort of clearinghouse for all UFO reports that reached NASA's attention. He thus had access to many of the best cases of the era. As a result, he was able to observe films that were made by professionals in the 1950s and 1960s. Among these was a film shot in 1952 by a Navy chief photographer, Warrant Officer Delbert Newhouse, while vacationing in Tremonton, Utah.

With two thousand hours of flying time as an aerial photographer and twenty-one years in the navy, Newhouse is obviously classifiable as a photographic professional with a specialty in reconnaissance. Like Dr. Hill himself, Newhouse appears to have been given a remarkable opportunity to record the operation of UFOs during the summer of 1952.

He was driving down a highway when he noticed some unusual objects in the sky. Immediately aware that they were outside of his very extensive experience, he stopped the car and took out his movie camera. Using a 3-inch telephoto lens and color film, he obtained a good record of the phenomenon. Because he realized the importance of what he was seeing, he adopted a professional stance. While the disks maneuvered in formation, he held the camera steady. When one left the group, he moved the camera ahead of the object, then let it fly through the frame so that he could get a record of its angular velocity.

Dr. Hill reported that he studied this film carefully, along with fighter pilots and other professionals. Nobody involved concluded that the films were of the usual suspects—aircraft, birds, or stars—or even marsh gas, a favorite debunking explanation at the time.[4]

So they were judged to be genuine unknowns, photographed by a professional in 1952. They represented concrete evidence, obtained at a level of confidence consistent with scientific demands for professional-level data input. But why did we not conclude, in 1952, that UFOs were what these professionals thought they were: intelligently guided objects? It is hard to see how science ended up in the position of rejecting evidence like this, especially when the Cold War was causing the American military to engage in a frantic search for new weapons of all kinds—unless, of course, the evidence was classified in order to enable a search for the motive power of the craft to be undertaken outside of Soviet scrutiny.

This was an extremely serious issue at the time. In 1949, the USSR had detonated an atomic bomb. In

---

[4]Ignis fatuus is the flickering light that results from the spontaneous combustion of marsh gases, produced by decomposing plant and animal matter.

1953, both countries exploded hydrogen bombs. A top-secret 1953 RAND study, now declassified, showed that American airbases were vulnerable to Soviet long-range bombers.

The United States, Canada, and Britain had a joint flying saucer project called Project-Y, which had as its objective the production of a flying saucer–type aircraft. Dr. Hill worked on the precursor to this project, using his observations of UFO tilt-to-control maneuvers as the basis of designs that eventually became the AVRO Flying Platform. A tilt-to-control design rests on a column of energy—or, in the case of a flying platform, air. It sits level to hover, tilts forward to accelerate, tilts backward to stop, banks to turn, and descends by "falling-leaf" or wobbling motions.

So not only was professional-quality film in the system, it was being used as the springboard for aeronautical design considered important enough at the time to be highly classified. Even though there is little documentation suggesting that propulsion experiments were also undertaken, it is hard to see that this would not have been done. The greater likelihood is that such work was also classified and remains so. The only reason that the flying platform studies were ever declassified is that they were not successful.

If—fantastically—the data really have been ignored just as the government claims, then we need to stop doing that, because we have at our disposal the capacity both to collect more and to evaluate it and can conceivably deduce how to engineer the propulsion system of the UFO from observation, if there is enough of it and it is properly documented.

Even though Hill did not duplicate the propulsion system, he made significant progress toward an understanding of the technology. He analyzed a number of cases where force-field effects were reported, such as people being affected by sunburns or other physical symptoms, cars stopped due to electrical failure, and, in one case, roof tiles being swept off a house. (A mysterious shutdown of a vehicle's electrical system and engine often seems to take place when a UFO is near.) Not only did he make it clear that the strange maneuvers of the UFOs made good physical sense if it was granted that they were operating within some sort of force field, he also came to the conclusion that this field must be what he called a "direct acceleration field." Hill proposed that this type of engine would be far better at developing thrust than the heat engine that we have been using for two hundred years. He called it the field engine and suggested that, because of the way the objects repel all mass, not just electrically charged or magnetic objects, that this engine must generate a field that can cancel gravity.[5]

Dr. Hill also addressed the matter of the plasma that seems to surround UFOs, stating that "there is really no secret as to what this illuminated sheath of ionized and excited air molecules is." Through an analysis of its characteristics, he identified it as an air plasma. He went on to say that "the ion sheath also accounts for some daytime UFO characteristics such as a shimmering haze, nebulosity of the atmosphere or even smoke-like effects. . . ." This description precisely fits the phenomena observed in some of the Mexican tapes made more than forty years later.

[5]Such fields are the subject of growing scientific interest, as indicated by the discussion of the technical aspects of field propulsion mechanisms in H. Puthoff, "SETI, The Velocity-of-Light Limitation and the Alcubierre Warp Drive, an Integrating Overview," *Physics Essays* 9, no. 1 (March, 1996): 156.

It would seem probable that this plasma is generated by the field engine, and therefore that a correct analysis of the plasma might lead closer to an understanding of the engine. Dr. Hill offered many observations on the possible origin of this plasma, concluding that it must be caused by the ionizing radiation of X-ray frequencies. This would certainly account for the deep burns experienced by the Mexican witnesses who were injured by the August 6 UFO.

Because of the aeronautical behavior of UFOs, Dr. Hill ruled out the electromagnetic field as a power source. It is not a static field, but one that, as it spreads at ultra-high speed, cannot be concentrated enough to generate useful thrust in the atmosphere.

When he looked at static fields as possible power sources, he found that the motions of the UFOs were consistent with the presence of such a field around them, as anything using a static field will obey Newtonian dynamics when it comes near objects or engages in flight maneuvers.

There are three types of static-energy field that might conceivably hold something up: the magnetic field, the electric field, and the repulsive-force field. In his analysis of which type of field might be involved with the objects, Dr. Hill narrowed his search to the repulsive-force field.

This did not mean that he rejected the many reports of electrical effects, such as the blanking of radio reception and interference with auto ignitions, but rather that he did not believe that these effects were signatures of the primary field that was being used to hold the craft up.

There is a popular notion that the motive power of UFOs must be a magnetic field that opposes the magnetic field of Earth. This cannot be true, because

Earth's magnetic field is parallel to the planet only at the equator. Because the so-called magnetic dip increases toward the poles, UFOs would have to maneuver at increasingly extreme angles as they left the area of the equator, and this is not seen to happen. In fact, by the time they reached the arctic circles, they would slide down the angle of Earth's magnetic field and hit the ground unless they greatly increased the power of their internal magnetic field. But this, in turn, would drive the object toward the pole, where it would eventually come to rest.

The question then is, can we determine what kind of force field might be capable of holding these objects up and enabling them to maneuver as freely as they are seen to do on the Mexican videotapes and films such as that made by Delbert Newhouse?

In 1967, Russian physicist Andrei Sakharov published a study suggesting that all of the general relativistic phenomena, including gravity and inertia, among others, could result from changes in the energy of the vacuum brought about by the presence of matter.[6] This went significantly beyond Einstein's own theory that inertia must be accounted for as a reaction to the gravity of distant galaxies, and raised an implication that, if inertia was actually dependent on the quantum-fluctuation of energy within the vacuum, then it might be accessible to engineering. For example, the vacuum could be mined for virtually limitless energy, and inertia could be exploited by the very kind of field-effect engine that Dr. Hall had proposed that UFOs were using.

---

[6]A. Sakharov, "Vacuum Quantum Fluctuations in Curved Space and the Theory of Gravitation," *Soviet Physics.-Dokl.* 12, no. 4 (1968): 3454–55.

Despite this, it is still difficult to imagine how even a field-effect engine could generate speeds faster than light. If it couldn't, then it would take millennia to traverse interstellar distances.

Lately, there has been a popular notion that a "warp" drive would solve this problem by bending space until any two points were, in effect, joined. Then interstellar travel would be instantaneous. In 1994, physicist Miguel Alcubierre showed in a delightful and elegant paper that one way inertia could be engineered was by expanding space behind a vessel and shrinking it ahead, effectively moving the ship faster than light.[7] But a recent study suggests that the amount of energy necessary to sustain such a warp is about ten billion times the energy locked up in all the visible mass in the universe.[8] According to *The New Scientist* of July 26, 1997, Alcubierre commented, "I'm not really surprised. I always thought the amount of energy needed would be ridiculous." So it would seem that alien fans who assume that the visitors must be hopping around in warp ships might need to find another assumption.

Or will they? In 1941 it was conclusively proved that man could never reach the moon because it would take a million tons of fuel to send a one-pound payload that far. But nobody considered the idea of a multistage rocket that would send only a small part of its total mass to the destination.

Einstein's general theory of relativity doesn't prohibit faster-than-light movement. What it prohibits is acceleration across the speed of light. If a particle

[7]M. Alcubierre, "The Warp Drive: Hyper-Fast Travel Within General Relativity," *Classical and Quantum Gravity* 11 (1994): L73.

[8]M. Pfennig and L. Ford, "The unphysical nature of 'warp drive' " *Classical and Quantum Gravity* 14 (1997): 1743. NY, 1997.

starts out faster than light, it doesn't violate the theory. One way around the barrier would be to move through a higher dimension where it doesn't exist. This possibility, suggested by a branch of physics called string theory, would work by gaining access to higher dimensions, which are compressed inside particles, and using them as a sort of shortcut. But these extra dimensions—there are ten of them—are more than a billion billion times smaller than a proton, and "inflating" them will also take a great deal of energy.

This would be another means of manipulating the vacuum, which, despite the problems outlined by Pfennig and Ford, may still be a key to ultrarapid movement over long distances.

Perhaps one of those phenomena might involve the ability to move through what is popularly called a wormhole, a structure that links two distant points in space, if it could be kept open long enough. To do this, we must learn to find, store, and manipulate exotic matter that has some very weird properties indeed.

These are almost unimaginably exotic possibilities. And maybe they *don't* work and therefore nobody is moving faster than light. This might mean that the visitors have come here slowly—and the probability that this is true has been the reason that skeptics have, for years, maintained that they could not be here at all. But the mathematics of interstellar travel at even a small fraction of the speed of light do not actually support the skeptical arguments. On the contrary, if there are any interstellar civilizations in the galaxy at all, it is logical to expect that they have already arrived here.[9] However, if they do not have the ability to

[9] T. B. H. Kuiper and M. Morris, "Searching for Extraterrestrial Civilizations," *Science* 196 (1977): 618.

travel faster than light, then it is also probable that their journey has been one-way but that they retain an ability to communicate with their home planet using some version of quantum communications that are at present in the experimental phase here.[10] Such communications would be based on the fact that particles that are said to be in a state of quantum entanglement both respond simultaneously to changes in either one.[11] Right now, we have been able to observe this phenomenon in particles as far as seven miles apart,[12] and there is no theoretical reason why this instantaneous "spooky action at a distance" as Einstein called it, would be in any way changed by physical distance. So if visitors have come here slowly, they may well also have carried communications devices containing half of many billions of entangled pairs, and therefore continue to enjoy rich instantaneous communication with home even though it might take quite a long time for a physical journey to be made.

During the time they have journeyed, they will have been victims of time dilation: On the ship, only a few years will have passed, but their home world will have gotten thousands of years older. If their civilization has fallen, maybe they are more deeply alone than we can possibly imagine, and perhaps this accounts for the profound sadness that close encounter witnesses so often report.

[10]B. Stein, "It Takes Two to Tangle," *New Scientist*, September 28, 1996, pp. 24–30.

[11]Malcom Browne, "Far Apart, 2 Particles Respond Faster than Light," *The New York Times*, July 22, 1997, p. C1.

[12]Dr. Nicholas Gisin of the University of Geneva and colleagues demonstrated this with paired photons. "Light's Spooky Connections Set Distance Record," *New Scientist*, June 28, 1997, p. 16.

There could be other methods of transferring a species across interstellar space that would work even if "classical" speeds are all that can be achieved—speeds in the low millions of miles per hour, for example. In the late 1950s, Dr. John Von Neumann, one of the pioneers of modern computer science, and called by the press "the smartest man in the world," postulated that there could be created something that has come to be known as the Von Neumann Machine.[13] Such a machine would be capable of duplicating the species that created it, traveling the universe until it found a suitable planet.

So even if there is to be no "warp drive," and even if interstellar travel is extremely slow, not only is it possible that somebody is here, but they might be in close touch with home despite the vast physical distances involved.

Even though the United States government appears to have possessed ample evidence that UFOs were real as far back as 1952, over the 1960s and 1970s it went out of the UFO business completely—at least, as far as the public was concerned. The Project Blue Book committee, chaired by Dr. Brian O'Brian and including Dr. Carl Sagan, declared that the UFO phenomenon did not threaten national security and that the committee could find "no UFO case which represented technological or scientific advances outside of a terrestrial framework." This was based on an assumption that interstellar travel was just too unlikely, an assumption that appears not to be all that supportable.

In retrospect, it is fair to ask if the committee's statement was a lie, given the fact that it should have

[13]John Von Neumann, *Theory of Self-Reproducing Automata* (Champaign: University of Illinois Press, 1966).

had access to the Newhouse film and should have been aware of Dr. Hill's work. He was well-known throughout the space sciences community as NASA's "UFO clearinghouse" by the time the report was published. And yet there is no evidence that he was even consulted. Given his credentials and the records and film he had available, his testimony alone would have been enough to compel the committee to come to an opposite conclusion.

Despite all this, the intelligence community and the Air Force continue to maintain that there is nothing wrong and aggressively to engage in the denial of UFO reports. In 1997, the CIA announced that it had used UFO stories as a cover for early flights of the U-2 spy plane,[14] but this still doesn't explain Dr. Hill's observations or the films he refers to. If UFOs are secret aircraft, then it means that as far back as 1962 we were in possession of vessels that could accelerate from a speed of one hundred to eighty-nine hundred miles an hour in four seconds.

This would mean that a part of humankind has technology so extraordinary that the rest of us are virtually a different, lesser species, confined to an over-crowded, dying planet while the others traverse the heavens like gods.

Frankly, it seems much more likely that UFOs have a nonhuman origin, if only because the technology they displayed back in the 1950s could have been used to bring the Cold War to a quick end, had either side had access to it, and this did not happen. What did happen—and what is happening—is indistinguishable from what would happen if aliens were not only here

---

[14]William J. Broad, "CIA Admits Government Lied About UFO Sightings," *The New York Times*, August 3, 1997, p. 12.

but also actively enforcing the secrecy that surrounds them.

As Dr. Hill's book makes clear, the government apparently did have evidence made by professionals that UFOs were real. It even invested in flying platform research that its own creator claims was inspired by observations of them, and at the time this research was highly classified. Whether the aliens—if that's what they are—and the government are hostile to one another, they agree on one thing: Both sides want the public to remain ignorant at the present time.

Now, why would that be?

Over the next two sections of this book, the answer to that question will become clear.

Part Two
CLOSE ENCOUNTER

Much madness is divinest sense
To a discerning eye . . .
Assent, and you are sane;
Demur,—you're straightway dangerous
And handled with a chain.

—Emily Dickinson,
"Much Madness Is Divinest Sense"

7:

An Emergency Situation

The evidence that UFOs are flying around in our skies is so extensive that it is reasonable to consider that these unconventional objects are in some way real, and that many of them seem to be under intelligent control.

The immediate question, then, is what sort of intelligence is involved—alien, human, or something else— and what does it want with us?

All sorts of arguments can be made for one hypothesis or another about what the visitors are, but there is little hard evidence to support any of them. What there is consists of a few brief videos of apparent aliens, some of the most famous of which may be fakes.

Nevertheless, it would appear that this intelligence has deposited a most unusual message among us, one that involves a compelling, possibly urgent, mystery. Very often, something happens to witnesses during encounter that leaves a total and complete blank that has been called "missing time." As somebody who has experienced it myself, I can attest to the fact that it is much more profound than simple forgetfulness. Missing time is different in the sense that you are left with a blankness, as if part of reality has been somehow removed. Memory can be lost, but I doubt if anybody who has experienced missing time would ever consider that this eerie inner absence is anything like normal forgetfulness.

Despite the barrier presented by missing time, an enormous number of people have claimed to have seen visitors and come back with some amazingly provocative memories. Just as waves of UFO sightings had been reported in the 1950s, in the 1960s people began reporting strange and intimate encounters with aliens. These reports have risen until, over the ten years since my own encounter and the publication of *Communion* in 1987, I have received nearly a quarter of a million letters claiming contact, with more than thirty thousand of them offering detailed descriptions of the encounters.

These letters present a completely new picture of the experience, one that has not yet been described by anybody, not the media, not UFO investigators, not the smattering of professionals who have the courage to deal with the subject.

There are three issues connected with these letters. The first is, do they originate in real experience? The second is, how, if at all, does some sort of filtering alter the memories? The third is the great mystery of close encounter, the fact that many witnesses report periods of time within their experiences that involve total amnesia. If we are ever going to understand this, we must bring light to that darkness.

Reading the letters and discovering their extreme strangeness, it became clear to me and my wife, Anne, that almost nothing is known about close encounter. Its complexity, its weirdness, and its amazing frequency suggested to us that we were literally looking at a message from another world that seemed to be relying on the witnesses themselves as its medium of communication.

Scientists tell us that we are dealing with dreams and hallucinations. The press agrees. The public, on the other hand, seems to suspect that the encounters are with aliens. Some behavioral scientists have theorized a perceptual level they call the "imaginal," which is more substantial than ordinary imagination but less so than physical reality.[1] But this work has never gone beyond the theoretical stage.

Unfortunately, the lack of authoritative answers has meant that hucksters and false experts have been exploiting public ignorance, and speculative cosmologies have emerged that not only treat the notion that aliens may be present as fact but even include detailed beliefs about where they are from and what they may be doing here. So powerful have these fantasies become that in March of 1997, a cult—most members aging and tired of waiting for "the landing"—committed mass suicide on behalf of their particular system of beliefs.

As we construct a picture of what people are actually reporting, certain things will become clear. First, this is the strangest thing that has ever happened. Second, compared to past descriptions of encounters with fairies, angels, sylphs, and so on, the modern experience is vastly more bizarre. Most of its imagery is, in fact, stunningly new. We are thus faced with the same problem that Montezuma's observers confronted when they were unable to communicate the real meaning of Cortez's attack to him until it was too late.

Having been able to examine so many thousands of narratives, I am in a position to construct a general

[1]Kenneth Ring, *The Omega Project* (New York: Morrow, 1992), p. 219: "Perhaps there is, after all, a third realm of the imagination in its own right, not as something unreal but as something objectively self-existent, the cumulative product of imaginative thought itself."

picture of what people actually say about their encounters, which is almost totally different from the
picture that has been built up in the press.

Not only that, the natural memory presented in the
letters is mostly different from the narratives that
emerge out of hypnosis. Even though there is a curious
symmetry to the natural recall, it is not the sort of
easily understood narrative of abduction and torment
that the hypnosis-derived stories suggest.

The one thing that I wish I could do and cannot is
to apply statistical analysis to the testimony. There has
never been a large-scale study done of the authors of
these narratives. It may even be that some of the letters
that I quote are hoaxes. But because every letter
quoted represents many others that are similar, at least
in overall structure if not in detailed content, this remains as representative a sample as I could derive
without professional support.

What is it actually like to have one of these encounters? From personal experience, I can tell you that
there is little in life with more impact. It has been ten
years since my first adult encounter, and I still remember it as vividly as if it was still happening. I think
about it, remember the sounds, the look of it, the feelings that I had. How many dreams do I remember
from ten years ago? None. My dreams have been forgotten, but that encounter is like a memory of meeting
the president or being in a plane crash: It has come to
rest in my mind as an extremely intense, entirely real
experience. Understand, I am not by this claiming that
it *was* real, only that it felt real then and it still does.

But what *happens*? What are the visitors like and
how do they act? Moreover, if they are really independent entities of some kind, then what are their motives, and is it safe or dangerous to be exposed to

them? And where are they from—another planet, another reality, or somewhere in the secret interior of ourselves? Can we ever identify them, or is it that we simply do not have the tools and the language to accomplish this?

One thing is certain: To properly address the issue of what is happening to people, we must abandon beliefs and embrace questions. The first belief to put aside is that close encounter, as we undergo it now, is a continuation of past experience of the unexplained. The fact is that the letters reveal something that is far more elaborate than what has been reported in the past. In this sense, they are like the reports of crop circles. Even though the first description of one dates from 1687, appearing in a woodcut from Hertfordshire, England, titled "The Mowing Devil," the crop circles of the past were trivial affairs compared to the extraordinary complexity of what appears today. And lest it be assumed that crop circles have been explained, they have not. Of course there are fakes. They're created every year, but even the best of them are distinguishable from the real anomalies.[2] The fakes are made with rollers, and the crops show evidence of mechanical crushing and bending. The mysterious ones—in general also the more complex and beautiful—are made in some unknown manner. The crop stems are bent, but not by pressure, because no breakage takes place. Even the gray film that coats growing stalks remains undisturbed, something that would be impossible if any conventional means of bending them was used. This does not prove that aliens are respon-

[2]"Clocking the Swirls of Summertime," *The Independent Long Weekend*, London, August 2, 1997, p 15.

sible. The use of unknown means suggests unknown origin but does not prove it.

The original descriptions of close encounter are, in a sense, as distinctive as genuinely mysterious crop circles. Even more telling, the arresting image of the large-headed alien with the huge black eyes that now appears throughout our culture was not present until recently. Although there exist a few suggestions in Sumerian and prehistoric Israeli art, and possibly from some cave paintings in Africa, this image was not part of the culture in any really large-scale way before the last few decades, or our art would be full of it.[3]

The close encounter experience, which has been the subject of a great deal of hysterical speculation and misguided reportage, is surrounded by false information. The first inaccuracy to address is that witnesses report seeing the same thing again and again, suggesting that some sort of organized scientific study of human beings by aliens is taking place. Witnesses do not report the same thing again and again, not even as a response to the lurid imagery that fills videos, books, and television shows.

And yet, dismissing the reports as hallucination doesn't work either. Multiple-witness contacts, which have hitherto been considered extremely rare, are actually commonplace and as such are, quite simply, indistinguishable from descriptions of real events.

It is obvious why the materials sciences have not studied the UFO phenomenon: Until now, there has been no material to study. But it is less clear why the behavioral sciences have not more carefully considered the condition of witnesses. Probably, the reason is that

---

[3]It first appeared on the cover of the June 1957 issue of *Fantastic Universe*, designed by Virgil Finlay.

most behavioral scientists assume that the commonly publicized abduction scenario is the beginning and end of the story—and thus that there is no story.

The *Chicago Tribune*, on April 23, 1997, published an article that amounts to a compendium of the commonly held assumptions.[4] According to the *Tribune* article, people who report these experiences are usually disturbed and looking into their past to understand why they feel that way. But the reality is different. Many of my correspondents describe events that have just happened to them, and few describe any mental disturbance beyond the fact that they are very naturally confused, curious, and sometimes frightened by what has happened.

That they are normal people is borne out by a number of studies of the broader spectrum of witnesses, none of which were referenced by the *Tribune*. Nor were all of these studies conducted by researchers sympathetic to the witnesses' claims. For example, in the November 1993 issue of the *Journal of American Psychology*, Nicholas Spanos reports on a study of close encounter witnesses. The study showed that such people are "neither psychologically disturbed nor especially fond of fashioning elaborate fantasies."[5] He theorizes that many of the encounters occurred during dreams that were mistakenly recalled as actual events, and others involved nightmares associated with sleep paralysis. To an extent this is probably true, but it does not explain the many encounters that start while the witness is wide awake, or the multiple-witness cases.

[4]"Spacing Out," Jeremy Manier, *Chicago Tribune Tempo*, April 23, 1997, p. 1.

[5]*Science News*, November 13, 1993.

The *Tribune* article goes on to explain that "hypnosis is invariably the preferred method" in dealing therapeutically with these disturbances, with the result that false memories are elicited. But most witnesses never get near a hypnotist, and in any case, it isn't at all clear that hypnosis is without value as a tool in memory recovery. In the hands of a skilled professional, it can obviously be useful. Unfortunately, close encounter witnesses who are subjected to it are often working with investigators who hypnotize them again and again until their story agrees with an accepted scenario, and do become victims of the misuse of the technique.

We will build our image of close encounter out of the natural memories of people who have had continuous recall of their experiences from the time they happened. Recovered memory and recall generated under hypnosis form a small part of the close encounter narrative actually available and will not be used here at all.

The *Tribune* article goes on to say that the typical abduction story "adheres to a script" involving the humiliation of the witness and featuring a ritual strapping to a table, followed by strange medical experiments and sexual intrusions.

Even if this sort of script were commonplace, which it is not, why would the UFO stories take such a frightening turn? Interviewed for the article, University of Washington psychologist Elizabeth Loftus suggested that "you get more attention these days if you tell a story with sex in it." This implies that witnesses are seeking publicity or notice of some kind. In reality, witnesses are so desperate that their anonymity be preserved that it takes requests to about ten people to find one who will allow his or her story to be told publicly—and then, for the most part, only if anonymity is strictly preserved. They have good reason for this reticence, too. I know of only a few witnesses whose names have appeared publicly who have not suffered tremendously as a result. Even a brief appearance on the radio or television can lead to a ruined life.

So the picture presented in the *Tribune* of the close encounter witness as a disturbed individual seeking attention, who has been further damaged by hypnosis, would not appear to reflect the vast majority of actual people reporting this experience. That it adheres to a script is deeply believed by some UFO groups. In the Mutual UFO Network's Information Center in Seguin, Texas, there is an illustration—engraved as if in stone and looking like an Egyptian frieze—of what is now believed to be the typical abduction experience. The human victim is carried by coldly robotic aliens into a UFO, placed on a table, and subjected to horrendous and inexplicable medical procedures.

But we get only a smattering of letters that describe this. The reason that it came to be assumed that this was the whole of the close encounter experience is that it was heavily publicized and is easy to understand: Alien scientists are studying us and exploiting us. They're cold and uncaring, emotionless, ruthless, and cruel. In other words, they are the enemy, the *other*— not so very different from the cold, often mechanistic imagery generated about outsiders by tribal cultures.

But if this scenario was not true, why would researchers who are making a sincere effort to understand what is going on assert that it represents fact? It is too easy to assume that they are simply incompetent or conspiring to create a false impression. Knowing many of them as well as I do, I feel quite certain that they are entirely sincere, and I would not doubt that there is something useful to be understood from this story. Later, one of the most compelling of the implant cases will turn out to be involved with the very sort of sexual assault that they claim is happening.

And if our close encounters are indeed with aliens, wouldn't they have an obvious motive for obtaining sexual and genetic material? If we found creatures on another planet, these are among the first things we would want for study. Additionally, we might very well breed animals from that planet for scientific reasons. Whether or not we would do the same with intelligent species we found there would depend on our approach to the ethical issues.

What appears, swimming up like some shadowy creature of the dark unconscious ocean, is very bizarre, but also—in an odd way—very logical. To enter the world of these narratives is to discover what appears to be the working of a nonhuman mind, or of a part of the human mind so hidden that it has never before gained a voice.

Individually, the stories are incredible. But taken together, they are beyond the incredible. Whether it comes from deep within us or from out among the stars, we are most certainly dealing with a communication from another world. Again and again, the letters present one consistency: The witness is challenged, often with devastating power, to look at self and life in a new way. The challenge cannot be ignored, because to do so is to surrender oneself to a descent into total psychological and spiritual chaos.

This, then, is the threat and promise of the close encounter experience, as recounted by thousands and thousands of witnesses: whether it is to be welcomed, borne, or fought, it must be faced. We must wake up and stop being passive to it. In doing this, we must also face its central mystery: What happens during missing time?

In *Communion*, I theorized that it may be what the force of evolution looks like when it applies itself to a conscious mind. I would suggest that this is probably the best of my many notions about the visitors, especially because it refers only to their effect in our world, a question we can usefully address no matter whether "they" are aliens or not.

Where are they from? Until we can begin to see the real magnitude of that question and cope with its complexity, it is probably better that we don't have any biological remains to lead us to the certitude that they are from another world.

What, after all, might one mean by the term "another world"? Obviously, that could mean another planet upon which has evolved a species with an ability to reach here. But it could also mean another *sort* of world altogether, one that swims in the ocean of our being, or one that contains us in the same sense that the universe contains its stars. It could mean something extraordinary about us as well, after all, could "another world."

Whatever it means, there is one thing about it that we *can* examine and, if we keep our wits about us, even understand. That is the message that has appeared among us and within us, in the form of all these letters from all these people, each of whom bears a tiny part of the whole enormous document. It is in decoding this message that we will probably find the first true answers about the motives of the visitors and get our first real hints of their true nature.

But it isn't simply a matter of collating letters and extracting "the facts." There really aren't any facts of that sort to be had, not yet. What is available is a sort of tool, one that can teach us how it feels to grapple with missing time and to cope with experiences that unfold on a larger-than-ordinary mental scale.

As we journey through this wild country, we will find again and again that the message points not toward the alien but toward the human: Who are we, who would react as we have to this strange intrusion into our lives and souls, at once hiding from it and displaying ourselves to it like testing adolescents?

If it is possible to find out, it would seem that it must begin with a careful examination of testaments like these.

8:

The Journey Begins

It is the wee hours of the morning, and all is quiet. Softly, swiftly, a shadow comes, passing above the houses, moving less quickly now, coming closer and closer yet, stopping, hovering in the night sky above one certain house, blotting out the stars. A sleeper sighs, stirs. Briefly, light shines down on the house. A dog grumbles, the sleeper begins to dream. . . .

And then, eyes fly open, the sleeper sits up, astonishment bringing a cry that is instantly stifled—

The mystery begins: Is the sleeper seeing figures of dream, or real, flesh-and-blood creatures . . . or perhaps something so strange that we are going to have a hard time even finding words to describe it? Hard, but because of those hundreds of thousands of people who have already tried, no longer impossible. We can weave their descriptions together to create a tapestry, shimmering with strange colors, suggestive of new meanings—a tapestry of language about things that we have not thus far named . . . at least not in any way that seems deeply true.

The visitors approach in many different ways. Often, it's studied and careful, especially when groups of people have their encounters together. But equally often, there is total, stunning surprise.

"I went to bed late and I reckon my head had been on the pillow for less than thirty seconds, when, for want of a better word, it exploded." Thus begins a testament that exemplifies one of the most characteristic manifestations of the close encounter experience: the overwhelming, devastating, and total assault on the deepest sense of being and worth.

Although the established picture of the experience is that it usually wakes people up and is therefore explainable as sleep disturbance, that is very far from true. Equally often, it starts when they are wide awake: "The next thing I remember is the breath being knocked out of me as I somehow went through the windshield of the car."

Even testimony as incredible as this is not all that uncommon. Incidents while driving usually happen on the highway rather than city streets, and the witness ends up unharmed but in possession of some extremely bizarre memories. Sometimes, when the encounter ends, the car is found to be miles from where it was when the experience started. Other times, it appears as if no time has passed at all.

Encounters often involve more than one witness and are indistinguishable from real experiences in their structure—although not their content. It was from such encounters, starting in the early 1970s, that the modern image of the alien with the long thin face and huge black eyes emerged.

One day in 1984, two friends were traveling together when "my car was completely immersed in light inside and my hair felt like it was standing up on my arms and head. Even my complete body seemed quickened now at this moment I know something is going on and the light seemed to be centered in behind us. As I started looking over at Fred, I noticed in the rear view mirror an image.

"There sitting in the back seat was this white beautiful creature with very bony thin arms, legs and rib cage, long skinny arms with very long fingers twiddling them while slightly turning its head looking us over. Its eyes were very large and tear drop shaped, its nose and mouth area were small. Eyes were very black, chin was prominent almost like the lower jaw of an ant. I knew instantly this creature was highly intelligent."[1]

The two witnesses stared at each other in amazement, and then they had a period of missing time. They have discussed the matter often over the years, but without coming to any understanding of what happened to them. It is possible, of course, to dismiss their experience as a seizure-related hallucination that was communicated from one party to the other by suggestion, but this seems disingenuous, in the sense that it amounts to rejecting it simply because it is too strange to accept.

At the same time, the question begs to be asked: What *did* happen in that car—if anything? As I said earlier, I have not personally investigated all of these letters, and its perfectly possible that hoaxes are involved. The problem is, as will be seen, they're *all* this strange—or stranger. Surely a hoax would unfold along more accepted lines, involving perhaps a vivid tale of being taken aboard a UFO and treated to the sort of interaction described in conventional abduction literature. After all, isn't the hoaxer's objective to be believed?

Who is going to believe a story like this, though? Two men are riding in a car that, after a bath of light from above, ends up with an edgy, finger-twiddling

[1]All quotations in chapters 8 through 11 are from letters sent to the Communion Foundation and used with permission of their authors.

alien sitting in the back seat? Perhaps the story should at least be entertained, if only because it contains so many elements that are hardly present in the published literature but are commonplace to the actual reports. For example, the alien seems to have come in right through the roof of the car. Just as it is not unusual for people to find themselves flying through windshields, roofs, and solid walls, it is also quite ordinary for the aliens themselves to pass through solid objects and to appear and disappear at will.

How such reports relate to reality is not known, but there is some interesting research (to be discussed in Chapter Twelve) that opens up the possibility that we may one day be able to differentiate between memories of actual, physical events and memories that a witness only thinks are real.

Encounters often involve groups of witnesses, and when they do, they often begin with the appearance of a UFO. Soon after, one or more of the people who saw it have a close encounter. However, it is extremely rare that the close encounter feels "normal." Witnesses begin to drift mentally; they seem to become almost hypnotized; they experience the sensation of static electricity tickling their skin, they have allergic reactions. But if these symptoms are seizure-related, then why would two people become seized at the same time, and why don't the cars involved get wrecked? And what about the imagery? In 1984, the particularly arresting alien image that was reported above was not yet commonplace. The letter does not say if either man had a preexisting awareness of it.

But it was around, certainly, in 1984. However, some of the most vivid alien imagery comes from long before the form had acquired a place in the culture. A typical example is this description of something that happened when this witness was five, back in 1954:

"Something came through the wall that looked like a man, but it was not human. Whatever it was, it had substance and was solid matter. It bent forward until its face, if one can call it a face, was only about two feet from mine. The most dominant physical feature of this thing was its long, thin nose and it had arms and legs that were thin as broomsticks."

If this was just a child's fantasy, then why aren't there descriptions of images like this from earlier eras? Did this form of fantasy just begin? In fact, this sort of imagery doesn't start to be remarked on in the psychological literature until the 1970s, when the mental health community was just starting to grapple with the alien encounter experience.

The experience develops in many different ways, and many do not involve the alien image at all. Hundreds of witnesses report, for example, that they see balls of light that seem to have conscious direction. They are a commonplace of the experience that links it to other visitation imagery. In many cultures, they are associated with the souls of the dead, and it will be seen later that there is something about the close encounter experience that is deeply involved with death and the dead.

Another initiating event involves the blow to the body. "As I lay on the bed sleeping, I was suddenly awakened by some kind of force which hit me right in the center of my chest."

Sometimes this seems to shock the witness into a wider view of reality, not unlike a Zen slap. One Zen practitioner, after reading *Communion*, said to me, "fifteen seconds with the visitors, fifteen years of meditation." I would not entirely agree, but certainly this is a blow that sends the mind off on a long, long journey into places where mystery, dream, and truth mix in a maddening but potentially fruitful brew of questions.

Sometimes the shock of the approach is even more impressive than the Zen slap: "They were dressed like 1920s thugs, and came into the bedroom with old fashioned Tommy Guns, aiming at me and blazing away. I felt the pellets bounce off my torso, and for several days I had pains in the chest. . . . They seem to delve into nascent fears, test a person, and then return with all kinds of amazing compensations."

So in part—and perhaps great part—this communication would appear to be about us. It starts with a stunning surprise, then builds from there upon the wreckage of shattered beliefs. What it seems to be about, on this level, is the destruction of the witness's faith in his or her assumptions about reality. One witness's head explodes, another goes blasting out through a windshield, a third is slammed in the chest, a fourth gets attacked with machine guns. In other words, the message is: wake up, the world is not as you thought.

But the delivery of this message does not end the experience. Far from it. At this point things get really strange and really provocative, because this is when the witness usually ends up facing the mystery of missing time.

Hypnosis has been used to try to access it, but so far this effort has suffered from the total lack of reference points. Given that there is absolutely no basic memory to provide a foundation, there is no way to tell if the recovered memories are real. To explore the issue further, it is necessary to add more dimension to the approach phase of the experience, because this is where many of the richest and most detailed material comes from. Here is an example:

"Directly in the middle of the yard was a large metal saucer-like vehicle. The vehicle was much smaller than I might have guessed.

"As long as I felt like an observer, I was content to watch this peculiar drama unfold. There were four or five small kids walking out of the ship onto the lawn. I can remember thinking that this was absolutely an amazing stunt that these individuals were pulling off.

"These kids were much smaller than I was and were no threat to me. I would estimate that they were probably the size of a five or six year old. They were wearing body hugging dull silver/gray suits that seemed to cover them completely from head to toe.

"Why did their parents allow them out so late? These type of thoughts were the prevailing ones in my mind at the time.

"The tiny occupants walked across the lawn heading toward the end of the driveway. They walked down the driveway and stood directly in front of me, but fifteen feet or so down from my window. I found it humorous that they would not be able to climb up to my window.

"As soon as I had presented this thought, I noticed two of them take something from nowhere and let the item unfold before them. I quickly saw that it was a ladder of some sort. I perceived it to be a rope ladder with metal hooks on the ends. I became completely amused at the simplicity of the tools which a seemingly advanced group of beings were forced to use to enter my domain. For sure this was an elaborate hoax.

"I heard the metal ends of the ladder as they gripped tightly on the window sill directly in front of my face. I saw them with my own two eyes right in front of my nose. My heart started racing as fear began to consume me. The tiny kids were about to climb up to my window, but why?

"I saw the fingers of the first to reach my window as they reached up to pull themselves up by the ledge. These were *not* people fingers. There were only four of them and they were a different color. They seemed to have a bulbous look to them.

"It was when the head started to peep up over the ledge directly two inches in front of my face that I lost it. The head was donning no helmet. It was completely hairless with wrinkles like frown marks across the brow line. The color was that of a dead person, kind of ashen. It was about to pull itself up to where we would be eye to eye when I became so terrified that I was no longer able to witness this scenario any longer. I flew out of the room screaming."

Usually, when people are awake during the approach, they feel a sense of menace and they flee or, if they can't, they struggle. Although I am trying to base this discussion on letters that are representative of the whole, I would like at this point to turn to one that is unique, because if it is true, the insight it offers is so valuable. I have met this woman, a teacher and a grandmother, a gentle and straightforward person. She told this extraordinary story, I believe, just as she remembered it.

"In 1976 I was vacuuming my living room floor at about noon. Suddenly I felt quite ill and thought I was going to vomit, so I sat down on the couch to see if the sick feeling would subside. I then saw that I was not alone; there were three strange little people standing alongside the couch, just looking at me. I froze with fear, as I had never seen anything like them before, not even in the movies.

"Two of them were short and fat, about four to four and a half feet tall, with broad faces and enormous black eyes, but with only a hint of where a nose or mouth might have been, almost like a pencil drawing. They had wispy bits of brown hair at the back of their heads, and they didn't have blue suits on like the ones you described in *Communion*; instead, they were wearing brown shrouds. These, I knew instinctively, were the workers. The other was female, thin and about five feet tall. She wore a black shroud and had black wispy hair at the back of her head. Her face was very elongated, with huge, dark, piercing eyes, and once again just a hint of where a nose or mouth would have been.

"The tall thin one started to speak to me with her mind, and told me I was to go with them. I answered with my own mind that I wouldn't go. Somehow, telepathic communication seemed perfectly normal at the time, and I felt quite comfortable communicating that way. This doesn't mean that I wasn't frightened—I was beside myself with fear."

As her mind came under the control of whatever was affecting her, she naturally experienced extreme terror. She describes herself as literally crawling toward the front door in her effort to escape. There she saw a vision of her husband. Gratefully, she embraced him, only to be dragged back. At that point her resistance broke and she gave up trying to escape.

From that moment on, there is no memory, not for hours. When her husband finally did arrive home, she could hardly believe that it was really him. He had been at work all day. It seemed that they had drawn an illusion of the most powerful figure she knew out of her mind and broken her will by showing her that they could overcome it.

Nothing has enabled her to recall one second of what happened after she was overpowered. She lost about four hours of memory, which seem to be completely inaccessible to recovery.

For the most part, the structure of the ordinary doesn't depart until missing time begins. In many cases, there are substantial numbers of witnesses, often whole families, involved together in the encounter. These encounters, especially when they start during the day when people are awake, are remembered in great detail. It is from the ultrahigh-level strangeness of this detail that my own suspicion that we are dealing with an alien presence comes.

"At about nine P.M., what I thought was a large car with bright headlights rolled down our gravel driveway." The witness looked outside but saw no car and so dismissed the incident—for the moment.

"We slept until about seven A.M., and when I was back at the kitchen sink after breakfast, I looked out the window to see a woman in a red windbreaker jacket enter the stables. She was wearing white pants and was holding a long stick in her hand.

"Then I saw a man jump off the pumphouse nearby. He was small, with brown hair, and seemed to bounce in a way that had no relation to gravity.

"Next, I left to do some marketing, and when I returned, my husband walked up to me and said, 'There are people in the trees! We've been trying to talk to them but they won't answer.'

"I looked and saw that whoever was up there had constructed some sort of platform.

"We went upstairs to look out of the bedroom window. I said to my daughter, 'Do you see what I see?' She said, 'Yes, Mom, there's two of them. What's that thing coming out of that one's head?'

"There was some kind of beautiful beaded antenna sticking out of the left side of the head of one of the beings. One of them looked slightly oriental, and the other seemed more caucasian, but smaller and with a brown mustache. One of them had on a remarkable piece of jewelry—it was a band striped in different metals of all colors: silver, gold, platinum, green, red, purple and black.

"Since they continued to ignore us, we went downstairs and outside again. I let out our Rotweiler dog. This caused a commotion, and I saw ten or twelve pairs of legs, all wearing white pants, scamper away up the hill. I let go of the dog and as I approached the house, I saw a woman who was the same type of being you describe in your books. She was dressed in a kelly green jumpsuit and was too long and thin to be a human being. She was climbing among the branches of one of the trees next to the house. I said, 'You have no right to do that without my permission, you should have asked.'

"Back upstairs, at the bathroom window this time, I was able to get a closer look at her. She was unlike anything I've ever seen. Her arms were long and unbelievably thin, and she had some sort of faun colored soft leather flight cap on, of the type that pilots used to wear in the old-fashioned cockpits of early planes. She was also wearing goggles from the same era, although the lenses were shaped to fit her large, slanted eyes. She had soft looking gloves on, and her jumpsuit was closed down the front with some sort of metal fasteners. She looked like she was engaged in filming, and aimed a black video-type gadget directly at me."

The witness's husband came in, but the being had disappeared. The witness then ran downstairs and out-

side, still attempting to get a better look at what was
going on.

"Then I saw the most incredible being that I have
ever seen. It was almost indescribable—a silver crystal,
moving mass of energy and light with the exact same
striped band of jewelry that I described before on it."

Later, the family felt unsure about this whole experience. It had been vivid at the time, but the high
level of strangeness made it hard later for all of them
to be certain that it had been real.

There was, however, a sequel that suggested that it
was all too real. "I got very ill after that visit. The
following week, I lost thirteen pounds. I needed two
liters of intravenous fluids the following Friday. My
littlest one has ground her teeth down, and pulls the
covers entirely over her head every night, but we're
more calm about it than we used to be."

So what happened to this family? A careful reading
of the letter suggests that there was a great deal of
missing time involved, and that whatever happened
was so stressful that this woman and her youngest
child were left with severe trauma.

Again, missing time. So the question must be asked,
is there any way to raise that curtain, because if we
don't raise it, we aren't going to be able to understand
what is happening to us.

And so the visitors approach, the sleeper awakens,
and we learn a little bit more. But the gate to the unknown is barely open. We can't yet guess what happens during missing time.

Or is that really true? With care and cunning, we
might be able to shine more light than one might think
into that particular dark corner.

9:

Beyond the Dark

The moment that human eyes meet visitor eyes, the world usually goes black. But not always. Not all of the assaults—if they are assaults—are successful, and a great deal can be learned from the people who actually fight off the visitors. This next series of cases offer a startling sense of continuity as each witness in succession penetrates the darkness a little more deeply. This first case is an example of the witness fighting off what was apparently an attempt at abduction. The witness had lain back on his bed only to feel, as mentioned in the last chapter, a sensation of his head literally exploding. He then went deeper into the experience, much deeper.

"After a few seconds, the vacuum of what used to be me was filled by an entity of total evil. This evil thing so terrified me that I wanted to start fighting, until I became conscious that I was unable to move my limbs. Although I was screaming to my wife to wake up and help me, my lips barely moved and the screams were whispers."

This state is characteristic of people in hypnagogic trances, a harmless, mildly seized condition that can occur during the process of waking up. In this state, the subject will often observe the "old hag," a hideous apparition that generally sits on the victim's chest. The condition persists until the individual manages to break the paralysis, whereupon the whole thing evaporates like a mirage.

In this case, the initial sensation passed as soon as the witness could move and scream—a situation characteristic of a waking dream and in no way remarkable. But what happened next is totally beyond explanation:

"We had decided to turn off the light and get some sleep, when we both said, 'What's that noise?'

"We heard a low humming sound. A quick glance at the clock told us it was two-thirty A.M. The humming soon changed to a deep, fast throbbing. It didn't sound like a plane, or a truck, or a car. It got louder and stopped right over the roof of the house, directly above our bedroom. There were no flashing or glowing lights, just a very loud thumping sound right over our double bed. We froze; what on earth could be on the roof?"

By now both of them were wide awake and terrified. When I met and talked to this witness, the fear that he had experienced on that night was still in his eyes, despite the years that had passed.

The next thing he knew, "Something invisible grabbed me by the chest and started pulling with amazing force. I felt like my soul, not my body, was being pulled up vertically towards the loud throbbing noise, and although I thought it would be futile, I screamed for Sally to lie on top of me. When she did this, the sensation of pulling eased a little."

What was being drawn out of this man? I have discussed it with him, and his impression was that the part of him that could think and feel was being separated from the physical part of his body.

"I was screaming and struggling against an invisible 'beam,' with my wife lying on top of me in my bed at

two-thirty A.M. What a sight we would have presented
if someone had walked in! It might have seemed funny
later, if it hadn't gone on for another two hours."

A shocking situation and indicative of just how persistent the close encounter experience can be when
somebody has been singled out. But, in this case, his
will proved stronger than whatever was hovering over
his house, and the attempt eventually ended. Toward
dawn, the couple fell asleep. Subsequently, this very
successful man has gone on to pursue his career without any further nocturnal interruptions.

It is not enough to say that some wandering demon
came along and tried to rip this man's soul from his
body. As Monsignor Balducci points out in the appendix, we can do better than to approach the situation
with assumptions like this that do not actually fit the
situation. It isn't even obvious that this was a negative
experience, because the witness became deeply aware
of himself in a new and richly rewarding way. He was
plunged directly into the mystery of the soul by his
experience.

Amazingly, even though this man stayed in his bed,
the story can still be continued. This is because this
precise thing has happened to other people at other
times, and not everybody has managed to fight off the
attack. So our original objective of recovering something from the missing time experience still has not
been defeated. Although the two had never met, this
next witness faced exactly the same experience as the
first one, except that his struggle against the pulling
force did not succeed.

"Then I was pulled up and through the ceiling head
first. I reappeared in a large room with a high ceiling,
or no ceiling. I seemed to be floating. I looked up and
saw long ropes hanging down, lots of them. They were

thick, maybe six inches around, and that part of the room was full of them. I was close to one rope and it looked like it had white cocoon webbing all over it."

It is not entirely unexpected that this extraordinary memory from the dark would be so strange. In all probability, one of the reasons that we cannot remember missing time is that what happens there is so bizarre and so hard to understand that it simply does not come together in a coherent enough way to form a memory. The witness is left with a feeling that something important has taken place, but he or she cannot form it into a structure. But not in the case of this witness. As the situation developed, his memory continued its penetration of the unknown:

"I saw someone across from me, about twenty feet away. He was white and misty and I knew it was a male. Someone was observing me close up on my left, out of my field of vision. As I became aware of this, I said, 'May I look at you?' The answer was, 'No, you may not.' It was female and also firm, as if talking to a child. I obeyed as if I was indeed a child.

"I started to turn to my left to see who it was that had spoken to me. As I did, I started to panic and screamed bloody murder. I saw the top of a bald white head, and holes for eyes."

With the advent of fear, the light of memory is extinguished. The next thing the witness knew, he was back in his bed and wondering whether he had been dreaming. But he at least took us to the portals of the cave, even though we have as yet shone no light on what happens in its depths.

This next event also took place in the predawn hours, which is the time when sleep is deepest, when most deaths and births occur, when our dreams are at their most powerful, and when most close encounters take place.

"I was trying to go back to sleep when I really felt strange. It was like I was being forced to close my eyes and fall asleep. I knew I was not dreaming. I fought this feeling and struggled with all my strength. It was horrible. I felt I was being taken, not my body but my soul.

"I remember that 'they' won and I couldn't fight anymore."

Like the woman who had been caught while vacuuming and the one who had been captured by the beings coming up the ladder, the next part of this interaction was a total blank. But this time a new wrinkle was added. So far, all of the encounters we have been discussing were one-time-only affairs. This case, though, proved to be different.

The witness reports that her experience began recurring almost daily. She continues, "I then became unexpectedly pregnant." The experiences became less during the pregnancy, but when she brought her daughter home, "the first night was extremely restless. I sensed evil, as if something was trying to get my baby. I stayed up all night praying by her side. I did wake up to see a short shadow at our doorway."

During her work as a nurse, she had a powerful conversation with a dying patient during which he suggested to her that she not fight. She decided to follow his advice, with fascinating results.

"Since he told me not to fight it, I don't. It's not so scary anymore. I let it happen. Just once, I remember hearing a female voice say, 'Come here.' It sounded either very old, or computerized."

"I have grown spiritually so much in the last eight

months. I now call the experiences a spiritual awakening."

Unfortunately, she does not tell us what precisely is creating her newfound spirituality, but she has indeed taken us a little deeper.

There have been whole books written about missing time and what it may contain. But most of these stories have either come from long series of hypnosis sessions or have been derived from channeled information. So this information seems even harder to take at face value than the more conventional memories and dreams reported here. And beyond these letters, there just isn't much that has been recovered in natural memory from those concealed hours.

So if we cannot penetrate missing time any more deeply without resorting to unproved memory recovery techniques, is it necessary to stop?

Actually, no. There is an indirect approach. As simple as it is, it also offers the twin advantages of continuing to stay with natural memory and to support it whenever possible with more than one witness.

It would seem that there are people who don't have missing time at all.

"My greatest experience was when I was walking home late one night from a friend's house. As I was crossing a bridge, I noticed something strange. I was glowing; everything was glowing. What looked like a glowing fishnet crossed the entire sky. To my left, upriver and above at about two thousand feet, something that looked like a giant manta ray without a tail sat motionless."

The witness sat on the bank of the river where he had been walking and watched the phenomenon from early morning until noon. Nobody else saw it—maybe because he was having a waking dream. But, then again, it was a very strange one:

"What appeared to be a blue glowing ball with sparks flying off of it hovered at eye level just barely out of my left field of vision, keeping a distance of about a hundred feet from me."

Encounter has a lot of peripheral effects, among them dark blue, fast-moving figures such as the woman vacuuming her living room saw, and, as this witness describes, glowing balls of light. They are generally seen in peripheral vision, and people often mention that they are somewhere to the left.

This suggests a neurological component involved in these observations that may well in some way be seizure-related. This is not to say that the observations are hallucinations but rather that the brain of the witness is being affected and his or her perceptual abilities interfered with.

After making the observations reported above, this witness proceeded on his way and found himself observing numerous people in the area who, as he puts it, "didn't seem to fit into the local culture." More disconcerting, they seemed to know him.

Behind this seemingly simple comment there lies an almost totally unremarked but not too surprising aspect of the experience: the implication that there is a human connection of some kind, that not all of the visitors are strange alien forms, but rather that people are often involved.

It is when people are involved on the "other" side of an encounter that missing time seems most often not to occur at all.

Even though some extremely strange aliens have been reported, any discussion of the forms the visitors take must begin with the human. From the beginning, there has existed this undercurrent of human involvement.

If there are aliens here, then it obviously wouldn't be impossible that they would be working with human beings. If so, then it is unfortunate that these people are also isolated behind a veil of secrecy.

In discussing the experience in terms of its human component, it is possible to go deeper than the mere fact that people are seen in the company of aliens. There's more to it than that—much more. For example, there is this sort of story:

"Suddenly I felt something smooth rubbing my open right hand, and when I opened my eyes I was surprised to find that a hybrid child was holding my wrist with both hands and rubbing the top of his head with my own hand! He was looking right at me and grinning, and for some reason this tickled me; he was so cute.

"There was also a normal little girl with dark brown, longish hair, wearing a dress with petticoats. She was about four, and was trying to pry open the fingers of my left hand. I asked the hybrid what he was doing and he telepathically said, 'I'm chewing purple gum.' "

This charming anecdote did not lead to any great revelations, but it does take our concept of the experience a step farther away from the stories of alien scientists here engaging in some sort of an organized study of humankind. It would seem that the imagery connected with close encounter is light-years beyond this. Certainly it doesn't fit our folklore in any meaningful way, beyond the fact that some of the visitors are small like elves and seem to possess the power of gods. But what they do—well, there isn't any folklore about fairies who chew purple gum.

But how does this relate to the quest to crack the shell of missing time? To answer that question, we can go a little deeper, into the stories that explore the connection between close encounter and death. By looking at these stories—which are generally absent from current close encounter literature—we may begin to see why the fears that surround the hidden hours are so incredibly deep.

"About twelve years ago, when I was six to eight months pregnant, I woke up and saw this white form standing beside my bed. It showed me something and I said, 'Hey, that's my kid!' I then felt a kick in my stomach. For a long time after that, I thought something was going to happen to the child I was carrying. As it turned out, during my ninth month, my five year old son was killed in an accident a few yards away from the house. I gave birth three weeks later."

The close encounter experience has been terribly trivialized by the attempt to force it to appear comprehensible and believable. It is not possible to understand, and it is awfully hard to believe—or even to theorize about what *might* be happening.

But stories connecting it with birth and death abound among the letters we have received, so it makes sense to follow them, as far as they may take us from present ideas about the form of the contact experience. By doing this, we come to the borderland between life and death—and what are probably some of the most powerful experiences human beings have ever had.

In the 1960s, a mother and her small daughter were driving by night across the Mojave Desert. "About two hours outside of Flagstaff, my daughter began to shout that she saw a spaceship in the sky." She looked in the direction that the child was pointing and observed "first two and then three lights moving rapidly in the sky, turning at ninety degree angles, pulsating and disappearing." She then pulled off the road onto a dirt track. They were sitting there watching the sky "when suddenly in front of the car there appeared a huge, dark and glowing object with a partial row of lights in the middle."

She then remembered her breath being knocked out of her and being pulled through the windshield of the car. She found herself in a large room with some very strange-looking people. She was filled "with a feeling of love or long-lost family; it was almost like a homecoming." Her daughter was not there, though, and this concerned her.

"They kept saying 'Welcome, welcome!' in my mind, and laughing. They then told me some strange things about human origins and alien intervention on the planet earth at various times in the past and future.

"There was a whole generation of beings that came to earth in the far past and took up earth life. They were from the family of Ranm. They said that was why the old god names were as they were on earth: Rama, Brahma, Ra, Abraham, etc., in order that humans might remember. But so much confusion set in that the names became designations for gods or heroes, and that wasn't the point at all."

Once reassured that her daughter would be fine, she "was strangely soothed and unusually happy." But not for long. She was told that they were in some way sorry about her daughter, but they did not say why. When she was returned to the car, "my daughter was in the back seat crying." She told her horrified mother never to touch her again. "I tried to calm her and ask her what had happened to her and she shouted, 'I'll never tell you! Leave me alone!' "

They then drove to California, the mother hoping that the incident would be forgotten. But, as is characteristic of close encounter witnesses, she soon began having difficulty sleeping and became ill. "My hair began to fall out and my mouth started bleeding, and I was exhausted."

Her daughter was suffering, too, and one night woke up screaming. When her mother calmed her, "she said very factually, 'Mommy, I'm going to die. The spaceship people told me so. They said little bugs had gotten into my body and they were sorry, but there was nothing they could do since I'm a little girl.'"

She then began to display symptoms as well: high fever and swollen joints. She was diagnosed with rheumatoid arthritis, but there was also concern that she had been exposed to radiation. They returned to their home in Texas, where "she was diagnosed with a very rare cancer of the nervous system, neuroblastoma, and it had metastasized, and she had just a few months to live.

"Before her death, she began to draw extraordinary pictures that were more advanced than a ten year old's, even though she was only three and a half."

This terrible event continued to have unusual repercussions in the grieving mother's life. After the child's funeral, a friend called from a city two hundred miles away, saying that she had to drive to see her immediately. "Without glasses, she was legally blind, but she drove anyway. She said that two nights before at about two-twenty A.M., she was awakened by a noise and then saw her roof begin to dissolve. In the air above, she saw a type of spaceship. Two tall beings appeared, and in between them was my daughter. They told her they hadn't been able to get through to me because of something, but to let me know that my daughter was okay and was with them! She thought at that point that she'd gone completely insane. I broke my promise to myself to never tell the story of the experience in the desert and told her what had happened that night, and we both cried and cried."

If this was the only such story, it would be powerful enough, but the fact is that it is one among a whole class of the stories that emerge when there is no missing time.

Another such event took place a few years ago in the southeastern United States. A husband and wife were sitting in their downstairs living room at about ten o'clock at night, with the elderly family dog sleeping on the floor between them. Even though he had already been walked, he suddenly became nervous and began to pace. The wife decided to take him out again.

As she opened the front door, two things happened simultaneously. The first was that an orange ball of light swept away from the house, disappearing across a nearby line of trees. The next second, the couple's ten-year-old son came running downstairs yelling excitedly that "little blue men" had brought his older brother into the bedroom, and the older boy had a message: tell his mom and dad that he was okay.

I was deeply moved when the man narrating this story to me over the telephone concluded it with the statement: "Mr. Strieber, our seventeen-year-old died in an auto accident last week, and we want to know if there's any way that this story might be true."

I talked to him for a long time, trying to be supportive without making claims that could not be substantiated. I could not tell this man that aliens with the power over life and death had brought his son to him to relieve the agony of grief that he and his family were enduring. But I could say that there were others out there like them, whose lives had been lit in just the same way by the strange and powerful light of close encounter.

Does this suggest, though, that human beings come into this world with some sort of a life plan, and that whoever is behind the close encounters understands this level of reality and can actually see and even adjust such plans? If so, then if they ever come out into the open, we can expect our lives and our world to change in some extremely fundamental ways.

Among them would be confirmation that the soul exists and probably also that it can in some way be touched by science. In the past, as scientific understanding has increased, the borders of what is considered to be supernatural have been pushed farther and farther back. What was witchcraft in 1650 was science in 1750, and, if the soul exists, I suspect that the same process will eventually include it within the boundaries of the known. So our science may someday also include a technology of the soul, and the curtain between the worlds of the living and the dead will finally be raised.

Then there will be no more missing time. But we need not wait in order to continue to explore it, because we have not yet come to the end of the letters. There are other mysteries, tales of sexual encounter and journeys to other worlds, trips through time and meetings with some very remarkable creatures indeed, and the most amazing stories of all, those that come to us from childhood, when our eyes were too wide open for us not to see.

10:

Innocence

Perhaps the reason memories from childhood are so rich is that our minds are more flexible when we are young and more capable of being open to what adults reject as impossible.

One witness wrote of a childhood adventure he'd had near Hamilton Air Force Base in California. "In a small gully we encountered a shimmering mirage effect that reflected the sides of the gully as mirrors reflect the sides of a magician's box. Going through the mirage, we found a large tunnel that led deep into the hill."

Once inside, this group of small boys with BB guns made an unusual discovery.

"The tunnel led into a landing area divided into four bays, equipped with a conventional bench at the back and a variety of metal parts hanging on the walls. We examined the benches, and then entered a large door that was fully four inches thick, approx. 12' high, and 7' wide. This size is the most important thing to recall.

"Entering the base proper, we were fully functional and free to go where we wanted, under no restrictions. A groove ran down the middle of the tunnel floor. This divided into four other grooves, one of which led to what seemed to be a landing bay."

They had extraordinary adventures, including seeing UFOs parked, what looked like a greenhouse, and an area containing alien babies. In the end, though, they began to suffer from a familiar problem.

"Finally, a box-like device moved out from behind the UFO, and my vision blurred and I got groggy.

"I noticed a weird, full-sized figure coming towards me like a robot with a red target painted on its chest. I found out later it is body armor. The target is designed to attract fire to the center of the armor, the safest spot. At this point I got really groggy.

"I came out of it surrounded by a circle of larger beings, heavier built, all staring at me every which way I turned. I panicked, and broke out of this ring to the tunnel where my other friends were. We tried to mount a counter-attack to get our friend (who was left behind), but panicked and ran outside. At a loss about how to get our friend, we hollered for him to come out several times. He finally did, but in a badly shaken state."

He had a vague memory of being told to "forget everything." "I awoke at sunset, with my friends kicking me awake and, slowly, we went home exhausted and totally unaware of what had just happened."

But he did not remain unaware. He made other visits to the base. "I also saw a conventionally furnished room, where aliens and humans were freely mixing with each other. They had human males working with them as 'front men,' so to speak."

Other children have had unexpected fun with their encounters: "In many ways I was a 'different' sort of child; for one thing, I was nocturnal, which led to my falling asleep at school a lot. I often told my parents that small doctors visited me at night."

This witness was often found standing on the doorstep of her apartment in the middle of the night, ringing the bell to get in. Once, at the age of four or five, she appeared there wearing only her underpants. Her pajamas were neatly folded on the foot of her bed.

But where did she go on those long-past nights?

The motif of schools and teachers is fairly common among childhood memories.

"We met in the garage at my grandfather's house, and I would sit out there for hours talking with a tall, thin gray lady with a pointed chin who told me to call her Grandmother. Grandmother put me through a kind of schooling. She taught me to use my mind and senses for telepathic and other communication. She showed me pictures of the earth from space and little video pictures of what would happen to the earth when I was about fifty. She was a loving, patient teacher. Her skin felt like very soft leather, and she had a pleasant but cheesy smell. She quit coming when my mother objected to what I was learning."

Later this witness touched on the possibility of re-contact and is still considering doing it. She believes that close encounter witnesses are volunteers, that others "literally don't see what we see," that the visitors are "not emotional, and their loving approach is not an emotional love," and that "they are here to help, as they define help."

But what is meant by help is not what we might expect. Rather than giving us plans to build a starship, the message of the encounter experience seems to be about us: Hidden behind the wall of missing time isn't some revelation concerning the aliens and their hardware but, rather, one that concerns us and our hidden—or forgotten—potentials.

One witness remembers two men from his childhood in the 1940s, who seemed perfectly normal, except for what they taught him, which was far from the usual sort of lesson.

"Milt asked if I'd like to learn how to fly. They would hold my trousers belt in back and we would run along and they'd let me go. I would go three to five feet, then I'd bite the sand. [This took place at meetings on a beach.] Then the other one would pick me up and send me back, all the time saying to me, 'Think no thoughts. That is important and necessary. Then float.' I could go twenty to thirty feet at times. It was great! I went at a rate of one to three miles an hour, I'd guess."

He also saw the two men going in and out of the sea in what he describes as a capsule that looked to him like a silver Airstream trailer. Inside the capsule, he once saw a being that looked like one of the visitors, with a narrow face and huge black eyes. His imagery, as it dates from before the idea of the flying saucer had been introduced into the culture, reflects shapes and forms that were familiar in the 1940s, such as silver trailers.

Witnesses often report that they are told that our world is "a school," and if we are coming into contact with vastly advanced aliens, it isn't unreasonable to consider that they might think of it in just this way.

"One of my first memories is of being in a classroom with other children. We were a select few. I was very happy to see my teacher, the lady on the cover of *Communion*. I loved her teaching. I was about age nine.

"My next clear memory is from age eleven. I remember being in her office. Her husband was also there. She had a radio on her desk that was playing my favorite kind of music. The three of us were dancing to this music."

Like so many who seem to live altogether outside of the constraint of missing time, the witness quoted above has seen her encounter experience evolve over her whole life. She recalls an adult meeting with her old teacher. "I then found myself in a well-lit hallway facing an old friend. She was standing in the doorway to her office." A moment later, she found herself back in bed. Then another lesson unfolded. "About twenty seconds later, I saw a small gray box in front of me. There was a hand over it, also gray. It was a clawed hand, and it held a silver wand. The top of the box was tapped once. This created a great wave of knowledge that went through me. Physically, it felt like a slow-moving ocean wave. In that wave was knowledge of myself."

Many witnesses describe a box. More than one has thought of it as Pandora's box, and perhaps that is not too far wrong, given what seems to be inside.

Many families report encounters across the generations, and I have numerous letters from parents describing things happening to their children that are similar to what they remember from their own childhoods.

"My earliest memory was probably from before the age of four, when I clearly remember being taken from my bed and led to a clearing near the bluffs overlooking our local lake. Someone was holding my hand, and I was frightened when it was put into another child's and I was told I was the one to complete the circle.

"As I did, the sky above us lit up so brightly that I was able to see all the children quite well. I realized that I didn't know any of them. They weren't neighborhood friends, but I felt a sense of connection, a family feeling, a sense of familiarity."

Her further memories are unclear. She recalls a soothing male voice telling them what she describes as "very important things about our future and the reason we had all been summoned to that place."

This is typical of the encounter experience: One is so often left with a sense that something tremendously important is happening, so rarely with any clear idea of what that is. In a sense, then, what we *can* say is that the experience creates powerful questions in people, questions that change minds, that open them and compel them to grow. It is thus a challenge of the deepest kind, probably viewed by the inner self as momentous. Depending on how widespread it is, it could conceivably be having a phenomenal hidden evolutionary effect on humankind—but how much greater that effect would be if we understood!

Another witness, now a state official, as a boy observed with his mother an incident of jets scrambling to intercept UFOs. His father was involved in the incident in an official capacity but would tell them little of what happened.

Afterward, though, the boy was deeply affected. Like another witness quoted in this chapter, and like me and many others, his experience was signaled by an increase in nocturnal activity.

"During this period, in the fifties, I began sleepwalking almost routinely." Often his mother would catch him, sometimes outside in the street. But not always. "I still remember these episodes to this day, and how the night felt, so vast." All he recalled of any interaction were vague memories of shadowy figures in the house, and he never had any encounter memories that were more specific. Despite that, this story illustrates the profound changes that can take place in a person after something as simple as a sighting. Some deep part of him began trying to go somewhere. Was he trying to meet the visitors, or to run from them? He never got to the end of that particular journey, and perhaps the fact that he didn't tells us a little more about what lies behind the curtain of missing time. If we have a soul, and the soul has a plan, then maybe we fear to see the blueprint. Perhaps looking at it would transform life's fertile spontaneity into a rigid drama devoid of surprise—would, in short, rob us of our reason for living.

In this sense, then, we would prefer the blindness of missing time, because we do not want to wake up to knowledge that would so damage us.

And indeed, sleepwalking is such a common motif that it would almost seem to be a metaphor for the limited contact that is available to us or that we prefer. "When I was a small child, my parents found me on numerous occasions sleepwalking in our neighborhood. Once on a family camping trip, my father failed to lock the camper door. Subsequently, he found me miles from our camper up on the mountain walking around in my nightgown. From then on, all doors were securely locked at night."

Another thing that childhood encounters are associated with is unusual intelligence and what appear to be changes in intelligence.

A typical example: "My son started reading at one year of age and started first grade with a seventh grade reading level. He has an incredible obsession with astronomy, just like you said you did when you were younger.

"He told me that he has been having abduction-related dreams . . . about ten or so in all. He's described visitors appearing in the room and talking to him. He's got a lot of fears, very much so, and in fact he's slept with my wife and I quite a lot.

"Once we were waiting for darkness so we could use the telescope when he decided to talk to me about the nature of time, space and 'aliens.' He basically went into an unprompted lecture to us. Pulling out a pad of paper and a pen, he went on to draw a matrix showing where humans exist on the scale of living things, both intelligent and non-intelligent, and pointed out how far we are from the visitors' level. He described abductions as an attempt on the part of the visitors to accelerate the process of development, bringing us closer to their level. He said, 'we are like babies in a baby carriage and the aliens are like a mother pushing us along. But they are pushing it very fast and we don't have a safety strap holding us in.'"

I knew nothing about this boy when I met him across a table at a book signing, but looking into his eyes was a startling, even electrifying, experience. He was shy, but those young eyes flashed with a brilliance that I often see in children who are close to this experience. I had the odd feeling that he somehow knew the secrets that we adults are struggling so hard to crack. It is possible for human beings, especially young ones, to know and understand more than they can put into words, and I am to this day haunted by the expression on his face. I was not surprised to get his father's letter.

Much useful information can be obtained from children who are being properly supported in their experience, by parents who do not ask excessive questions, draw too much attention to their stories, try to impose religious beliefs on them, or deny them.

It's difficult, because there is a tendency to want to explain things to kids, emerging naturally out of our desire to protect them, relieve their fears, and satisfy their curiosity.

Parents often find themselves dealing with this experience under the most difficult of circumstances. There are cases where the whole family is under the pressure of visitation, and there are symptoms of implants present as well. This is a dreadful situation to have to cope with alone, but such is the social ignorance and superstition surrounding close encounter that parents have no idea how to get help. Although it is difficult, an effort can be made to find a nonjudgmental caregiver if professional support is needed.

It is especially hard to cope with the experience when powerful and sensitive matters such as birth and death are involved, and this is very often the case. The close encounter experience unfolds at the points of greatest question that human life possesses: What is the meaning of a life? What happens when we die? What is a human being?

"We saw UFOs all the time," writes one parent, describing events that happened in the 1970s, when her children were young. "My second son dreamed he was taken to a base for UFOs."

They then had an incident occur at about eleven at night that unsettled the whole family. "I started to take a step [toward a window] when there was a brilliant flash of light. It lasted a very long time. Before I could move, my son exploded out of his room at the top of the stairs and my daughter came pounding down the upstairs hallway. They were both demanding to know the same thing: 'what was that?'

"This is what we discovered: we had lost upward of an hour of time. Where did it go?"

Later, this correspondent may have received an important clue, one that leads to the conclusion that the amnesia might come not only from the confusion and deep threat that lie behind missing time but also from the fact that what happens there is on a much larger scale than ordinary life—a scale that is so large that it is hard for the human mind even to sample it, let alone grasp its full meaning. Powerful feelings are engaged when somebody comes face to face with it, that sometimes lead the witness toward a painful sense of having been raped, but more often in the opposite direction, toward insights that encompass even the secrets of the future, and as such seem to be almost dangerous to remember.

In our attempt to unlock missing time, we have journeyed far from the factual matrix that should govern any book about hard evidence. But if we are to take a realistic look at what people are reporting, it is important to digress in this way. The shocking relationship between these stories and hard fact will be dealt with soon.

Even so, something occasionally happens in the hallucinatory world of close encounter that seems to draw us a little closer to the facts.

A witness who was attending a school function met somebody for the first time whom she felt strongly she had seen somewhere before. He felt the same way, but they couldn't place each other.

As they lived in different towns, they kept up their new—or renewed—acquaintance by mail and over the phone. After the school year ended, they visited. "Suddenly I found myself asking if he believed in the visitors. 'I don't want to talk about it,' was his response. The fear in his voice was chilling. Then images began streaming through my head. They were of him as a child, asleep on a couch in a house I had never seen. I was terrified, I couldn't stop talking, the words just came out. I described the room he was in. Jacob said, 'I hated that room because those ugly little children would come in and take me away!' He was crying and I was shaking uncontrollably. This went on all night." They eventually went to bed in separate rooms where my correspondent's situation became even more shocking.

Believing that the event had ended, she closed her eyes. As soon as she did so, she had an experience similar to the one frequently reported by others, with a being seeming to intrude into the darkness of her mind.

"I saw a tall, thin figure with huge inky black, liquid eyes. She (it seemed feminine) was bathed in a pale blue light. She reached a thin arm toward me."

After her initial shock, she came to feel that this creature was not really hostile to her. It seemed then that her friend's fear was somewhat misplaced, and she entered the fairly large group who feel that the visitors are in some way trying to help us. Whether this is true or not, they are certainly putting us under pressure, and pressure is often a very productive state. The next letter illustrates the sense of being educated and pressured at the same time that is characteristic of many stories:

"I may have been ten when I woke up to find myself sitting in a rectangular room. A blackboard was across the wall. There were only long benches to sit on. These benches were full. Maybe four benches contained forty kids, all the same age. Everyone was sitting with their spines stiff from terror! Then I saw why.

"An insect-like humanoid entered the room. He was the teacher. His skin was gray and ugly, with an over-sized brain cavity. He seemed nude and was bent over, trying to keep his head up. I was terrified. I really went stiff when I saw it stop writing on the blackboard and turn to look directly at me. He seemed really angry, really hating me. (New student?) His face was weird: no mouth, a little nose and big eyes, not black or Asian. He had no hair anywhere. Also, he needed a walking stick to walk about."

There is something at once terrifying and hilarious about this story, with its image of a fearsome alien hobbling about on a cane. But the thought of those children, literally "stiff" with terror, suggests a darker interpretation, that they are being placed under pressure so ferocious that we can hardly even bear to face it.

And yet we *are* facing it a little. Gradually, as we come to see that we can do this, no matter whether the close encounter experience represents a dialogue with aliens or a new kind of dialogue with ourselves, it is still filled with all sorts of valuable potentials.

This next witness is another person who had his childhood experiences in the 1930s and '40s, long before there was extensive alien imagery in the culture. As so often, his experience was intimately involved with the largest issues of life and death.

In 1935, he was suffering from pneumonia, at that time a dangerous and often rapidly fatal disease. "One evening right at dark two beings came to the windows in an elongated envelope. They and their conveyance were like Northern Lights, and they asked me to go with them, and each took a hand. When they touched me it was like being lightly tickled, and very pleasurable. [This sensation is commonly described.] I couldn't see them as being like us. The odd part was that you could see through them, but they were there and we talked without sound."

The imagery described here accurately expresses the

same sort of encounter that is reported today, with the difference that the choice of words such as "elongated envelope" for "flying saucer" are obviously from a time before today's catchphrases were known. And now we would describe talking "without sound" as telepathy. But since we have no more idea how this is done than we do what a UFO is, maybe these earlier, more neutral descriptive phrases are actually more accurate. In any case, this experience evolved to a level that is rarely reached but seems close to the very core of encounter.

"They took me to a huge pavilion where pairs were waltzing. My impression was that the males were dressed in black with white trim. The females were dressed the opposite way. There was no ceiling, but crystals hung above and made music beyond comparison that sounded to me like wind chimes."

He had three visits to this place, on the last of which he received a message. A female asked him why he was afraid of the dark, then told him "that both the light and the dark are my benefactors, and they would make them equal. She took a crystal and placed it in the palm of my left hand. For a second it resembled the Star of David, two triangles, then melted and ran between my fingers."

So the witness is taught on his third trip something about the nature of the three forces: positive, negative, and equalizing, that Buckminster Fuller years later would describe as the building blocks of the universe.

We are dealing here with a communication about the most fundamental forces of nature—the positive and negative energies that dance together to create the friction on which reality itself depends. If it were not for this dance, repeated from the subatomic level to the moral, there would be no life, and life would be devoid of choices, and what now seems filled with purpose and meaning would be blind and empty and dead.

He had physical consequences that were oddly related to the metaphoric ones. "In a few weeks it became apparent that my night vision had changed. My eyes would adjust to allow me sight when it was pitch black."

He also became nocturnal, and whatever had taken an interest in him quickly began using that to its advantage. Late one night on a Boy Scout trip, when he was the only one left awake, he found himself watching undulating shafts of light that fascinated him. "The shafts of light began a strange movement, and there was my envelope, and something like an oval cylinder; it just seemed correct to go into it. In an instant there was the pavilion, but the 'others' were not dancing. They seemed to be conversing, but not with me, when a lady asked me to 'step on the dais' because I was their 'conductor.' "

He asks, "What is the purpose of the 'conductor?' My being is as common as the earth."

Perhaps that is exactly why he was so exalted in the fantastic world that conceals itself within the mind and soul and the dancing universe that embraces us.

11:

Worlds Beyond

It could be that scale is the essential problem with this communication. Our difficulty understanding it may be because it is being delivered in thoughts that are on a larger scale of time and meaning than we are used to. Since we can understand it at all, though, it would also seem that we can rise to it and close the gap that its presence suggests must exist between ourselves and the visitors.

Even given the small amount of decoding that can be attempted, it seems reasonably clear that this message has the coherence, subtlety, and grandeur that one would associate with the marvelously rich consciousness of somebody old and brilliant, but it also contains a logic so strange that an alien origin does seem possible. Again and again, the voice behind the letters speaks: The world is not what it seems, it is greater, stranger, more wonderful than you dare to see.

If the visitors are really aliens and are communicating with us in this way—not only using the sky as a theater but also using the mind—then wouldn't they have deposited information about their own world somewhere along the way? This would be such an efficient way of helping us to narrow the question of what they are, and thus work faster to close the gap that is keeping us apart, that it seems inevitable that the witness reports would abound with this sort of information. And they do.

"We went to a beautiful planet, (I think it was another planet) that was very hot. It was hard to breathe. I remember seeing a flower and wanting to pick it up. They said not to because it could harm me. We were on what seemed to be a mesa. It was filled with vegetation, but no insects and no animals were present. My friend remembers picking a fruit off of a nearby tree that resembled a pomegranate. The grays said we could eat the fruit, it wouldn't hurt us. We were told to scatter the seeds when we were done."

This couple are deeply involved in the encounter experience, the man having had contact for nearly thirty years. On the occasion described above, they recall going on a three-day journey that ended with a return to Earth on what appeared to them to be a spaceship. Then they made a discovery that will surprise nobody involved in this experience. "According to the clock we were only gone for a half hour of our time. How could that be?"

We are beginning to understand the physics of time, and in recent years it has become clear that movement through it is a theoretical possibility.[1] But physical? Perhaps, but at present it seems that we could affect movement through time only "by manipulating matter and energy in the most extreme and fanciful manner."[2] But *something* happened to these people. Is it a shared fantasy or dream? If so, what caused it? Or did they actually physically go to another world over three days that were somehow compressed into half an hour?

---

[1] J. Leake and S. Rajeev, "Hawking: We'll Be Able To Travel Back In Time," *London Sunday Times*, October 1, 1995, p. 1.

[2] P. Davies, *About Time* (New York: Simon & Schuster, 1995), p. 248.

Given how little we know about contact, it would be inappropriate to make a decision based on the logic of reality as we now understand it. What if the visitors are five hundred years in advance of us? We can't imagine what they might be able to accomplish in terms of alteration of consciousness or even movement through time. Look at our world as it was five hundred years ago: No one had ridden in a car, flown, listened to a radio, or felt refrigeration. The world of five hundred years ago was almost unimaginably less capable than our own.

But who is to say that the visitors are only five hundred years ahead of us? What if they are billions of years in advance of us, if they have had consciousness since before earthly life even began?

What might they be? What might they have accomplished? The possibilities are breathtakingly limitless.

Whether journeys like the one just described actually happen or not, a desert-like landscape is so frequently mentioned in the letters that it is worth considering that it might be a real place. Often, the desert is red. But whether the visitors are the Martians of fiction and legend or not, it seems clear that they aren't from the Mars that we see today. But it is also true that the planet once had flowing water, and there also exists a certain amount of evidence that simple life-forms might have existed there in the incredibly distant past.

Mars probably died about the time life on Earth began, and it just doesn't seem possible that evolution to consciousness could have taken place during the early part of the solar system's life, given the experience of Earth, where it has taken three and a half billion years for it to evolve.

Surely, also, if they had been here over all of time,

we would have noticed them before this, and that simply has not happened. And yet the universe is a very
strange place, and all of our understanding of the time
it takes evolution to unfold comes from a sample of
just one planet.

Not only does the desert recur as a motif in the
stories, cities are often seen, and there is in this material also a curious consistency.

"I was standing in the middle of a red plain. The
ground beneath my feet was dust . . . like what I imagine moondust would be like. There were no rocks, no
chunks of anything.

"I appeared to be in the middle of a street. There
were large, tan buildings running up and down this
street, in all sorts of strange configurations. They were
not elaborate at all—just very angular. On the whole,
they looked like Spanish missions, if those missions
had been designed by Salvador Dali. They were made
of some crenellated metallic material that on first
glance looked like adobe.

"The sky above my head was white. Not bright
white or cloudy white—it was more like the sky
glowed, like it had some innate property of light.

"On the street were dozens of the 'gray' creatures.
They appeared to be gliding back and forth up and
down the street. They gave off this feeling that I was
sort of distasteful to them. I felt big and dirty and
ugly."

The visions of the desert planet go on and on. Here
is another:

"This dream involved a repeated scene from inside
a low-flying vehicle, of a desert landscape below.
There seemed little or no perspective, but speed was
slow enough to allow a good view of an absolutely
vegetationless desert landscape, of reddish brown

color. I somehow associate a school with this desert
location so old that our best efforts to measure its age
would be totally inadequate."

However, this is not the only image that is reported,
and a distant planet perhaps in another age is not the
only place that is described. People have had other
experiences with time.

"We flew over this weird looking landscape. It
looked like the trees turned into grass, we were going
so fast. When we slowed down it was evening. Almost
as though we had traveled an entire day. I looked
down at this log house and saw this woman as she
nervously waved to her husband and two children,
who were heading away from the house in a buck-
board being pulled by two horses. I looked at this lady
who was wearing this old, worn and dusty dress with
a dirty white apron around her waist. The next thing
I remember, I'm standing on the ground near where
she's hanging up her laundry. The interesting thing is
that like these visitors, I, too, am wearing a hood. I
remember she looked around one of the sheets she was
hanging up and screamed."

Not a particularly surprising reaction, certainly, as
a pioneer wife confronts an unknown far greater than
anything she could possibly have imagined. But her
ordeal was not over yet.

"One of them said that this lady's condition was
worse than he thought, and she would have to leave
with them if she was to live. Next thing I know, I'm
looking down on this house and watching her husband
and children as they come home. I can tell he's calling
for her. As I watch him head into the house, the children look up and see the vehicle we're all sitting in,
but by that time the husband is in a panic because he

can't find his wife. I don't know what happened to this lady after I was dropped off."

I made an effort to find out if any record of such an incident exists from the past. The problem is that the reader does not know where the incident occurred, and if there is a past record, it is lost in a newspaper archive or buried in a pioneer diary in a museum somewhere.

Another witness had an experience that may have been related to movement through time and also leads us to an exploration of yet another aspect of close encounter: the confrontation with the double.

"I was riding down a highway in my town when I looked across the median and there was someone waving rather frantically in the westbound part of the lanes. I took a left, deciding to see who it was.

"I pulled over into a Dairy Queen, and he took the second entrance in. We were driver side to driver side, headed in opposite directions. Then it hit me.

"The closer we came to each other, the bigger his smile and the brighter his eyes got. HE WAS ME! He just smiled, waved slowly, passed me by, and took off!"

He drove a very similar car as well. The witness never saw him again but is doubtless a haunted man.

There are many wrinkles to the time-travel theme. "I walked up to an old white, wood-frame house. A small boy about ten with blond hair came out to talk to me. I asked, 'Where's your mother?' and he replied, 'She's gone right now.' He went back into the house. It then dawned on me what had happened. I had gone back in time, to see myself as a child and to see my mother. It felt like I really had gone back in time, or anyway everything looked right."

Does all of this mean that time is not the fixed,

immutable reality that we assume, but that we can somehow free ourselves from it? If so, what an amazing blessing that would be—and also, in a sense, what a tragedy.

If we could travel through time, we would lose something of our species' childhood, because we would come to know everything that was true about us and everything that was not. Huge areas of the past, now rich with mystery and wellsprings of cherished belief, would cease to be in question.

In a sense, every time we answer a question, the world gets a little smaller. A hundred years ago, radio was a breathtaking mystery, a spark dancing with promise. In this age, it's commonplace and not very interesting, as the leading edge of communications science is already beginning to explore quantum entanglement as a means of sending messages that would be able to travel unlimited distances instantaneously.

Another witness had a number of dramatic UFO sightings in the company of friends and family members, that evolved into a dream glimpse of another world and an unforgettably powerful message.

He and his mother were together at the time. "We saw what started out as a bright light that started to get bigger. We realized that it was coming closer. It stopped and did nothing but hover for a few minutes. Then the most beautiful 'spikes' shot out from it. Some were short and others were long." The spikes changed color from white to purple as the UFO rotated. They then heard and felt a hum and went out on their porch to observe more. "We didn't see a bright light. Instead, we saw a large black disk. As it flew over us, we saw what appeared to be lights, or perhaps windows, all along the outside of the craft." It then went away, and the two of them calmly reentered the house and retired for the night—the sort of inexplicable response that characterizes the experience.

He then began to have a dream "of somehow being told the world was about to end and I was one of the many who were chosen to go to another planet to survive.

"We were led to a cliff at dusk, and a big spaceship of some kind came down to rescue us. The next thing I remember is walking through the streets of this place with the other survivors. The buildings were small and square, one story stucco or clay. We were led to a building where two robot-type beings told us that the planet was where we'd be living and we would be the rulers, guided by them."

Reading this, I was once again struck by the consistency of so many of the letters about other worlds. Only a few mention tropical or temperate places. Most have the desert motif, and stucco or adobe buildings predominate to such an extent that one wonders if people are reporting visions of a real place.

Along with the appearance of impossible and wonderful beings, time travel, meetings with the dead, and journeys to other worlds, warnings that our own is soon to end are a commonplace of the close encounter experience. There is many a witness waiting for the moment when the ships come in waves to collect the chosen and take them to some other world.

Warnings such as these, along with the plethora of seemingly impossible experiences that accompany them, do not necessarily signal a great change in the physical world. What they most certainly do signal— quite indisputably so, in fact—is a profound change in another world, one that is at once more durable and fragile than the physical—the world of the mind. And this is true whether the architects of the experience are aliens or not. In fact, if they are not aliens, then it is even more true.

In the high summer of the Roman Empire, during one of the most peaceful eras in history, the Roman world was filled with portents of doom and undercurrents that seemed to indicate that the whole meaning of the world, as it was then understood, was wrong. Millennial preachers scoured the empire proclaiming that the end was coming by fire and the wrath of an angry God.

Given that we are still waiting two thousand years later, it would appear that God is not as easily angered as was thought. But the classical world was certainly ending, soon to be engulfed in the tide of compassion and fervor that marked the rise of Christianity.

The reason the Romans felt doomed in the midst of plenty was that they could instinctively see that the imbalances inherent to their empire's structure would eventually destroy it.

It is this sort of an ending that we are facing now, and I think that our mind, at a very deep level, understands that the modern economy, dependent as it is on perpetual growth for its prosperity, is coming to a crossroads. Either we find a way to expand into space on a massive scale, or growth is going to stop.

One of these things has to happen, and either one of them is going to change our world fundamentally, making it within a hundred years completely unrecognizable to us.

And so we are in much the same position as the ancient Romans were. We, also, live at a time of fundamental change, and the content of the close encounter experience, with all its warnings and portents of devastation and its completely new look at reality, is, at least in part, a response to this.

Still, the experience involves enormous issues of perception. Put simply, are any of these stories factual? I am tempted to take a stand on behalf of some of them, because they involve multiple witnesses or seem to have happened to people in completely normal states of mind. What else would an honest, normal woman who looked up from her housework to find a bizarre team of aliens watching her report except the truth?

Combined with the fact that there are UFOs flying around in the skies, it seems that stories like this should just be taken at face value. If not, then there has to be some compelling reason, something stronger than denial based on the improbability of the situation. In general, when perfectly ordinary people offer reports like these in a world that is filled with evidence of UFOs, it seems illogical to assume that they must be false.

But the stranger the stories get, the less easy it is to be certain about them. So we have to decide, where do we draw the line? Certainly most of these memories are consistent, at least in one way: They are consistently strange. The one thing that links the story of the family who arrived at their country home to find aliens leaping around in the trees to that of the terrified child who ended up in a classroom with a mean-tempered old alien teacher on a cane is strangeness. Both stories are impossibly absurd, and yet both are being reported by perfectly rational people in normal memory.

If we are to conclude that all of these stories are nonsense, then we must also conclude either that thousands and thousands of people sent me hoax letters, or that something is wrong with ordinary human memory. But might it not also be interesting to entertain the notion that, as Dr. Carl Sagan suggested, real aliens would be almost unimaginably strange?

In all of these stories, there is a curious sense of impossibility and reality intermixing in some way, a kind of mad stew of meanings and implications—in other words, a thread of chaos woven into their very texture that threatens to destroy the whole fabric.

One thing is undeniable: Contact can leave witnesses in a fruitful if uneasy state, filled with questions too provocative to ignore and too bizarre to answer. Like the paradoxes of philosophy and the unanswerable koans of Zen, the very impossibility of their memories urges the minds of the witnesses toward change, with the result that those who do not become locked in fear report spiritual awakening.

We are curious creatures, and I think that it is time that we let the close encounter experience beguile us a little instead of rejecting the mystery as either too silly to bother with or hopelessly inaccessible to solution.

Before continuing on to a discussion of the physical evidence that supports the reality of these memories—and that evidence is as appalling as it is compelling—I would like to explore some of the issues of perception that attach to the close encounter experience and may explain some of its strangeness and how to make it become more consistent and clear.

If there are aliens here, why would they combine the spectacularly public airborne theater of the UFO phenomenon with the secretive theater of encounter—a penetration of the individual so deep that it involves nocturnal raids not only into our bedrooms but into levels of our mind that we generally cannot reach ourselves?

If this represents some sort of an attempt at contact, then these two activities may not be contradictory at all. They may both be expressions of the same central policy, which would be to enable us—or compel us—to include imagery of our visitors in the group of assumptions and perceptions that we refer to as reality. This would be to help us acclimatize ourselves to their much larger scale of thought and learn to integrate the rich new reality that they represent. Aliens or no aliens, the next phase in the evolution of mind is likely to take consciousness to the point that it is no longer dependent on time to structure meaning but is centered beyond both space and time.

So we have defeated missing time to a degree and even gone beyond it. We have seen the outlines of a coherent and quite incredible communication. But we have also seen a lot of obvious dream material and some that seems seizure-related.

Where, then, are the facts? If somebody is trying to say something, why don't they just say it instead of depositing it in our unconscious like this and making it so difficult to understand?

It may be that they are being as clear as they possibly can. And it also may be that we possess effective tools that are finally going to enable us to get things into focus.

12:

Yes Or No

What can possibly be made of stories like these? Why would normal people be generating such incredibly bizarre tales out of their ordinary memories?

Is it because aliens are here, and aliens—real ones— are just as strange as we thought they would be? Or is it that expectations built up within the culture have led the fantasy-prone to recast ordinary nightmares into hallucinations of alien contact?

Behavioral scientists have offered many theories of why certain people might come to believe that they have had close encounters. Until the Spanos study (discussed in Chapter Eight) and others like it, there were theories that witnesses must be fantasy-prone or boundary-deficit personalities, or persons otherwise marginalized and given to occult interests.[1] Multiple-witness cases were explained as instances of group hallucination induced when a number of fantasy-prone individuals came together.

The terms "fantasy-prone" and "boundary-deficit" both describe individuals "whose ability to distinguish between imagination and reality is diminished relative to a 'normal' individual."[2] Such people have a ten-

---

[1]R.W. Balch and D. Taylor, "Seekers and Saucers: The Role of the Cultic Milieu in Joining a UFO Cult," *American Behavioral Scientist* 20 (1977): 839–60.

dency to alter memories, combine subconscious and hallucinatory events into fantasies, and to experience imaginary events "with the same vividness and emotional impact of reality."[3]

A 1988 study by Ph.D. student Julie Parnell involved more than two hundred participants in a UFO conference.[4] Two personality tests were administered, the Minnesota Multiphasic Personality Inventory (MMPI) and either the 16 Personality Factors Test (16PF) or the Adjective Check List (ACL). Like the Spanos study, this one did not find evidence for psychopathology.

In my case, the Bender Gestalt, the Wechsler Adult Intelligence Scale Revised, the House-Tree-Person Test, the Thematic Apperception Test, the Human Figure Drawings Test, and the Rorschach were all administered to me by Dr. Maryellen Duane on March 7, 1986, a few months after my December 1985 close encounter. Among the findings were that I was a bright individual who "appeared to be under a good deal of stress," was suffering from fatigue, and "appeared to be very frightened and to feel powerless." She saw "a good deal of inner turmoil" and was concerned that my stressed condition not compromise my ability to separate fantasy from reality.

I did not show any evidence of being a fantasy-prone personality, though, and the general high level of stress and turmoil that I displayed seems consistent

[2]T. E. Bullard, "The UFO Abduction Phenomenon: Past Research and Future Prospects," *Proceedings of Treat II,* ed., R. E. Laibow, R.N Sollod, and J. P. Wilson, pp. 59–83.

[3]Ibid., p. 80.

[4]J. O. Parnell, "Personality Characteristics on the MMPI, 16PF, and ACL of Persons Who Claim UFO Experiences" (Ph.D. diss., University of Wyoming, 1986).

with the picture presented by victims of post-traumatic stress disorder (PTSD). "A fantasy origin for PTSD would be a novelty, because all prior experience indicates some external source as the cause," according to Bullard.[5] But stress disorder also appears to cause a tendency to fantasy, so it is conceivable that alien fantasies could arise as a secondary consequence to explainable stress factors.

In part, the results of my personal tests were what has led me to adhere strictly to the notion that the close encounter experience—especially my own experiences—should remain open to question until there is absolute proof of origin. I continue to stand by that belief, although the physical evidence to be presented in the next section must stand as a possible indication that the time for neutrality is passing.

Many psychologists quite logically take the position that any memory that contains elements that are unexplained by present theories of reality must in some way be incorrect. This position originated when it was discovered that the claims of people reporting satanic ritual abuse could not be substantiated by investigation, and that there were cases of claimed child abuse that the parents felt certain had never happened.

Eventually a group of accused parents came together, founding an organization called the False Memory Syndrome Foundation. Its assertions about the distortion of memory have been taken by the media to mean that all unusual memories must be false, whether they were repressed or not.

On May 23, 1993, in the *Middletown Record*, reporter Joseph de Rivera explained, "in March of 1992,

---

[5]Bullard, "UFO Abduction Phenomenon," p. 81.

the False Memory Syndrome Foundation began collecting cases of parents who reported that they had been falsely accused on the basis of 'memories' recovered during therapy." He went on to report that memories recovered in so-called trauma-search therapy, where the therapist searches backward from a presented disorder to find the trauma that caused it is fundamentally flawed. "The problem with this reasonable-sounding procedure is that a patient in distress is vulnerable to influence by suggestion."[6]

Of course, it is important that innocent people not be incarcerated for crimes that did not happen, but at the same time, it is not at all obvious that we understand memory well enough to conclude that there is no such thing as repression.

Although the validity of the mechanism of the repression of traumatic memory, primarily in abuse cases, has been questioned by some psychologists, reports of such repression have been present in the psychological literature for years.[7]

On November 23, 1996, an Associated Press story was filed about a woman who had been attacked and gang-raped after a college Halloween party.[8] She remembered nothing about it until fellow students started telling her that there was a videotape of the crime. It turned out that five men had raped her and taped themselves doing it. The victim is seen in the

[6]J. de Rivera, "Memories That Aren't Really True," *Record*, Middletown, New York, May 23, 1993, p. 53.

[7]J. Briere and J. Conte, "Long-Term Clinical Correlates of Childhood Sexual Victimization," *Annals of the New York Academy of Sciences* 528 (1984): pp. 327–34.

[8]Ed White, "5 Accused of Raping Student, Taping Attack," *Atlanta Constitution*, November 23, 1996.

tape to be physically helpless and was said to be
drunk. She did not even talk to police until five days
after the event, when pain from her injuries triggered
her memory.

But would her memories of the content of the attack
have been accurate if they had been recovered by
trauma therapy instead of videotape? If trauma can
alter and derange memory, they may not have been.
There have been theoretical attempts to explain how
false memories can be generated, most notably by Elizabeth F. Loftus in *The Myth of Repressed Memory*.[9]
She theorizes that suggestion can end up being assim-
ilated and perceived in the same way as real memory,
and that a complex mixture of cultural influences and
confused childhood perceptions can be accidentally
molded by well-meaning therapists into bizarre structures that essentially mirror their own fears. It seems
to me that an inexplicable attack on an adult might
well be misinterpreted through a similar process of culturally induced distortion.

As there is little to no evidence that the more lurid
descriptions of satanic cults reflect actual groups that
operate in the real world, there must be truth in what
Loftus says. In *Remembering Satan*,[10] Lawrence
Wright demonstrates that satanic rituals recalled by
members of a family involved in an abuse case simply
did not happen. Unless all the investigators were also
satanists, the family had not remembered whatever did
happen—if anything—correctly.

Could it be that bizarre memories—even those that
are never repressed—are simply distortions of other

[9]E. F. Loftus, *The Myth of Repressed Memory* (New York: St. Martin's
Press, 1994).

[10]L. Wright, *Remembering Satan* (New York: Knopf, 1994).

types of trauma? If so, then why are otherwise normal people doing this?

One of the problems psychology has faced is that no clear mechanism of distortion has been identified. This has led some researchers to go so far as to conclude that all seemingly impossible memories must be wrong, that if bizarre memories of satanic cults are provably false, then it's safe to conclude that even more bizarre close encounter accounts must be false as well.

The fact that close encounter memories have been thought to be inaccessible without trauma therapy that usually involves hypnosis has made them even more suspect. Anyway, who would believe for a moment that anybody saw aliens in the trees or got abducted out of the living room in broad daylight by a giant telepathic insect? Or take my case—four books full of one impossible story after another.

It is reasonable to ask a simple question: Are there *any* facts associated with these memories? I can point to the many multiple-witness cases and to the structure of most of the memories, which would be perfectly believable if they didn't involve aliens. A man reports that he was educated by a crotchety old nun on a cane and all the children were afraid of her. A normal memory, accepted at face value, completely believed. But if he reports the same thing, except that the teacher was a crotchety old alien on a cane—well then, that's a different story entirely. We laugh. We dismiss it. Completely disbelieved.

The mind can deceive itself. False memories can even be induced in a laboratory setting. In fact, it has been decisively proved that people often distort memories of past events. But to the extent that a flock of birds, say, becomes a troupe of tree-climbing aliens—

to a whole group of people? Or a husband and wife misremember a passing airplane as a demonic force trying to separate soul from body?

Memory has been shown to change over time but not to this extent. The February 1997 *Journal of Psychiatry* reported a study of Operation Desert Storm veterans that showed that their memories of traumatic events changed in the two-year postwar period.[11] Although there was no way to tell if the original memories were accurate in the first place, forty-one veterans recalled events two years later that they had not originally reported, and twenty-seven did not remember events that were in their after-battle reports.

The study found further that veterans displaying the most serious symptoms of post-traumatic stress disorder showed the greatest amount of memory distortion. This is noteworthy, because it suggests a relationship between the level of distortion of the memory and the seriousness of the stress that accompanied the precipitating incident.

Interestingly enough, the extremely bizarre nature of the close encounter reports by this measure becomes a chillingly powerful argument that the witnesses are remembering something—even though inaccurately—that they not only perceived as real but that also delivered an ultrahigh level of trauma.

According to the story in *Science News*, Dr. Bessel van der Kolk of Harvard Medical School viewed the Desert Storm study as inconclusive. "This is an article about people's willingness to report traumatic experience to strangers," he said. "It says nothing about the

---

[11]B. Bower, "Combat Vets Show Shifting Trauma Memories," *Science News*, Vol. 151, February 15, 1997, p. 102.

critical issue of whether these recollections are in fact reflections of reality."

And so the central issue remains: How do we tell where reality stops and fantasy starts? Interestingly, if it can be proved that close encounter recall is based on real, physical experience, then it is less likely that the sensory parts of the memories will be distorted than intellectual ones such as the battle reports that were used in the Desert Storm study. In *Psychological Trauma*, Dr. van der Kolk proposes that traumatic events that are first processed as sensations or feelings may be preserved differently from intellectualized material. He notes, "Clinicians and researchers dealing with traumatized patients have repeatedly observed that the sensory experiences and visual images related to the trauma seem not to fade over time and appear to be less subject to distortion than ordinary experiences."[12]

But if close encounter is physically real, then we must also contend with the fact that the physical sensations involved may be seriously altered, just as the witnesses report. It may be expected that extraordinary distortions occur, possibly beyond anything that has yet been studied. But until we know how the mechanism of distortion works, we cannot filter out the fantasy.

However, there are a number of avenues of approach that suggest that science can make real progress toward the creation of just such a filter, because of the fact that memories can be evaluated biologically. This is connected to brain-imaging research, an area of exploration that has gained enormously in re-

[12]B. A. van der Kolk, *Psychological Trauma* (Washington, DC: American Psychiatric Press, 1987), p. 258.

cent years because of the development of the PET scanner, which enables researchers to observe the brain while it is actually at work.

Two studies, conducted independently, suggest that severe and repeated sexual abuse in childhood actually damages a part of the brain called the hippocampus, which is a sort of switching mechanism that organizes and integrates memory. These studies were reported at the May 1995 meeting of the American Psychiatric Association by scientists from the University of California at San Diego and Yale University School of Medicine.[13] Apparently, severe trauma may unleash hormones that injure the hippocampus, thus leaving a measurable signature of abuse in the brain of the victim. It should be noted, however, that not all victims of abuse exhibit this change, and a study conducted by McGill University scientists on twins suggested that, in men, there may need to be a genetic disposition for the change to show up. Nevertheless, it would seem possible that other forms of abuse may also leave signatures in the brain—scars, as it were, that prove that something bad actually did happen to the victim.

Obviously, though, that gets us only partway down the road, if it develops that damage to the hippocampus will occur only in some trauma victims and not in all. But there is yet another study that might eventually enable us to sort the whole thing out.

In 1996, research was reported by a team of Harvard scientists led by Dr. Daniel Schacter[14] that suggests that the brain actually processes false and real

[13]B. Bower, "Child Sex Abuse Leaves Mark on Brain," *Science News*, Vol. 147, June 3, 1995, p. 340.

[14]P. J. Hilts, "In Research Scans, Telltale Signs Sort False Memories from True," *The New York Times*, July 2, 1996.

memories differently, even though the witness may believe that all the memories are real. For example, a true memory of hearing a word will induce brain activity not only in the hippocampal area but also the left tempoparietal area where the brain decodes sounds. If the word was only believed to be heard, there will be no left temporal activity because no sound was ever decoded.

If this research proves out, it would have dramatic implications in the whole area of memory studies and would open a new door into the mysterious memories and life experiences of the close encounter witnesses. Dr. Schacter was quoted by the *Times* as saying, "we believe we have a clue now about how false memory works."

In addition, Dr. van der Kolk reports, "Contemporary biological researchers have shown that medications that stimulate autonomic arousal may precipitate visual images and affect states associated with previous traumatic experiences in people with Post Traumatic Stress Disorder but not in control subjects."[15]

It is this biological approach to the problem that is most likely to lead to a solution. If real trauma is present in the close encounter witness, it is going to have some sort of a biological signature. And conceivably, using the technique proposed by Dr. Schacter, we may be able to construct a true narrative out of witness testimony, if it proves to have its origin in real trauma. This would work by reducing the testimony to a series of very narrow yes or no questions, each of which

[15]B. A. van der Kolk, "The Body Keeps the Score: Memory and the Evolving Psychobiology of Posttraumatic Stress," *Harvard Review of Psychiatry* 1, no. 5 (1994): 253–65.

related to one of the physical experiences reported. Then, by determining the way the brain processed the answers, we could isolate the parts of the memories that were based on factual events. For example, if a witness believed that he had seen a shadowy figure in his bedroom shortly before a missing time experience, it might be possible to determine, by observing which parts of the brain process the memory, whether a visual image was actually present.

Using such methods, a picture of the close encounter experience could possibly be constructed that is based entirely on whatever factual realities lie behind it.

But the research that has been done so far has been limited to simple false memories induced in the laboratory, where witnesses were deceived into believing that a certain item had been in a set when it actually was not there. Whether it will be also applicable to extremely complex memories remains to be seen, but it does seem to hold out significant promise.

We can hope that, as science begins to come to terms with close encounter, it will realize that it has many tools that it can apply even to the anecdotal evidence with a reasonable expectation of useful results. And then at last this phenomenon will leave the realm of confusion and fear and fiction, and find its true place in the area of human experience we consider to be real.

It would be wonderful for close encounter witnesses if some progress could be made in understanding their memories. From personal experience of it, I know how overwhelming the stress response can be. The most debilitating problem is sleep disturbance, which often becomes chronic. Although I no longer suffer from the problem, I experienced "guarded sleep" for years after my first encounter. Associated with lack of sleep is depression, which can be devastating. An inability to trust others and strong separation anxiety that emerges whenever a loved one so much as leaves the house are also symptoms shared by close encounter witnesses and sufferers of post-traumatic stress disorder.

What distinguishes close encounter from ordinary high-stress experience is another group of symptoms altogether, and because they are so different from other stress-related symptoms, it may be inferred that whatever induces close encounter memories is no garden variety stressor.

What basically happens is that the witness's whole sense of reality explodes. People become psychic, they begin to believe that they can see into the future, they take spontaneous journeys through time, they begin to see vivid images in the region of the brain known in folklore as the "third eye," they levitate, they believe that they take on the appearance of alien forms for periods of time, they acquire wisdom and new compassion, their children become preternaturally brilliant, they take journeys out of the body, they become healers, they acquire relationships with the dead, they become deeply concerned with the welfare of the environment.

They begin to feel that their sexuality is involved, they come to feel that they are breeders of some sort, they begin to think that they have relatives living on other planets, they believe that they acquire ongoing relationships with the aliens who visit them.

Fortunately, not everybody has all of these side effects, but few people come away with none of them.

When we understand why the experience causes people to think that they have changed in these ways, we will also understand what it is that is happening to them. And then, perhaps, we will begin also to understand something of the mind that seems to be behind all the wonder and terror of the experience. And no matter the origin of that mind, whether it is alien or from right here at home, that is going to be one extraordinary discovery.

If the mind of the alien does not originate between our own ears, then there may be some interesting physical reasons for the perceptual distortion that appears to occur, that goes beyond stress-related issues.

If a nonhuman intelligence is responsible for what is happening, then there are likely to be problems involved in the process of interaction that are fundamentally different from any that we have experienced before. It is not obvious that contact will ever be a smooth process.

In fact, *if* it is happening, then there may be a complex and subtle mix of reasons for the perceptual problems that are occurring. First, it is unlikely, once fact is separated from fantasy, that what remains is going to be particularly believable or easy to understand. The bizarre combination of the sublime and the gothic that characterizes so many experiences, for example, is likely to conceal motives and expectations that are very different from our own. More than that, the secrecy that seems central to the whole contact process must be a major contributor to witness confusion.

Even beyond these problems, though, there is the issue of whether perception will be deranged by the mere process of encounter. There are indications from physics that the observer plays a role in the actual construction of reality. In his seminal book on quantum physics, Dr. John Von Neumann shows how quantum theory indicates that the observer may have an active part to play in the creation of reality.[16] Von Neumann says that physical objects would, essentially, not exist in any definite form if an observer was not perceiving them. Reality, when not being observed, exists as a sort of wave form of possibilities called a superposition, which acquires definite form only when it is observed. We never perceive the true texture of the universe, and can never see it, because everything we observe turns into the forms we are wired to see.

Although there has been a lot of controversy about this idea, the problem of the observer in quantum physics has not yet been solved. If it is true that the observer's expectations somehow govern the shape of reality, then close encounter could conceivably be an extremely difficult process.

I and thousands like me have found close encounter to be psychologically devastating, impossible to remember clearly, and full of perceptual distortion. Dream mixes with reality. Things that seem physical one moment become hallucinatory the next. Aliens change before our eyes into the very images of our worst fears. What appear to be living creatures become intermixed with our nightmares.

In other words, when we try to interact with them, we experience an outbreak of perceptual chaos. Could it be that this is what happens when two differently wired observers attempt to turn the same possibilities into a reality coherent to them? If so, then the fearsome pressure on the ego that takes place during encounter would be explained, because it would be experiencing a situation that would be doubly frightening: It would appear to the ego that a deeper, more

[16]J. Von Neumann, *Mathematical Foundations of Quantum Mechanics*, Trans. R. T. Beyer (Princeton, N. J.: Princeton University Press, 1955).

total annihilation than the individual had thought possible was at hand. Of course, it would all be an illusion: No matter whose consciousness prevails, it seems
probable that the superposition is going to resolve into
the same physical appearance. This is because,
whereas there is evidence that the resolution of superposition into matter may depend upon the observer,
there is no evidence that the process of observation
itself governs the structure of the universe.

So if there isn't an actual battle going on between
the two minds to create different realities out of the
same universal stuff, then this psychological side effect
must be controllable. Even if the physical content of
the world is somehow at stake, we still have a weapon
available. This is because understanding itself would
be a powerful form of control in such a situation.

I have had many close encounters. Despite my best
efforts, I have on only one occasion been able to alleviate some of the internal chaos. I did this by performing an inner movement of my attention that I
learned over many years of meditation. I moved my
attention out of my personality, which felt as if it was
coming unanchored and about to be destroyed, and
concentrated it on the sensation of my physical body.
This brought the situation nicely into focus. During
the few moments that this lasted, I saw four rather
tired looking people, quite small, wearing dark blue
clothing. Their faces were sloppily smeared with a
greasy substance of the same color. It was night and
the blue material seemed intended as camouflage.
There was a period of perhaps two minutes during
which we simply stared at one another. Then they left,
moving quickly, their coloring making them seem to
disappear. But there was no trick to it. They did not
evaporate like smoke. They moved off into the dark.

UFO Photos

This appears in a single frame of video shot by John Bro Wilkie over Los Angeles. (JOHN BRO WILKIE)

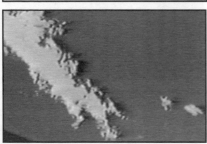

This object dives above the roof of the house, flexing like a living body. Its entire motion takes place in under a second. (TIM EDWARDS)

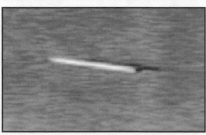

"Platform" videotaped by Tim Edwards. Its estimated altitude was 50,000 feet, and it was more than a mile long. (TIM EDWARDS)

Structure taped over Edwards's house. This is not a distorted video image. It was low and close, moving at high speed. (TIM EDWARDS)

The UFO videotaped over Mexico City on August 6, 1997. The best and most thoroughly authenticated video of a UFO presently on record. (JAIME MAUSSAN)

Implant Photos

1. THE STRIEBER IMPLANT STUDY

March 1988, MRI scan of Whitley Strieber's brain showing unknown bright object in right temporal lobe (left side of picture).

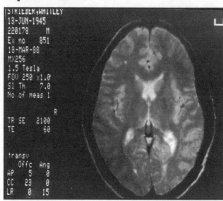

Object in sinus of witness.

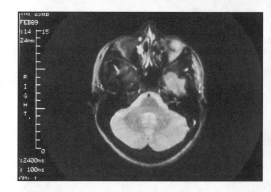

Object in sinus of second witness.

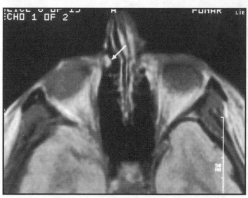

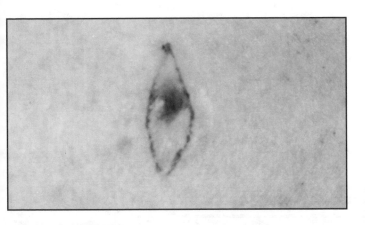

2. THE LEIR SURGERIES
A typical implant as it appears under the skin before removal.
(MICHAEL PORTONOVA)

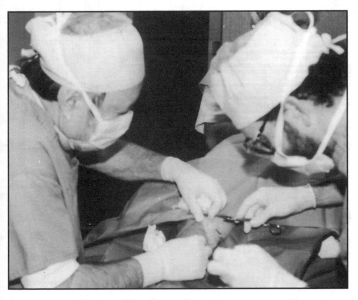

Roger Leir and his surgical team removing an object from the leg of Alice Leavy. (MICHAEL PORTONOVA)

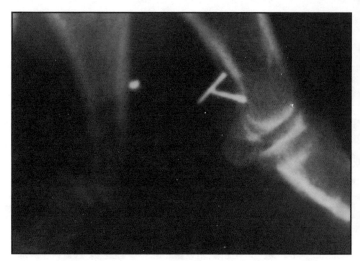

X ray of T-shaped object and "canteloupe seed" in the foot of a witness, found not to be a surgical inclusion. This object has a core of apparent meteoric iron.

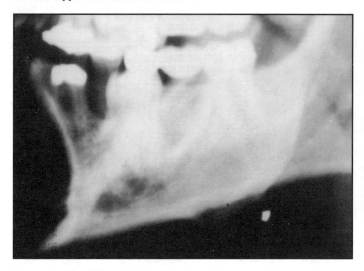

X ray of object found in the jaw of a defense worker.

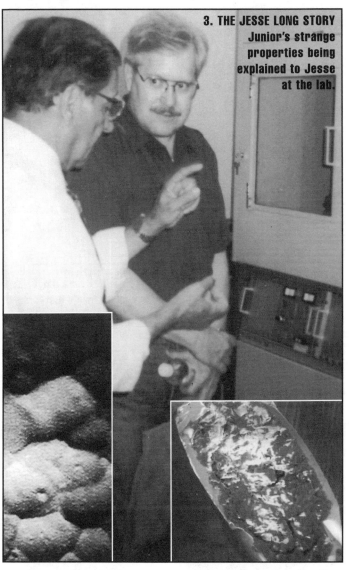

3. THE JESSE LONG STORY
Junior's strange
properties being
explained to Jesse
at the lab.

Electronmicrograph of
Junior's cobbled surface.

Proteinaceous inclusion in
the tip of the object.

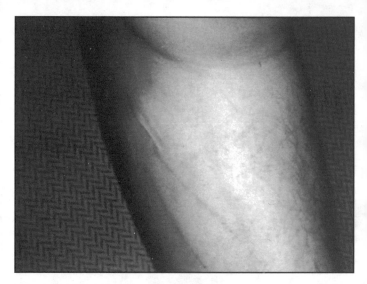

Scratches from an abduction-related attack that took place four years after Jesse's implant was removed and caused him to need emergency room treatment for shock.

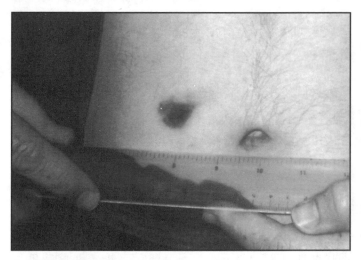

Triangular abduction-related injury on Jesse's abdomen that also occurred after his implant removal.

There is obviously much that can be done to understand the degree to which the close encounter experience is real, and the biological evaluation of memory looks especially promising. This is going to become particularly important, because, given the possibilities just explored, and what unfolds in the next part of this story, it seems urgent that we gain the clearest possible understanding of what the close encounter witnesses are trying to tell us. It could be, after all, that what is happening to them today will be happening to the whole world tomorrow.

Part Three
HARD EVIDENCE

The Lord shall preserve us from all evil;
He shall preserve our souls.
The Lord shall preserve our going out and our coming in,
From this time forth, and even for evermore.

—Psalm 121

13:

Early Days

It was a winter night so silent that it seemed to bear a sort of innocence. But it was not an innocent moment, because I had just woken up and I couldn't move. Instead of enjoying the sweet, contemplative quiet of the country in the deep hours, a helpless commotion of fear made me want to run. I was paralyzed and helpless despite the fact that something was being stealthily pushed up my nose. Then I heard a terrific crack between my eyes, and the world went black.

The next morning, I woke up exhausted, as if I had been struggling and fighting all night. There were even spots of blood on the pillow. But Anne hadn't been disturbed, and nobody else had been in the house. So it must have been a dream . . . except by February of 1988 I had been through too much: I knew the stories other witnesses told of getting strange little objects pushed deep into their sinus cavities. Typical of the reader comments was this one: "I protested as much as possible, which can't be much when they coerce as you know, and then they stuck something up my nose."

Because of reading letters like this, I thought *maybe* it had been a bad dream, but it also made me frantic. Clearly, my most logical strategy was to undergo a thorough physical and neurological examination, which would include both a CAT scan and an MRI scan.

The day after the incident, I began experiencing fearsome cluster headaches, so there was ample medical reason to undergo the tests. I did not tell the neurologist about my experiences, although the doctor who referred me knew the story.

The neurological exam revealed mild bilateral asymmetry, with the left side of my body being somewhat more developed than the right, but nothing to suggest the presence of disease. On March 16, 1988, I had the CAT scan. The finding was completely normal.

I then proceeded on March 18 to the MRI scan. The results were somewhat different. "Occasional punctate foci of high signal intensity are located in the cerebral white matter of the frontal lobes bilaterally, as well as the left temporo-parietal region."

The neurologist did not view this finding as a matter of concern, and indeed, no evidence of disease process related to it has emerged over the nine years since the test was conducted.

However, another MRI scan specifically of the nasal cavity conducted in 1989 revealed some deviation and apparent scarring consistent with a mild insult to the upper part of the left nostril. No discrete objects were observed in any of the tests.

I might also note that the phrase "increased signal intensity" in an MRI scan means, to us lay people, that a greater reflectivity is being observed from a given area. This return could be because of deposits of some kind, such as calcifications in soft tissue, microvascular disease, the dead nerve tissue that results from loss of the myelin sheath, or, conceivably, a foreign body. Unfortunately, it would be unlikely that an exact diagnosis could be achieved without more aggressive testing, even exploratory surgery, and only a serious medical problem would justify such a course. So the matter was left there, and I had to be content with knowing that something *might* have happened on that night. But if it had, and something had been inserted into my brain, then was my mind being influenced, even changed? What was happening to me, to all of us? I was beginning to feel that the harder I tried to find the answers, the more difficult the questions were becoming.

When I questioned my doctor about whether something could be introduced into the brain through the sinuses, he responded that this would be the easiest way to get to the temporal lobe—which is, of course, the seat of consciousness. However, it would be medically extremely dangerous, because of the danger of carrying bacteria-laden debris from the nasal cavity up into the brain along with any surgical instrument that was introduced from that direction. So I was left to suppose either that it was a dream or that whoever had done it had greater command of antisepsis than we do, because there had been no infection.

I decided, in 1989, to undertake a study, through the Communion Foundation, of people who reported intercranial implants, whether through the nose or by other means. At the time, I had no idea that two witnesses, Betty Stewart Dagenais and Jesse Long, were both struggling out on the West Coast with implant issues of their own, and it would not be until 1996 that I discovered what had happened in their quite shocking cases.

I felt that we should do MRI scans of people who had reported brain implants or nasal intrusions and see if we could gather evidence that was more definitive than what had been obtained in my own case. We looked through our file of letters and soon found a number of witnesses who reported one or both of these symptoms.

Some of them had, like me, already been disturbed enough by what they remembered happening to them to seek medical attention. One witness who had experienced pain in her ear and head after an encounter, leading to full-scale migraine, had an MRI scan with a result that sent a chill down my spine:

"There are several small areas of increased signal intensity present in the white matter in the frontal areas bilaterally, with three bright signals seen on the right side, measuring about 4 to 5 mm. in size. A 6 to 7 mm. bright signal is seen in the frontal white matter on the left side, with small punctate lesions anterior to this. These are in a periventricular location. Also two areas of increased signal intensity are seen in the white matter in the temporal lobes, one on each side." The doctor concluded that the areas of increased signal intensity were "suspicious for demylinating disease in a young individual." (The witness was in her forties.)

This was a virtual carbon copy of my own finding. Did it mean that we both shared the same exotic disease, one that might cause vivid hallucinations? I was eager to get an answer to this question, but my research was unavailing. So-called unknown bright objects are found in about 1 percent of all brains scanned, and the finding is usually considered innocuous, although it may be associated with chronic fatigue syndrome in some cases—but not in mine, as I have always had a normal to high energy level. This finding has also been seen in patients with myelin-related diseases such as multiple sclerosis, which occurs when an unknown process destroys myelin and

causes the nerves it encases to die. But the demyelinization associated with MS presents a characteristic
pattern of destruction centering in certain nerves associated with motor control, and that was not present
in either scan. This is why the other witness's radiologist noted only a "suspicion" of possible demyelenat-
ing disease and mine did not mention it at all. The
defining factor is that neither of us has shown symptoms of such disease over the years since the tests were
done.

If such returns from an MRI scan are not caused by
demyelinization or another disorder, another possibility is a foreign object. Back in 1989, a number of witnesses had reported expelling BB-sized objects from
their nasal cavities, but at that time I was not aware
of any that had been collected, so exactly what these
reports meant I could not determine.

Like me, the witness who sent me this other MRI
report had experienced severe headaches. So, assuming
that she was not suffering from a disease, then what
might be the matter with her?

She had vivid memories of a machine of some sort
being placed against her forehead, and had woken up
to find that triangular areas of her eyebrows had lost
their hair, and red dots like small puncture wounds
had appeared in the center of the hairless areas.

"I began waking up in the morning with bare
patches in my eyebrows. The bare patches were in the
shape of triangles. I used an eyebrow pencil to cover
them—but after months of this, I thinned them out."

She experienced a disturbance to the peripheral vision in her left eye, a symptom that she shares with
other witnesses. When her doctor told her that the unknown bright objects in her brain were behind her eyebrows, she was horrified. She has a rather clear image

associated with her apparent implantation. She remembers seeing a group of tubes coming out of a
white base. The ends of these tubes were ringed by
small lights and had needles in the center that she believes produced the marks in her eyebrows.

"While lying flat on my back the white base is
placed above my head. The tubes are flexible, the tiny
lights are white and warm. Once they are in place the
needle slowly penetrates into my skull. It is done very
slow in order not to crack the skull."

One can well understand why she complained of
headaches.

She ends her letter, "for some damned reason I am
connected to the unknown—the hidden. And we all
know that man hates what he cannot understand. So
where does that leave people like us? Dissected, prod-
ded, hated."

One thing about my proposed MRI study concerned me. It was that witnesses were reporting that
the small objects being expelled from their noses were
metallic. My problem was that magnetic resonance imaging places the patient in a powerful magnetic field.
If there was something metallic embedded in an organ,
there would be a danger that the magnetic field would
cause the object to move. Obviously, this could result
in injury, maybe quite serious injury in the case of a
sensitive organ like the brain.

I did not want to abandon the study, but I also did
not want anybody to get hurt.

My decision was to concentrate on people who had
already had MRI scans with no consequences and to
preinterview the potential subjects carefully, so that I
could be certain that they understood that there was
a certain level of risk, however remote. I was surprised

to find that absolutely nobody even considered dropping out of the project.

The way we found witnesses was to announce the project in the Communion Letter, which we were publishing at the time, as well as to cull our correspondence for people who provided descriptions of objects being put up their noses or otherwise introduced into their cranial areas. We concentrated on the brain largely because it didn't occur to us that there might be implants elsewhere in the body. I saw this as an intrusion into the seat of consciousness, and to me the brain was the place to go to find the evidence.

The letters that came in began to form a picture, and it was a disturbing one. "I was abducted and missing for five hours when I was between eleven and thirteen, some twenty-odd years ago. A few years ago I had an MRI scan done twice on my head. The doctor had no explanation for me for what the spots were that showed up on my brain."

This was another witness with spots in the temporal lobe, a finding that was beginning to become familiar to me.

One possible explanation I ruled out was that these were imaging artifacts—glitches in the scan caused by the equipment. There are many image artifacts associated with MRI scans, such as movement artifacts, flow artifacts, and central point artifacts. Movement and flow artifacts appear as fuzzy or smeared areas, but central point artifacts are bright dots of light. The radiologist I was working with said, however, that they are easily recognized and were not what we were seeing.

I cannot claim that there is a large-scale pattern of people who display unknown bright objects in their brains reporting close encounters, because the studies necessary to determine this have never been attempted. But certainly such an effort would be worthwhile. It would also be worthwhile to find witnesses willing to submit their bodies to postmortem autopsy, in order to determine exactly what has happened to their brains.

One witness sent us two diagnostic reports on his brain. The first said, "Skull X ray—Foreign body of possible metallic origin noted in the mid-brain." The second was slightly more informative: "X rays show a small metal object in the temporal right lobe causing temporal lobe syndrome." The skull itself showed no sign of any trauma, and no entry point for this object was observed.

This witness was having a complicated response to the presence of this object, which could have involved either close encounter or hallucinations or both. In any case, we very sadly could not include him in the MRI study, largely because of concerns about the effect of the magnetic field on what had already been identified in X ray as a metallic object. In addition, the radiologist was concerned that his X rays might show other disease process in the brain and felt that he should remain under care at home.

I felt tremendous sadness when I finally wrote this witness telling him that he could not participate in the program, but the danger of causing the metallic object to move was just too great. This is why witnesses who want to find out if their brains contain objects should always begin with X ray. Usually, metal shows up clearly on X ray, and if such a thing as this witness had is present, then an MRI scan should be attempted only if the doctors involved still feel that it is indicated.

Another witness sent us material showing that she

had something near her pituitary gland. But was it a growth or an unknown object?

This witness, Dr. Colette Dowell, has been mentioned by various UFO researchers and featured on the television program *Encounters*. On February 2, 1986, Dr. Dowell had a CAT scan of her brain and pituitary. The finding was that she had a normal pituitary, but "there is, in addition, a 3 mm. non-enhancing nodule in the left lobe which could represent a microadenoma." The key word here was "could." It was not a definitive diagnosis, which was why we were interested in looking more deeply into this case. What would the much more detailed MRI picture show us?

Dr. Dowell had experienced a disappearing pregnancy with no apparent miscarriage at age fifteen and suffered from menstrual difficulties. As menstrual and other problems of the female reproductive system can be caused by pituitary adenoma, these complaints were what led to her CAT scan.

She wrote us, "Since I was a teenager I have been experiencing 'UFO' dreams. I do not know the origin of these paranormal experiences." She stated that, from an early age, she felt watched. She reported, "I felt there were two Colettes, one from this planet and one up in the stars."

She further notes, "in 1988 while camping in my van near Chesapeake Bay, a vibrating energy permeated my vehicle and continued through my body with the focus being my third eye or pituitary region." This led to an even greater sense of clairvoyance. She had numerous abduction dreams. By 1989, her alien-related thoughts and apparent experiences so distressed her that she consulted a number of psychiatrists. But tests revealed a personality within normal range.

Dr. Dowell may indeed have a pituitary adenoma, as she has experienced other symptoms associated with this disease, including vision disturbances and galactorrhea, or lactation outside of pregnancy.

The anterior pituitary, which is the location of the object, is like a glandular clearinghouse. In it, hypothalamic neurohormones regulate the creation and secretion of six major peptide hormones, which are then secreted in bursts, or in circadian or diurnal rhythmic patterns. Enlarging adenomas can cause many symptoms, the most obvious of which are headache and visual disturbances. False pregnancy is not a symptom of pituitary adenoma.

As Dr. Dowell was one of the most interesting and articulate of our candidates, on June 6, 1989, an MRI scan was undertaken on her. To minimize the number of slices taken and thus the cost of the scans, candidates were asked to indicate the area where they thought they had an implant. Most indicated the sinus region, but Dr. Dowell's scan was done, for obvious reasons and at her insistence, in the pituitary area.

The impression was, "A 3 mm. zone of high intensity within the posterior sella turcica, as noted correlating with the patient's demonstrated micronoma." At the time, the radiologist felt that the object observed on the MRI scan and the one revealed by the CAT scan could be two different objects, but he eventually concluded on his report that they were the same.

Dr. Dowell's MRI scan has had quite an extensive amount of review over the years, as certain abnormalities associated with it have continued to suggest that it might not be an ordinary adenoma after all. Among those reviewing it have been four physicians, three psychiatrists, and two ophthalmologists, as well as a panel of five neuroradiologists from the Cedars-Sinai Medical Center.

Only one of these doctors would identify this as a normal-appearing situation, and he refused to identify it as an adenoma, instead stating that it was within normal range for an MRI scan of this area, and no disease process was present at all. The others would not offer opinions. The problem is that on an MRI scan, an adenoma does not usually appear as a 3-mm punctate zone. A small zone of high signal return is more often associated with calcium or other nontissue deposits, and the doctor who would discuss it said that it appeared to him to be a calcification.

Some UFO researchers have identified Dr. Dowell's object as an implant, but its nature has never been determined, any more than it has been definitively determined that the unknown bright objects in the brains of other witnesses have been put there by somebody and have not occurred naturally. Dr. Dowell is adamant that its true nature is unknown.

I talked to Dr. Dowell on September 4, 1997, and discovered that she was no longer having the vivid experiences that had been with her for so long, and there was an interesting reason for this. Like some of the other witnesses mentioned in this book, she was diagnosed with disturbances in her peripheral vision. In her case, these were thought to be a side effect of pituitary adenoma. Oddly, her medical records show that this has turned out to be a transient symptom for her. Unless the adenoma is removed, it is unusual for a symptom like this to disappear in such a case. But Dr. Dowell has had a study done that showed her peripheral vision to be normal after two examinations that showed otherwise.

She provided me with the medical records confirming this. On August 20, 1990, she was diagnosed with bitemporal quadrantanopsia, the vision dysfunction typical of pituitary adenoma. On March 29, 1994, she was again tested, and the visual field was found to be unchanged from 1990. The presence of the probable adenoma was again confirmed by another MRI scan. At this point, surgery was obviously becoming an option. Then, just ten days later, on April 4, 1994, she was retested to validate the previous test. The report states that the "results indicate no visual field defect—unexplained improvement."

Dr. Dowell has also ceased to lactate abnormally and has not had any of the sudden "jolts" of energy in her forehead region that used to disturb her so frequently. She states, "This is not to say that my symptoms won't appear again, just that they have subsided."

Dr. Dowell has experienced an unfortunately chaotic diagnostic history. Some of the doctors have even claimed that her scans were normal, despite symptoms like abnormal lactation and visual disturbances that are typical of pituitary adenoma.

It seems possible that the object observed in the CAT scan and the one in the MRI scan are indeed two different things, and two of the doctors agreed that this was so. But were either or both objects implants? There is no way to know. So she has been left to wonder whether she is an abductee with an implant that can be seen—at least at times—near her pituitary, or is simply suffering from a conventional abnormality that for whatever reason has a rather unconventional presenting appearance.

This case illustrates a fundamental medical problem that will crop up again and again as I narrate the further history of possible implants and certain ones—for there are some whose existence is beyond question. This is that we need and do not have an appropriate array of tests not only to diagnose these objects but also to identify their effects and functions.

Fortunately, not all stories are as hard to end as Dr. Dowell's. I would hope that some thought might be given to testing Dr. Dowell further, using some of the techniques suggested in the Communion Foundation's proposed implant study protocol.

But those are today's issues. Back in 1989, it was with high hopes that I continued to gather witnesses for our MRI study. Dr. Dowell's object was inaccessible because it was buried deep in her brain. These other witnesses mostly had memories of nasal intrusions.

I could hardly sleep the night before the tests began, I was so excited at the prospect of finding an implant at last.

14:

The One Within

Before I report in detail on those studies, I must add yet another dimension to the picture that we are painting of this bizarre situation.

It is easy to conclude that implants must be tracking devices or mind control machines of some sort, put in us by aliens. But recall that Dr. Dowell, as a child, felt that she was not entirely of this world—that she was actually living two lives at the same time, one on Earth and another as an "alien" among the stars.

She was not alone. In point of fact, this blurring of self is experienced by many close encounter witnesses, and it would seem appropriate to introduce it into the discussion during the survey of implants, lest we forget that one thing that the questions raised here do not have are simple, pat answers. But if implants don't do conventional things, then what else might they do? Even if they are tools of communication, it could be of a very extraordinary kind.

The deeper you mine the close encounter experience—always refusing to submit to the temptation to rush to explanations—the richer and more profound are the questions that it returns. There is a subtle but continuous suggestion that the experience involves some sort of inhabitation or—less distressing—a kind of blurring of normal and alien selves. Given the incredible stress of encounter, it really isn't too surprising that there would be unusual side effects like this. Other highly stressful experiences can lead to similar personality disruptions.

Witnesses are left with the sense that the visitors are somehow inside them, or using some means to look through their eyes, or dwelling in their bodies, or living parallel lives to them in other worlds. In some cases there are physical sensations involved, and witnesses will report that they feel as if part of their vision is being stolen, and they somehow perceive less of the world than they did before their body began to be "shared." In other cases, like Dr. Dowell, they feel as if they are in two worlds at once.

Occasionally, a witness will find that he or she has suddenly changed physical appearance and actually looks like an alien. Incredibly, this shape-shifting phenomenon is also sometimes witnessed by others.

One night a witness woke up and found that his arms were long and thin, and he felt light and seemed to be pulsing with the delicious electricity that eastern traditions identify as kundalini. He discovered that, in this state, he could fly. He went upstairs to his son's room and woke him. The boy seemed delighted to see him and acted as if he was greeting an old friend. Next morning, though, things were different. The boy remembered the experience vividly but as a nightmare. He recalled the "alien" as a monster that had flown around his room like a giant bat.

Another time, a witness cried out that the visitors coming near her were so ugly. One of them placed a blue-gloved hand on her wrist and said, "My dear, one day you will look just like us."

A member of the psychological community came out of the bathroom one morning and found his companion terrified. "You changed all of a sudden into this weird being. Your body was really thin and your arms were long and thin also. You had these huge eyes with a slightly larger head." At the time, the witness says, his friend knew nothing about my books. He changed back to normal, but does not report if the relationship survived.

It would obviously be inappropriate to jump to the conclusion that people are literally turning into alien forms at times. But something quite unusual must be happening in these cases. Whatever it is, it does suggest that there may be some sort of more active participation on our part, perhaps one we cannot articulate clearly, probably because it represents action being taken that is far from our conscious understanding of our own natures. It is a reminder that, whenever you ask the question "Who are the aliens?" you must ask in the same breath, "Who are we?"

Other witnesses have reported being told, "We will come from within you," and one was given the particularly haunting explanation, "It is me within thee."

Although this might refer to an aspect of the experience so strange that we simply do not have enough information even to begin to describe it accurately, it might also mean in a completely straightforward way exactly what it says, which is that the first confirmed alien artifacts are going to be found inside our own bodies.

Back in 1989, we gathered our witnesses for the MRI project, and one by one they went through their scans. Three of them displayed completely normal scans, but four did not. Here are the findings and the stories behind them.

This first examination was of a witness who had reported a recent nasal intrusion. The MRI revealed a "slight increase intensity in the right turbinates." This was assumed to be "suggestive of recent minor allergic changes or upper respiratory infection," and the MRI was judged normal.

We were all frustrated with this scan, because, although it showed that the nose was irritated, there was no return of an object or sign of trauma.

The witness comes from a family that has recorded dozens of close encounters since the early 1960s. The fact that there was so much multiple witness in this case was what had drawn my interest in the first place. Though I would have loved to get physical proof, in those days I was still vacillating about whether this was at its core a previously undetected hallucinatory phenomenon. For me, the implant project was in part a search for abnormalities that might induce seizure. I was considering, for example, the possibility that allergies were involved, largely because of the terrific allergic responses that I and some of my friends who had encounters at my cabin had experienced when the visitors came close.

Could it be that the allergies triggered the visitors, or was it the other way around? A secondary aim of the MRI project, then, was to see if there might be, for example, a connection between restricted airways and close encounter events. It is thought that airway flows might affect brain activity, and we considered that this might be a useful area of exploration.

The first witness also reported a number of childhood encounters with apparent nocturnal intruders, coupled with missing time and nosebleeds. The father had experienced intruders and nosebleeds in his childhood as well and had comforted his son by telling him that these things were normal for children. The witness's childhood intruder experiences and nosebleeds took place in 1967 and 1973, in an area of the country that had notable UFO flaps in both of those years.

The case was somewhat compromised because much of the material was dream recall, but it was strengthened by the fact that the witness and his father had seen a UFO while together.

After seeking out a psychologist to help him deal with his memories, he discovered that his sister also had a lifetime of encounter recollections, which she had recorded in a diary without discussing them with the family. He discovered that the dates in the diary coincided with his own memories and dreams, so the case was reasonable.

In the end, though, it did not offer much more than had been available before: lots of suggestive detail, now including the fact that there was nasal passage irritation in a man who believed that he had experienced nasal intrusions. But there was no object.

The second of these witnesses scanned had also reported a nasal intrusion. Her MRI report stated: "inflammatory changes in the paranasal sinuses. Otherwise normal examination." Once again, there was no object present.

I might note here that inflammatory changes like these are a very common MRI finding. Think of how many times people have a slight cold or allergy and irritate their nasal passages just by blowing too hard, and you can see how impossible it was to draw any hard-and-fast conclusion from such an observation.

Still, we now had two people who reported nasal intrusions, and both had irritated nasal passages. In neither case was there any sinusitis present. So these results were actually slightly supportive.

The next study, also of a witness with a memory of nasal intrusion, offered something a little more tangible: "Small polyp right anterior ethmoid cell. Evidence of mild inflammatory changes within the nasal turbinates."

I thought, at last. All we had to do was to remove the polyp and dissect it. Either it was an implant or it wasn't.

The ethmoid cell is located in the ethmoid bone between and below the eyes, at the root of the nose. Given where the needles were believed to be going, an object in this area would be a possibility.

However, the radiologist was not looking for something as easily identifiable as this. The polyp returned like organic material, not metal. Medically, it was trivial and probably the result of allergy. It could easily simply disappear on its own. Even if it didn't, it wasn't causing any sort of symptom or giving the patient any discomfort. It was not, in short, a candidate for surgical removal.

So it had to be abandoned as possible evidence, and we all became very frustrated people. The witness wrote, "Aside from learning that there actually is something in my head, I learned from you guys how important it is to keep a sense of humor about this."

Reluctantly, we brought the MRI study to a close. We had nothing but suggestions and implications, and when we did find a possible surgical candidate, we could not fulfill enough conventional criteria to justify the attempt.

As the clouds of autumn gathered, I found myself in a lonelier position than ever. I had been publicly branded as a cult leader and compared in print and on television and radio to the murderous fanatic Jim Jones, who orchestrated the mass suicide of his entire following. For the most part, the public recognized this lie for what it was, and a television poll showed that ninety-five percent of the viewers of one program did not believe it. Nevertheless, there are always a few eager to hate, and the afternoon after these charges had been repeated on one of the national breakfast programs, I was assaulted in Washington National Airport by being spat upon.

I slipped, in 1989, from being sad and frustrated into a state of clinical depression. The visitors were still in my life. Letters were pouring in. There were fantastic UFO sightings being reported by the Belgian military and civil air authorities. And I had been inches from proof that what I regarded as a desperate but totally rejected emergency was really happening.

I was frantic to break down the fortress of secrecy that has kept the average person ignorant and helpless, to restore my own reputation, and, above all, to trigger the explosion of scientific inquiry that would follow any disclosure that aliens were really here. I wanted it, but as I looked up into the dark of the night, I thought that it was really very far away. How would I ever make any progress? Where would I go from here?

I could not do anything but wait. Time alone was my friend, but time also worked against me, in the sense that, if the visitors were becoming progressively closer, they might eventually overwhelm all of us. To lie in bed at night knowing that you were being falsely turned into a national pariah even as the visitors came slipping through the dark was not easy.

And then there was always the horror of being alone with it. What if this was something evil, and implanted people were controlled people, lost to the power of a force as malevolent as it was incomprehensible?

At times I deliberated finding a surgeon willing to do an exploratory on me and extract one of the bright objects in my brain so that it could be dissected. But what if it was only a cluster of dead tissue? And who would do such a surgery whom I could also trust?

I didn't want to take the risk, and in this, I was not alone. Unknown to me, a witness in Washington State was going through very much the same thing. Betty Stewart Dagenais had experienced contact for many years. This contact had involved a phenomenon that witnesses call "toning," which are sounds that range from things like the raspy burr of digital transmission to series of discrete beeps heard in the head or beside the ear.

I had noticed a few instances of such toning in my own life but nothing that I could describe as recurrent or easily identifiable as an artifact of the encounter phenomenon. In my case, the reason was that I was diagnosed with tinnitus in my left ear in 1976, the result of damage from a truck backfiring near my head. This resulted in a slight but continuous ringing and could also have caused transient sounds. Another cause of such sounds would be circulatory. Such sounds would normally not involve beeps but rather a high-pitched noise building to a peak and then subsiding. A tumor pressing against the aural nerve might also be to blame, either for continuous or transient sounds. Normally, psychological factors do not enter into this, but with all the fear connected with the close encounter issue, I would think that it would be possible for people to experience normal sound transients and then proceed to hallucinate episodes like discrete beeps, relating them to imagined contact experiences.

But Mrs. Dagenais's contacts were too extensive for that, and, in her case, there would soon be physical evidence that suggested a connection between the sounds and her encounters. She had a lump in the pinna, or outside structure, of her left ear that she associated with a close encounter. At the time, I was only vaguely aware of the possibility that objects might be found other than in the nasal cavity or the brain. Budd Hopkins had suggested that a certain type of small scar was associated with close encounter, but we had no way of verifying this at the time.

The scars were called scoop marks because of the fact that they appeared to involve a removal of tissue just below the surface of a small area of the skin, most often on the calf, causing the epidermis to sink. I had never seen one on a witness, and at the time it did not occur to me that they might be associated with objects placed in areas of the body that were more accessible than the cranium.

Betty Dagenais had a very different sort of problem. In 1986, she had been told directly by her abductors that she would die if she had the object in her earlobe taken out. So she endured her encounters as best she could, the way most people endure them, in silence, alone, and without any real help.

I do not possess a record of her encounter experiences, as she never wrote me or communicated with me. I don't know if she knew about my books.

Mrs. Dagenais was obviously deeply concerned about what was happening to her, though, and as we get into the stories of implantees whom I do know and have interviewed, I think that it will become clear why this would be so.

In 1989, Betty Dagenais died of natural causes. There was no question that her death was in any way unusual. She left instructions that her ear was to be autopsied. This was done, and the material extracted from it remained with her family until 1994 when its existence came to the attention of some interested parties. On January 6, 1995, Mrs. Dagenais's dark, one-millimeter-diameter implant was subjected to electro-microscopic analysis by an engineer, and found to be made of aluminum, titanium, silicon, and traces of other minerals. He commented, "Titanium could be used in a transmitter or receiver, as could aluminum." A quality control technician with a specialty in electronics was also questioned about what a device consisting primarily of those elements might be used for. He replied that it "would be a transducer and can be used to transmit signals." He was not told that the device had come from the body of a close encounter witness.

To my knowledge, this was the first implant that was ever subjected to laboratory analysis. But, although interesting, these results cannot be called conclusive. The reason is that the object has an imperfect pedigree. It was not kept under controlled conditions after it was removed from Mrs. Dagenais's body, so it could be that what was examined and what was removed from Mrs. Dagenais are not the same objects. Even though there is no evidence of this, it would obviously be better if objects were analyzed immediately after their removal. This is especially important if their composition is ordinary.

Also in 1989, close encounter witness Jesse Long, a distant cousin of Amelia Earhart, was coming to the end of more than thirty years of enduring what is without a doubt one of the most wondrous and terrible human experiences ever recorded. This diffident, careful, and altogether remarkable man has recorded what he remembers of his lifetime of encounters in an amazing manuscript, as yet unpublished.

Unknown to me and to practically anybody else, Mr. Long had presented himself at a doctor's office to have an implant removed from his shin that had been inserted when he was four years old. Fortunately for all of us after it came out, he kept it against a time when it might be analyzed. In this case, it is less important that the object remained untouched by science for all those years, because of what has been found.

15:

Dr. Roger Leir's Discovery

Jesse Long's remarkable object remained unexamined until 1996, and between 1989 and 1994, to my knowledge there was nothing of significance done about implants by anybody.

"Psychic surgeons" claimed to be able to remove them, and some even charged fees for this service. Abduction researchers said that they existed but that they turned to powder or disappeared when extracted because the aliens didn't want them analyzed. So they became rather mythical, a sort of Holy Grail.

I went through those long, frustrating years struggling with my continuing experience, persecution that would not stop, and consequent depression. I was haunted and hunted at the same time.

Although after the MRI study I gave up hope of ever finding a physical implant, not everybody did, which turned out to be fortunate. In June of 1994, UFO investigator Derrel Sims of Houston met Roger Leir, D.P.M., at a conference in California. When Mr. Sims became aware that Dr. Leir was something quite rare, a medical professional who was also interested enough in the UFO question to be a member of the Mutual UFO Network, he told him that he knew some witnesses in Houston who believed that they had implants and might want to have them removed.

Roger Leir is among a small company of scientists

like Dr. Hill and Dr. John Mack who are too curious about the world around them to dismiss the unlikely as impossible. And like the others, he is a good scientist. He was interested because he wanted to know if there was anything real to the witnesses' claims. He saw that he had an opportunity to conduct a test.

He made an offer to Sims: If the people involved would fly to California at their own expense, he and a colleague would make all the necessary arrangements and perform the surgeries at no charge.

Up until this time, it does not appear that there had ever been any formal attempt to remove and then study such an object. With the exception of the work done on Colette Dowell, the results of our MRI study had never been published. The only object that might possibly be considered an anomaly was the one in Dr. Dowell's head, and there was a good likelihood that, despite all the questions about it, it was a pituitary adenoma. The existence of the Dagenais and Long implants was hardly known, and they had not yet been studied.

But witnesses claimed—swore—that this happened to them. And if there were actual implants, well, that would be a terribly important thing to find out. Perhaps because the area was so unknown, Leir was intrigued. His approach was, "Let's see if there's anything there."

It turned out that X-ray images had already been obtained of objects in two people. One individual had two objects in her left foot, another had one in his left hand. Both of these people were close encounter witnesses, and both felt that the objects involved had been implanted into their bodies by aliens.

It must be added at this juncture that an immediate objection is that it isn't all that uncommon for foreign objects to become embedded in feet and hands. So maybe these were just innocuous objects, a bit of gravel that came to be under the skin of a hand during a fall, a small piece of iron that got into a shoe and worked its way into the foot, or, in the case of a T-shaped object, a surgical inclusion.

If they were naturally occurring objects, they would either have been rejected or, if the body could not accomplish that, been encapsulated. Sometimes an encapsulation can involve tissue, but in general it also involves the deposition of minerals around the unwanted material. A surgery would answer the question of how the body had responded to the objects, not to mention making material available for analysis.

There are obviously any number of things that can work their way under the skin, especially of a hand or foot. Graphite debris left when a pencil lead pierces the skin would be the closest thing in external appearance, for example, to an implant. Commonly, pencil lead leaves a mark under the skin that can remain for years as a faint gray discoloration. It is medically trivial, and not in any way comparable to these objects, which were much larger and also deeper than a pencil lead would ordinarily be found.

If not a pencil lead, then the objects could be bits of shrapnel or other debris—nailheads, bits of gravel, any number of things.

According to the witnesses, they had entered in the following ways:

The woman recalled an encounter and abduction that had taken place nearly thirty years previously. But at the time she was not aware of any object being placed in her body. However, when her foot was X-rayed in connection with an unrelated problem, the returns for two unknown objects in her left big toe had appeared. She could not recall any accident that might have driven these objects into her foot, and they were large enough to have caused quite noticeable pain and trauma. So she had become concerned that they were connected to her close encounter, and she wanted them out.

Dr. Leir could see from the X ray that the objects seemed to be metal. They were deep in the tissue of the big toe, one on each side of the bone. One appeared to be small and seedlike; the other was a distinct "T" shape that he at first assumed had been placed by a surgeon. But there was no scar and no surgery was reported by the witness.

The second witness had quite an unusual story to tell. At the age of six, he had observed a basketball-sized object floating in the air in an open space behind his house. As he walked up to it, the thing had exploded, leaving him with the feeling that a fragment of it had been embedded in his hand. No wound remained, and nothing was done.

When, as an adult, he was X-rayed, he was surprised and disturbed to discover that there was actually something there. The strange incident was the only thing that had ever happened to him that had involved a possible injury to his hand.

Over the course of the next few weeks, plans were made to carry out the surgeries. Leir presented these X rays to a radiologist, who confirmed that they appeared to be of metal objects.

Prior to their meeting at Dr. Leir's office, neither of these witnesses had come into contact with each other. They had not, for example, been involved in the same accident, or been exposed to similar metal fragments in a shared work situation—or any work situation, for that matter.

Dr. Leir and his colleague, a general surgeon, were aware of how controversial these surgeries might turn out to be and were concerned about creating a very high-quality record of the proceedings. As a result, all of the operations were recorded on video, and the excised objects were also photographed at the moment of removal. There were a number of witnesses present, among them Alice Leavy, the state section director for the Ventura–Santa Barbara MUFON, whose own case would later become one of the best documented on record.

The general surgeon who was present and did all above-the-ankle procedures and the witnesses will not be named in this discussion. The surgeon doesn't want to expose himself to the danger of license-related attacks such as those that have occurred against other professionals who have expressed a public interest in this subject, including Dr. Leir himself and, of course, Harvard professor Dr. John Mack, whose book *Abduction: Human Encounters with Aliens*, brought him challenges both to his professional credentials and his tenure.

There were a number of other people in attendance at these surgeries. The surgical nurse was Denise Messina; the video photographer was Mike Evans, who also holds a degree in nursing. Jack and Ruth Carlson created a paper record of the event. The closed-circuit television system that allowed the surgeries to be witnessed from outside of the operating room was devised by Bert Clemens.

Among the witnesses in that room were Derrel Sims, Alice Leavy, and the coordinator of the event, Janet Warnick.

I mention the names of all of these people because I want to make it as clear as possible that these surgeries were not performed in isolation. Careful records were kept, and each step of the procedures can be seen on the video that was made. This is important, because it can be observed that there was no scar tissue above the objects before the surgeries, and the objects were actually brought out of the wounds and displayed on camera, proving that something was really removed.

The patients were processed in a manner that had been carefully planned. First, a full medical history was taken. Next, the patients were asked to provide as complete a history of their close encounter experiences as they could. They were then interviewed by a psychologist.

Prior to surgery, new X rays were taken and reviewed. Also at that time, small quantities of blood were removed from each patient for the purpose of creating a transport medium for the objects that would soon be excised. The blood was then centrifuged and the serum extracted. An anticoagulant was added to the serum, and the medium was ready.

The first patient, who had the two objects in her toe, was then taken into the operating room. Even using the X ray as a guide, it took more than an hour to locate the first object. In and of itself, this is not unusual when attempting to excise objects from deep tissue. However, despite hypnosis performed by Sims, who is a certified hypnoanesthesiologist, and extensive anesthesia to the toe, the patient began to respond to the probing, reporting bursts of pain. With this problem controlled, further probing of the area revealed a small gray object. At the moment that it was excised from the surrounding tissue, the patient reported another burst of pain.

Dr. Leir has had extensive experience removing foreign objects from the foot, and he reports that this type of reaction occurs when the object is involved with a nerve. The disturbance to the adjacent nerve fibers will overcome even heavy local anesthesia. However, this response is sufficiently unusual that the additional risk of general anesthesia is not indicated in surgeries of this type.

Once it was removed, Leir found that the tiny object was enclosed in a very dense membrane. He was surprised to discover that this tissue was so tough that he could not remove the object from the structure enclosing it even with aggressive use of a scalpel.

Leaving the object still encased in the membrane, he turned his attention to the other side of the toe. This too required a lengthy dissection, and the patient was similarly sensitive when the object was finally located. It was enclosed in the same type of dark membrane as the first object.

One of these objects was tiny and hard, about the size and shape of a cantaloupe seed, about two millimeters in diameter. The other was T-shaped, as it had been on the X ray, and somewhat larger, around three millimeters on a side. This object had the appearance of something that had been constructed out of two straight pieces.

The incision was then closed, and the surgery on the second patient soon commenced. This surgery proceeded similarly to the first, with the patient immediately reporting discomfort when the object was probed.

This object was strikingly similar in appearance to one of the objects that had been removed from the first patient, as it also resembled a cantaloupe seed and was about the same size.

If these were the result of accidents, how could it be that two people who had never met would end up bearing such similar objects in their extremities? If these were identifiable bits of debris this would not be hard to understand. But there was no obvious way to identify them, and in all of their quite extensive careers, neither surgeon had ever seen anything like them.

The combination of the fact that these objects were present in these people, and that two of them were nearly identical, is obviously compelling and disturbing evidence. Although it does not prove that aliens were responsible, it strongly suggests that the objects were artificially inserted into these people by somebody.

It developed that the membranes were almost as strange as the objects that they enclosed. After they became dry they weakened and it was possible to remove them and send them, along with surrounding tissue, for pathology study. The biopsies were performed at a local lab, which was informed that the tissue had been dissected from the area around some foreign bodies, which had also been removed. The lab was given no information about the unusual situation.

It was confirmed that the sensitivity of the patients to the surgery was due to the fact that nerve tissue had somehow grown to surround the objects. One of the reports stated that the fragments submitted contained "fibroconnective tissue and fat demonstrating peripheral nerve and pressure receptors." This growth of nerve tissue is a very unusual finding.

The membranes themselves were formed out of superficial rather than deep tissue. As the body does not possess genetic instructions that enable it to create skin deep inside muscle tissue, it is hard to see how these membranes could have grown naturally. In any case, they were the probable reason that the underlying objects were not rejected.

At this point, a misfortune occurred, as funds could not be found to carry out analysis of the recovered materials. I was not aware that the surgery had even happened, or I would have immediately offered to undertake this work.

Thus it was not until nearly a year later that the objects were actually placed under analysis. The benefactor was the National Institute of Discovery Sciences (NIDS), which is managed by former United States Army nonlethal weapons specialist Dr. John Alexander.

NIDS contracted with New Mexico Tech to do a study, and the following battery of tests were applied to the objects:

DENSITY IMMERSION USING TOLUENE
MECHANICAL PROPERTIES ANALYSIS
X-RAY SPECTROSCOPY
SCANNING ELECTRON MICROSCOPY
X-RAY DIFFRACTION ANALYSIS
ELECTRICAL/MAGNETIC PROPERTIES ANALYSIS

Two of the three samples were found to be essentially similar in density, the third one lighter. One of these was then broken. A core was observed of shiny metallic material. The lighter sample, which had been the T-shaped object, had no core. There was a dramatic difference in hardness between the samples. The seedlike objects were as hard as quartz, while the lighter T-shaped one was as soft as calcite.

The two seedlike objects both had insulating outer shells that were composed of iron, phosphorus, and calcium, with small amounts of chlorine present.

The lighter sample had a very complex structure and composition. Its small, harder areas were essentially similar to the heavier objects. The more extensive lighter material consisted of iron, silicon, phosphorous, molybdenum, chlorine, sodium, and calcium, with a trace of copper.

The cores of all the objects were found to be iron-carbon, probably ferrite, as the sample was ferromagnetic.

The lab initially had not been told anything about the possible origin of the materials. Later, they were informed that they had been dissected during surgeries. In a letter of opinion, they offered the hypothesis that the object might be made of meteoric material and suggested a number of different meteorites that had displayed similar contents. It was noted that iron meteorites contain a small amount of nickel, but the fact that this was not present in these objects could be due to their being fragments of a larger sample.

It was also hypothesized that an iron sliver embedded in the body could cause a calcification reaction, and that the mineral cladding observed might be due to this. In any case, the minerals would have prevented tissue rejection even if the membranes did not. However, what meteoric iron was doing in the hands and feet of these people is not known. If they had been struck by micrometeors, then there would surely have been scar tissue. And the T-shaped object, obviously not a surgical staple or nailhead or something else common, seems to be a construction of an unknown kind, made from unusual materials.

A year later, another group of surgeries were held, this time involving three patients including Alice Leavy.

My wife, Anne, and I were among the many witnesses to these surgeries, and observed them on closed-circuit television. As I watched the monitor, I found myself quite overcome with emotion, and the attendant psychologist very kindly took time out to help me. Even so, I was unable to remain in the room and had to go out for an hour simply to collect myself. The reason I felt such powerful emotions was that I have been trying so long to get science and society to admit the existence of the close encounter problem, and the idea that we might actually be closer to this excited me but also made me feel very aware of the injustice associated with the scorn and abuse that close encounter witnesses endure.

I saw Dr. Leir and his colleagues as heroes, and time has only made me more sure of this opinion. As I write this, Dr. Leir has finished his own book about his work, titled *The Aliens and the Scalpel*, but I cannot yet report that it has a publisher.

There were three surgeries performed on the afternoon of May 18, 1996. I witnessed one of them on the closed-circuit monitor and observed a second in part on the monitor and in part firsthand. I watched this one through a window in the door of the operating room because I wanted to be able to say that I had personally seen the object extracted. I saw it being probed for, found, and drawn out.

In addition to video, still photography was again used to record these surgeries. Like me, I have no doubt that the doctors were concerned that there would be accusations of some sort of sleight of hand. I satisfied myself, in one case, that the surgery was absolutely normal, and the photographic record proves that the others were no different.

Given all the witnesses and the visual record, questioning that these operations happened, it would seem to me, would be a way of putting off the real question that they have raised: What are implants and why are they being found in people's bodies?

The particular surgery I observed personally was one that I considered to be of paramount importance, that of Alice Leavy. At the time, I had no way of knowing what would happen in Alice's life later, but there were already two reasons why I considered this surgery so important.

The first was that Alice's first awareness of the existence of the implant had come during a hypnosis session. Unlike the other patients, she did have a small scoopmark scar above the area where the object was found, but she had no memory of what caused this injury.

So in Alice's case, this surgery would to a degree test the question of how well hypnosis worked to find the facts in close encounters.

This type of hypnosis, where the witness is regressed to find evidence that is totally absent from natural memory, is the most severely criticized. But in this case, the efficacy of the hypnosis was immediately challenged with X ray, and it was found that an apparent foreign object was present in the area concerned. And then the object was removed.

So it appeared that hypnosis did have an efficacy here. Without it, Alice would never have suspected that an object was present, as the small scar was innocuous and there was no indication of any lump under the skin.

There was another reason why the case was so important. This was the location of the object. It would be highly unlikely that a foreign body would get lodged deep in a calf muscle, unless the person had been a victim of shrapnel from an explosion, or had experienced the end of some kind of projectile breaking off in the tissue, or been hit by a bullet or BB. But Alice had never had any such injury.

Of the three surgeries performed, one involved excision of a triangular metallic object from a man's jaw, and two involved BB-sized grayish-white balls being removed from the legs. The metallic triangle from the jaw area also was covered with a membrane similar to one that covered an object Dr. Leir had removed from another patient's neck in an undocumented surgery.

So far, none of the objects removed has appeared to be particularly unusual. All are made of known materials. What is strange about them is that they were in these people at all.

What happened afterward was in many ways even more stunning than the removals themselves. I had wondered what might happen when an implant was taken out. If it had been inserted by aliens, would they react to what had been done?

In early December of 1996, I followed up the surgeries with a phone call to Alice Leavy. How was she doing? Fine. Had anything unusual happened after the removal?

Some people had felt as if they had lost a sense of intuition when their object was removed, but Alice was glad that hers was gone.

In her own quiet way, she then shocked me almost speechless by saying, "They came back and stayed for six days."

What in the world did she mean?

Thus begins the story of the Camarillo, California, sighting sequence. At 4:55 in the afternoon of December 2, 1996, an object was observed about fifty degrees up in the northern sky by a member of a family friendly to Alice. This object might easily have been an early star, but it was observed to be moving slowly, either rising into the northern sky or coming closer to the viewer, it was impossible to tell which.

It emitted a pure white light and was not in any way similar to aircraft, which could be seen in the area at the same time. Sunlight reflecting off their fuselages had a reddish hue.

At 5:10 P.M., the object changed color, from pure white to reddish-peach, suggesting that the setting sun was at least in part responsible for the light. But the thought that it might be a balloon was ended when, a moment later, a small pinpoint object of the same color appeared below the main object, moving downward. Soon, small puffs of some sort of substance began to be emitted from the top of the larger object, a process now familiar from the Mexican videos and Dr. Hill's discussion of it as a plasmic effect. Then another small object separated from the main object on its left side. The two objects moved in tandem, then disappeared in what looked like a puff of smoke or mist. The sighting ended at 5:12.

The witness reported this event to Alice Leavy, and she arranged for a group to visit the location the next afternoon, armed with a video camera and still cameras with telephoto lenses.

The object appeared at 4:46 P.M. It was more defined than the evening before and had a spherical appearance. After some problems, video recording commenced. At 5:09, the object became reddish. Then a tiny dot of light was observed through binoculars to emerge out of the top of the larger object and move away from it. This was not visible on the videotape, however, due to the lack of detail resolution.

The object then changed, becoming a vertical chain of smaller objects that soon vanished. This transformation was recorded on the video, and much detail was captured by the still cameras as well, including the satellite objects exiting the large object.

I have seen some of the still photographs and can verify their remarkable combination of clarity and impossibility. Being that the object's actions were observed by half a dozen witnesses, both through binoculars and with the naked eye, and recorded on video and photographed at the same time, it is hard to maintain a case that they are anything that can be explained. After analyzing the video, Jerry Barber of Sunland Video Productions thought that the object, when it moved, might have accelerated at five thousand miles an hour.

So Alice Leavy, from whose leg one of the most inexplicable implants was removed, a few months later ended up witness to one of the best documented UFO sightings in recent United States history.

Of course, it is impossible to tell if this represented an attempt to communicate with her, but given the ultrahigh-level strangeness of everything else in the UFO and close encounter world, the possibility must at least be entertained.

But perhaps the lights in the sky have nothing to do with the implants in people's bodies. Up until the Camarillo sightings, the witness testimony itself offered the only link. Still, the case is far from perfect. We don't have any convincing video of a witness being taken aboard a UFO and only one that may even show an alien. Not only isn't there any physical or visual evidence that witnesses and UFOs are connected, there is no direct evidence that aliens are involved.

So how can we be sure? The answer is that we cannot, not just yet. The objects that Leir removed shouldn't have been in the witnesses, true, and that some that came from unrelated witnesses were identical is startlingly suggestive of intentional implantation, but the only way to determine that they were put there by aliens would be to prove that they were of non-Earth origin. So we know that they didn't belong where they were found but not who put them there. And we are far from knowing why.

Even the fact that Alice both had an object removed and then ended up being treated to a fabulous UFO sighting could be coincidence. I don't think that it's possible to say that the sighting can be explained in any normal manner, not given what is on the videotape and the photographs, but there is no nonspeculative way to relate it to the removed implant.

Still, it is also true that Alice experienced a dramatic increase in close encounter activity after the implant was removed, something that has also been reported by other witnesses. Alice was kind enough to share some entries from her personal journal with me, and I will let her tell the story of what happened to her after her surgery.

"July 11, 1996. I felt different since the surgery. No longer had the drive I once had to investigate UFO abduction. Just felt different. That evening, around 11:00 P.M., I started to get a bad headache. Unusual. On the right side of my face behind my temple and eye. I took a pain killer. (Aspirin-Free P.M.) I went to sleep around 12:10 P.M." Her husband and one of her two daughters were also asleep. The second daughter was watching television in her room. "Sometime between 12:15 and 1:00, she noticed her TV having double images on a few channels." She then turned off her TV and went to sleep at 1:00 A.M. The following events then unfolded: "Bill [Alice's husband] says that at 1:05 A.M. he awoke as a bright white light was shining into our bedroom. He thought it was time to get up and get ready to go to work, as it was so bright. He sat up in bed, looked at his clock—it was 1:05 A.M. He thought, 'Oh, good, I can go back to sleep, it's not time to get up.' He then looked at my side of the bed, and noticed that the covers were pulled back and I was gone."

He assumed that she was in the bathroom or something, but she reports that the medication made her sleep heavily all night and that she had no memory of getting up. The feeling of illness and exhaustion that she next reports will be familiar from some of the close encounter stories reported in Part Two of this book. "When I awoke my right ear hurt, and it was wet inside. All day I was very ill. I had an earache in my right ear, a headache and my stomach was very upset." They also found that their dog had apparently panicked during the night, to the extent that it had scratched three large holes in the carpet in their family room, something that it had never done before.

These sorts of disturbances, with their vague implications of some sort of an outside factor being responsible, are very typical of what many witnesses report. Usually, they must be set aside as probable dreams and misperceptions, but in this case, the presence of the implant means that we could as easily be looking at fragmentary memories of a very real intrusion of some sort. But who came, and why?

It is going to require a methodical and scientific study to answer these questions. Since there are thousands of witnesses with implants, and many ready right now to submit to surgery and donate their objects to science, it would seem logical to seek a harvest of them. Still, because they suggest a reality that is so very far from the expectations of science and society, the tendency to continue to ignore the problem will persist. False and sabotaged research may be produced to facilitate continued rejection of the data.

Even if the objects are made of ordinary material, it may be that they contain extraordinary technology that we cannot detect. For example, if somebody had been given a transistor to analyze in 1915, he or she would have been able to report on its composition but would have had no idea of its function. It would not even have been possible to determine that it had a function. We may well be in the same situation with these objects.

It would be persuasive, I felt, if there existed an implant made of unusual materials, or showing obvious signs of the presence of technology that we do not understand. So for me the question became, could it be possible to find an object that not only was extracted from a close encounter witness but was also a mineral or technological mystery?

Meet Jesse Long and his friend Junior.

16:

Jesse's Story

It is a summer afternoon in 1957, in the small country town of Rogersville, Tennessee. Jesse Long and his brother, Johnny, are playing in their yard when a man in a dark uniform gestures to them from the edge of the woods nearby.

Modern children would have reacted by running. But America in 1957 was a different place, the more so in rural areas. The boys, age five and four, look curiously toward the man. When he gestures to them with a long rod that he's carrying, they go over to see what he wants. Jesse is a little uneasy, so he takes John, who is seventeen months younger, by the hand.

The man leads them into the woods.

Soon they arrive at the top of a small hill, where stands what Jesse remembers as a little round house. The man then points the rod at them. It emits a bluish-white light, which paralyzes them. At this point, Jesse feels fear.

In the house, the boys are separated. Johnny is taken into a room where he finds toys. He plays with them, watched over by what appears to be a giant insect like a praying mantis. He does not feel fear for himself, but he does hear his brother screaming and crying in the next room.

Jesse is not having such a benign experience. He has come face-to-face with a tall man, very thin but human looking, with unusually large but otherwise normal eyes. He is told to remain calm and that they don't want to hurt him. Figures he cannot see work around the lower half of his body. He experiences pain from his leg, and he screams and cries.

The next thing he knows, he and his brother are back in the sandbox where they had been playing. They had both been told not to talk about it, and this is a more than normal suggestion. They want to tell, in order to get comfort and reassurance from their parents, but they cannot. Somehow, this terrifying and bizarre experience is simply swallowed by these two children.

It is not, however, reconciled, nor is it forgotten. Both of them remember the encounter.

John, who is an artist, as an adult built a sculpture of a giant praying mantis and lives in a house constructed to resemble the round house on the hill.

Afterward, Jesse becomes fearful. He is so scared at night that he often hides under the covers. For him to sleep, the window at the head of his bed must be shut and the curtains drawn.

I first heard of Jesse Long in 1996 from a friend, special effects artist Steve Neill, as one of a number of close encounter witnesses who went public and as a result experienced damage to their careers. I had told Steve of my new plans to begin analysis of materials and do controlled studies of implants, plans that were inspired by the Dagenais case and the work of Dr. Leir and Derrel Sims.

Steve said that there was a man in Los Angeles who possessed an implant, and that when it had been removed from him, he'd had the surgery photographed and videotaped.

I called Jesse Long and found that he did indeed

possess this object, along with the videotape and photographs of the removal. As we talked, I quickly realized that this was potentially a good case with which to begin my new effort. It had two interesting elements: a second witness who had natural memory of the event, and a physical implant to back it up. But it wasn't perfect. In a perfect case, there would be adult witnesses to the abduction as well as an implant that had been removed under controlled conditions and then placed directly into the hands of analyzing scientists.

Despite these weaknesses, on the mental ten-scale I had originally developed to help me evaluate letters, this case was a seven, which was extremely high. Most cases are a two or a three. Five would be the highest number so far achieved.

A one is a dream memory corroborated in some way by physical effects. An example would be somebody dreaming that he or she had contact, only to find a day or so later that there were confirmed UFO reports in the area. A two would add some kind of physical side effect to the encounter, such as a bloody nose. In a three case, there would be waking memory instead of or in addition to the dream memory. Four adds parties to the abduction, such as two people in the same family dreaming the same dream. In a five, they have shared waking experience. Six adds observers who independently see UFOs in the area during the abduction. Seven adds other conscious witnesses who observe aliens. Eight adds evidence such as an implant observable under the skin. In a nine case, there is extensive conscious encounter added to an extracted implant. In a ten case, the implant would be extracted under controlled conditions and immediately transferred to a lab.

Beyond that, and off the scale, would be proof that the implant could not have come into the body naturally, and the final proof would be an implant that demonstrably could not have been manufactured on Earth.

Talking to Jesse, I got a very positive impression of his sincerity. But I also know that sincere belief may support false memories.

I was rather surprised to learn that his implant had been removed as long ago as 1989 and that he had not been able to find what he regarded as a satisfactory situation for it to be studied. He'd had two offers, though, one apparently from NASA and one from a private foundation. The NASA offer had come to him in a completely unbidden telephone call. He did not even know how they had gotten his name. They offered to fly him to Houston, but he was too unsure of the situation to respond positively. The private foundation wanted the implant but did not want him to come along with it and would not tell him whether they would release the results to him.

So the object had stayed in a small case on a chain around his neck, held there day and night for seven years.

Mr. Long was without personal resources to conduct the study on his own, because, since 1989, his career had been virtually destroyed. In that year, after the object was removed, he had begun to talk publicly about his situation. No sooner had he appeared on a fairly obscure public access television show than his formerly thriving business as a script supervisor began to decline.

I have heard this tale of woe so many times from witnesses who go public that I always suggest in the strongest terms that they remain anonymous.

There are many reasons for the persecution. Local skeptics groups actively engage in persecution of witnesses. UFO groups who do not agree with a witness's interpretation will do the same, as will religious groups, especially fundamentalists. There may be government intervention at times.

I am not much of a conspiracy theorist, but I do believe that a combination of cultural bias and even small amounts of active persecution can destroy lives and careers, because I have seen it. In point of fact, I do not know of a single witness who has gone public in the United States and not suffered economic and social hardship as a result.

Mr. Long's profession of script supervisor is quite competitive, and I have no doubt that his public statements were used against him. A script supervisor needs to be clearheaded, and the suggestion that he might have some sort of a mental problem was probably what devastated his career.

On another level, it was interesting to me that we had undertaken our MRI study in 1989, Betty Dagenais's implant had been autopsied in 1989 and Jesse's object had been removed in 1989. Only now, in 1996, was anything more being done.

Why had all this time passed with nothing happening? I had been through a devastating depression, suffered a financial attack that led to the loss of my famous cabin and almost to my suicide, and had only gradually rebuilt my life. I don't know what happened to the Dagenais object during that period. Jesse's implant had remained in his immediate possession.

In 1995, I was in San Antonio a good deal, and I had met Catherine Cooke, the head of a local organization called the Mind-Science Foundation. This foundation had been created by Tom Slick, a wealthy oilman who engaged in the first scientific search for the abominable snowman, and sought to bring science to the study of rejected phenomena such as psychism. Slick also founded the Southwest Research Institute (SWRI), and I realized that it was conceivable that Mind-Science, with its mandate to explore the frontier, and Southwest, with its fabulous scientific resources, could work together to study implants. There would be resistance, of course, but I felt that, with Cathy Cooke's support, I might be able to make a little headway.

Cooke enthusiastically agreed to help fund the Long study, and we were soon ready to fly Jesse to Texas.

Southwest Research Center is divided into two parts: the non-profit Biomedical Research Division and the Southwest Research Institute, which is not-for-profit and subsists on contracted research for government, industry, and the individual. We would be buying analysis from the Materials Sciences Division of Southwest Research Institute which would not be asked to make any commitment about the object. In any event, most of the scientists involved in the work didn't know where it had come from, and the staff member scientist involved, Dr. William Mallow, was never asked his opinion about UFOs.

Before I can turn to a discussion of the results of our studies, and why they made this such an incredible case, it is important to complete Jesse's story. For it is somewhere between the physical evidence and narratives like this that we are likely to find the beginnings of a real answer to the question of what UFOs and the close encounter experience may mean.

So far, nothing that I have told of Jesse's experience has been from memories extracted with hypnosis.

These are things that Jesse remembered in natural memory.

I have seen two childhood photographs of him. Jesse appears to be extremely uneasy. When I showed one of the pictures to a specialist in child psychology, she said that Jesse appeared to be grief stricken. Since he was not in grief when the picture was made, she thought that it might indicate that he was depressed.

This is not a usual state for a child and could well be related to an effort to conceal what the child regarded as a frightful secret. In one of the photographs, Jesse is touching his shin, in what he reports became an almost compulsive childhood gesture.

Jesse's next strong memory of something unusual is a vivid experience of flying over Florence, Alabama, the town to which the family had recently moved. He did not feel that this was a dream, not even at the time, but he also could not understand how it could be anything else.

The next winter, this harassed child became frightened of Santa Claus, because he could get into the house when people were asleep and nobody could stop him. Fears of the Sandman, the Easter Bunny and such sometimes seem to occur in children who are having trouble with the close encounter experience and may be related to memories of the figures they see and the apparent ease with which they gain access to the child.

When Jesse was twelve, a dreadfully disturbing event took place: Shadowy figures began to show him babies and tell him they were his children.

It is hard to think of anything more upsetting for a little boy just beginning to cope with puberty. I have never heard of a child fixating on a fear like this, or even dreaming about such a thing—nowhere except inside the close encounter experience.

Later, we will explore further the way that the experience connects to sexuality and genetics, because no discussion of it can be complete without reference to these two areas.

It is difficult to know how, as a child, Jesse really felt about these experiences. He is too gentle and straightforward a man to express much raw emotion, but when he said to me, "I was scared," I felt a wave of sympathy pour through me.

What external force would do this to a child? What child would have a nightmare like this?

His experiences continued. He would recall seeing craft flying above the streets of the town and be terrified that they were coming for him.

The matter did not end with the close of childhood. In college, he saw a light come down from the sky and land in a field behind his house. He went out to see what was happening—only to find himself suddenly turned around and walking in the opposite direction, with no way to explain what happened to half an hour of his life. He had been walking toward the light, then experienced missing time and found himself walking away.

Of course, the time is not missing. The victim's memory is what is missing.

The picture Jesse presents is one that is very typical of people who are troubled by their encounters. It is hard to distinguish between the behaviors and feelings reported in many such cases and stories that might be told by a child who was trying to cope with repeated nocturnal visitations by an abusive human intruder by imposing imaginative reconstructions on acts that are too terrifying or dangerous to remember accurately.

In Jesse's case, though, the display of the babies stands out. It is an unusual memory for a child, even one whose mind is trying to screen conventional abuse with more palatable memories, or dissociating from the abused part of the self.

Long continued to struggle in his adult life. For the most part, he remembered what he referred to as "silhouettes," small figures moving very quickly in his house.

Through all of this time, the strange object remained embedded under the skin of his leg. Occasionally, there was mild irritation, but he made no effort to have it removed.

He moved to Los Angeles and began his career. As a member of the union, his future seemed secure. He was coping as best he could with his strange dream life and also living with wild mood swings and many other symptoms of a high level of stress that did not appear to have any clear source in his life.

He remembered a good childhood and was still in close touch with other members of his family, including his parents. Around this time, John built the house in the woods that was shaped like a UFO.

In 1989, Long read Budd Hopkins's book *Intruders*. He was startled by the similarity between his own memories and some of the stories told in the book, and he wrote Hopkins a letter describing his experiences.

At this point, a skeptic would say that he took a step into the fantasy world of the abduction researchers. And previously any responsible party would have to say that, at the very least, his reading of a book on the subject by a writer like Hopkins or myself would quite possibly reconstruct disturbed but essentially normal memories around the imagery of alien abduction.

But things are changing, and Long's case is one of

the first to reflect this change. Not only did he have his memories, he also had the object in his leg.

Hopkins referred Long to a support group in Los Angeles, and he eventually ended up working with Yvonne Smith, who has devoted her life to helping people who suffer from what I believe ought to be called contact trauma.

According to members of her group whom I have talked to, Yvonne has been successful in relieving them of stress. She uses hypnosis, and although it is effective in helping them to come to terms with their emotions, whether it is also an effective mnemonic tool is still an open question. As is suggested by the case of Alice Leavy, it is probably better than has been suggested by those who would deny the validity of the whole close encounter experience.

Some of the problems with hypnosis have been dimensionalized in a recent study conducted by Dr. Joseph Green, a psychologist at Ohio State University, and Dr. Steven Jay Lynn, a psychologist at SUNY Binghamton. They reported on their study at the annual meeting of the American Psychological Association in August of 1997.

In the study, forty-eight students who had passed a susceptibility test that showed them to be highly hypnotizable were divided into two groups. Prior to regression, thirty-two of the students were warned that hypnosis could lead to false memories and told that it could not make people remember things that they would not ordinarily remember. Sixteen students were given no such warning.

The students were asked to select an uneventful night from the previous week during which they had experienced normal sleep with no recalled dreams. Under hypnosis, they were asked if they had heard a loud noise at four in the morning. Afterward, they were again asked this question.

Forty-four percent of the students who had not been forewarned reported that they had indeed heard it. Only twenty-eight percent of those warned made such a report.

This suggests that false memories can be induced in hypnotized subjects simply by asking questions. Also, though, people warned that this may happen may have an easier time discriminating.

I know Yvonne Smith both personally and by reputation, and I can say with assurance that she would never intentionally lead a witness. In fact, most researchers using hypnosis are well aware of these problems and compensate for them as best they can.

We cannot know, however, the degree to which the volatile situation and the hypnotic process may combine together to induce inaccuracies in witness memory. It is also clear, though, that regression offers both positive therapeutic effects for witnesses and may possibly be uncovering some very real experiences.

Nevertheless, extreme care has to be taken, and when a witness enters hypnosis, a line is crossed. This is especially true when the witness's natural memories are vague or even nonexistent. But that was not Jesse's situation. He went into hypnosis with a considerable store of intact natural memory.

In his work with Yvonne Smith, Jesse found that his uncertain experiences of the little "silhouettes" that came for him in the night concealed a great deal of suppressed memory, and it was extremely disturbing. He remembered instances of forced extraction of semen and being frequently shown children who were claimed to be the offspring of these assaults.

This led him to decide to have the object in his leg

surgically removed, and this was done in May of 1989. There were no complications, and the surgery took only a few minutes. The object on the tape and in the photographs looks very much like the one that Jesse showed me in 1996. Although I cannot say that it is the same object, some quite shocking discoveries about it have made what happened to it in the years between 1989 and 1996 less important. No matter where it was during those years, and when it was put into his body, it is one very strange object.

A few months after it was removed, he had a horrendous experience, remembered in full consciousness, in which his visitors reappeared, apparently searching for the object. Not finding it, they left a painful injury in his leg in the form of a hole burned by a bright light, apparently a laser.

An event that took place in 1992, some years after the removal, suggests that the excision of the object had not ended his experiences. This happened in Atlanta, during the filming of a feature for which he was doing script supervision. It had been a long time between films, and he considered himself extremely lucky to get this job.

He had been provided with an apartment for the duration of the film's location time in Atlanta, and one night he was awakened by a noise. He found himself paralyzed. He could see that there were shadows standing in the room. Terrified, he tried to protect himself, but he could not move. He was somehow transported to another location and placed in a reclining chair with his feet raised and his head back. A moment later a woman so thin that she appeared to be in an advanced state of starvation came onto him. As he puts it, "I began to feel and see that a sex act was taking place."

He pleaded for her to stop. He was so frightened and revolted that his struggles finally overwhelmed the paralysis enough to enable him to grab the woman's shoulders and push her off his body.

Up to this point, nothing in this situation is beyond conventional explanation. The "old hag" attack is a commonplace of psychology, a type of hypnagogic hallucination first described more than a hundred years ago. In a normal situation of this type, the breaking of the paralysis would cause the apparition simply to disappear. The victim, shaken and horrified, would eventually return to normal sleep.

In this case, though, that is not what happened. Paralysis did not cause the apparition to disappear. Instead, the woman fought fiercely, clawing Jesse's left arm as he thrust her away from him.

There was no further memory, but upon awakening the next morning, his attention was immediately drawn to a group of scratches on his left arm. Unlike the "old hag" nightmare, which is usually vividly remembered the morning after, Jesse had only a confused jumble of memories, much more like a trauma victim immediately after an assault or accident.

He and another member of the crew habitually took a walk together after breakfast, and this morning he showed her the marks. That afternoon, they were watching second unit film footage taken from a helicopter that had been flying at treetop level. While watching this, Jesse suddenly recalled being removed from his apartment and going up into the sky.

This unlocked a flood of memory, which came back so powerfully that he had a panic attack and collapsed. A 911 call was made, and he ended up in an emergency room with a diagnosis of shock.

Even though his work on the film was completely

satisfactory, rumors about the incident got around Hollywood, and since then he has been hired only on rare occasions.

Did Jesse have a nightmare that was exacerbated by hysteria caused by his exposure to the UFO community? If so, why did it have such a strange structure, leave physical traces, and come into memory when triggered by a mnemonic? This pattern fits spontaneous recollection of memories suppressed by trauma, not nightmare.

We do not know exactly what happened to Jesse Long. There is at present no way to be certain what parts of his story are fact. More than that, even when we are able to determine which of his memories his brain processes as real, physical events, we will just be at the beginning. This is because memories are not naked records of events, they are interpretations.

To find out the truth, we are going to have to locate a base in fact that is founded in an understanding of what actually happens to people like Jesse.

It is no longer responsible to dismiss a story like his as a disturbance that is probably due to child abuse that the victim has been induced to misinterpret to be alien abduction.

The reason is simple: Jesse's implant.

17:

"Junior"

In the introduction to this book, I quoted Dr. Carl Sagan's famous challenge, outlining what science needs to make the whole issue of UFOs and aliens worth studying. Among the things he said would be needed was, "material of absolutely bizarre properties of many sorts—electrical conductivity or ductility."

As part of my proposal to Catherine Cooke and Dr. William Mallow that their foundation engage in a study of implants, I suggested that the first object to be studied should be Jesse's implant. Initially, we laid ambitious plans to undertake a program that would start with witnesses who still had implants in their bodies, then extract these objects and study them under the kind of controlled conditions that could lead to the publication of papers in the peer-reviewed scientific press.

However, the Mind-Science Foundation is both small and not directly concerned with the essentially physical issues that surround the question of implants. Its small size made the board wary of the liability implications of a human subjects study, and there was the question of whether its charter directed it to enter this area.

A letter from Dr. William H. Stone, chairman of the Scientific Advisory Committee, sent to Ms. Cooke and other members of the board, stated, in regard to the implant project, that they had "ranked it low in terms of adding to the knowledge base of 'mind science.'" It went on to say that "the issue of liability was raised by every voting member of the Committee."

If studies like this are to proceed beyond where they are now, it is going to require commitment from organizations whose charters charge them with solving problems like those that an implant poses. These problems are very complex and involve everything from the behavioral, memory, and mental health issues brought by the hosts, to their overall physiological condition, to the detailed state of tissues surrounding the object, to the obvious materials and technological issues connected with the object itself.

It is obviously not within the purview of a small foundation devoted to studying the human mind to undertake such a study, but it is to be congratulated for at least taking the project seriously and attempting to find a way to do it.

It is well within the Communion Foundation's chartered aims, but again, to do the study on a large enough scale will require greater resources than it possesses. Also, because of all the controversy and the extremely high level of resistance from science, the study needs the support of more established institutions.

Such institutions must not allow a cultural bias against the possibility of an alien presence being responsible to stop them. I have often met open-minded scientists who end up jumping through hoops to avoid this one possibility. All possibilities must be faced head on.

I met Jesse Long for the first time on June 18, 1996, when he drove to San Antonio with the object that he calls "Junior." He was not willing for it to leave his sight, not even to be brought by courier to the lab. So we had agreed that he would accompany it personally to San Antonio and stay with it as it moved from equipment station to equipment station, being tested.

When I first saw it, I was quite disappointed. Jesse kept it in a round plastic container on a piece of dark foam material, and it looked like nothing more than a sliver of glass. I had already interviewed him on the telephone, and I was quite familiar with his case, so my immediate thought was that this was just an ordinary sliver of glass, and I was looking at a possible case of child abuse that had been distorted into memories of alien abduction by a combination of cultural forces and the subject's inability to face the truth.

I almost suggested to Dr. Mallow that the tests not proceed. The Mind-Science Foundation had kindly provided the funds for the testing, and I thought that it was my responsibility to cut their losses. Mallow, however, who has been with SWRI since 1954, immediately noticed things about the object that piqued his interest.

For example, even though it appeared to be glass, it held an unusual pliancy, and there was a faint clouded effect that interested him.

The following tests were applied:

SCANNING ELECTRON MICROSCOPE EXAM-
   INATION WITH SPECTRAL ANALYSIS
FTIR (INFRARED) SPECTROSCOPY
X-RAY DIFFRACTION

As we went into the darkened electron microscope area, I recalled my youthful fascination with this astonishing technology. I was looking at an instrument that could see almost to the atomic level, and I was suitably awed.

It operated effortlessly, and the journey down to the surface of Jesse's object was, I believe, the most extraordinary that I have ever taken.

Dr. Mallow's report described the object as follows: "A glass-like fragment resembling the shard of a broken bottle; about 1.5 cm. long, 3 mm. wide tapering to 1 mm. at the tip, and 1 to 1.5 mm. thick; colorless and slightly clouded when viewed against a black background. The narrow tip appears to have been broken and blunted as opposed to a fine point. The 1 mm. cross-section of the tip appeared dark when viewed at an angle or directly."

There was no reason, at this point, to believe that this was not exactly what it appeared to be—a glass shard, completely trivial. However, as the electron microscope looked more closely, some unusual details began to emerge. "The narrow tip contained a carbonaceous inclusion, dark and globular in form, at approximately 1000X magnification."

This material appeared to be a tiny quantity of dried blood that had been forced into this well-defined indentation in the tip of the object. Could the tip of this thing be structured? Were we looking at accident or design?

More work needs to be done to determine this. What can be said at present is that it did not appear like the irregular tip of an ordinary glass shard. In addition, there was a groove running down the body of the object from the tip, and it seemed possible that one edge of the object's surface had been sharpened and then melted in order to smooth rough edges. But these were just initial observations.

A more definite piece of odd evidence was observed:

"The wide end of the shard contained a bulbous and spheroidal outcropping suggesting rapid cooling of a liquid or a melt."

If the strange condition of the tip and the apparent attempt to melt rough edges were both taken together, did it not suggest that this object was not a glass shard at all but something manufactured? If so, then we could be looking at something that had been purposely built to penetrate the skin.

There were a couple of features about it that were already interesting in this regard, the main one being that there had been no attempt by Jesse's body to reject the object. Normally, foreign objects will be rejected by the body, either floated out the entry wound or, if that isn't possible, then encapsulated in minerals that will enable the rejection process to stop.

The object had remained in Jesse's body for thirty-four years without being rejected but had come out completely clean. It had not been encapsulated at all, which meant that it was not recognized by the body as a foreign object.

There was only one reason why the object might have caused this kind of response: It had to be made of a substance that the body does not reject. There is one, called Bioglass, which is a glass formula developed in the 1970s for use in dental implants that the body recognizes as bone and does not reject. However, the body integrates Bioglass, so why, after thirty-four years, was this object still free?

Since Jesse had definitively claimed that the object had been in his body since 1957, I would have been very concerned if it was, in fact, Bioglass. To me, this would raise a suggestion that this object had been manufactured much more recently than 1957.

I said nothing about any of this to the lab personnel.

Their tests were thorough. If it was Bioglass, they were going to find that out when they did comparative work on the spectroscopy and identified the formula.

The scanning electron microscope's spectral analysis was not unusual. "Silica dominated the spectra with calcium, magnesium, and some potassium, sulfur, iron and zinc in very low levels." Nothing odd there except the sulfur.

"The X-ray fluorescence, which can penetrate the mass, revealed a very remarkable composition. I was astonished by the levels of calcium, phosphorous, and most surprising, sulfur in this specimen. No known glass or transparent ceramic was available in the 1950s with 6% phosphorus, 22% calcium, and certainly not with sulfur at any measurable level, let alone 22.42%. A 1970s patent for Bioglass does resemble the implant, except for the sulfur content."

This was confusing. If the object was Bioglass, then where had the sulfur come from? Maybe it was responsible, in some way, for the fact that the object had not functioned in the body in the same way that bioactive ceramics do. What happens when a bioactive ceramic is inserted into the body is that the surface of the ceramic forms a biologically active layer that works as a bonding interface with the surrounding tissue. And not only do bioactive ceramics bond, the bonding layer can be stronger than the implant material itself.

None of the eleven different formulas for bioactive ceramics, including five Bioglass formulas, contained any sulfur. There was also a small amount of potassium (1.10 percent) found in Jesse's implant, which is not part of these formulae.

So this was interesting, and Dr. Mallow suggested that another set of tests be run. Prior to doing that, however, it was discovered that the object was smaller than the minimum required size for the X-ray fluorescence instrument that had been used to detect the sulfur, so that result probably was not reliable.

Without the sulfur, the formula was conceivably close enough to Bioglass to end the story of this implant. This is because what had happened to it during the seven years between 1989 and 1996 now became all-important. Unless we could say that we knew for certain that this was definitely the same object that had been in Jesse's leg since he was a child, the only possible conclusion would be, "Bioglass, probably manufactured sometime after 1970."

What disturbed me about drawing this conclusion, though, was the extremely aggressive and unpleasant nature of Jesse's story. If his perceptions were accurate, then somebody had been exploiting him in a brutal manner. I did not want to allow an excess of skepticism to deprive him of his one tangible piece of evidence that the torment that had followed him throughout his whole life was real. If I did that, I might end what chance he may have of receiving the support, or at least the sympathy, of society.

The fact that Jesse's abductors had been so secretive and that he had been routinely subdued, with no effort made to convince him to comply voluntarily meant to me that there was a strong possibility that what was being done to him would turn out to be unwanted even if it was explained.

Anybody engaged in an activity like this would take pains to conceal the least shard of evidence. So, did the subtle hints of manufacture mean that this was a piece of technology in disguise, and we were on the point of discarding it because we were being deceived by what was, in effect, an attempt to camouflage it as something ordinary? This bit of glass would have been discarded as unimportant by any doctor who might have removed it during Jesse's childhood. Now, without the sulfur, we were back to Bioglass. But there was a second inspection of the object conducted in December of 1996, largely because of Dr. Mallow's insatiable curiosity about materials. Since he had not found the correct formula the first time, he wanted another crack at it.

This time, scanning electron microscopy, X-ray diffractometry and, despite the previous problems, X-ray fluorescence would be employed in analysis.

It had been determined that X-ray fluorescence could be used even though the object was very small, as long as there was some adjustment made for the readings that would be obtained from the part of the X-ray beam that reflected back from the surface on which the object was placed. So when the test was run, a blank was also run using only the mounting component as a reference, and the values obtained in this test were then subtracted from those in the test containing the object.

This resulted in a reading that was similar to the reading obtained from the surface scans run off the electron microscope and left no further doubt that sulfur was not a component of this object.

Under X-ray diffraction, the object was confirmed to be amorphous, not crystalline. But we had a further interesting issue appear this time, again suggesting some sort of manufacturing process. "An orange peel effect at 140X, which is not typical of fused silica or a glass shard, was observed."

The lab broke a number of glass jars and examined the breaks microscopically, and could find no instances where this texture occurred.

Further efforts were made to induce normal glass to exhibit this surface effect. "One shard was caustic treated using 10-normal sodium hydroxide, boiled for 30 minutes, and another acid exposed for a short period (1–2 minutes)." This was done to see if artificial biochemical aging could produce the effects. No such structures appeared.

Could it be, I asked on reading the report, that these structures might have appeared if we had aged Bioglass?

Then I was told that the new, more accurate readings showed that the formula was not Bioglass at all. In fact, there were some very strange features about this formula, the first one of which was that, since it wasn't Bioglass, why hadn't it been rejected?

The object was actually stranger than it would have been if the original formula had been correct. And then it got even stranger.

The ordinary glass shards were subjected to scanning electron microscope examination and "induced such severe charging and scatter, they could not be photographed or analyzed." This is absolutely typical of glass and occurs because it does not conduct electricity. For such substances to be examined by SEM, they must first be coated with a superthin film of gold. This is standard operating procedure in a laboratory.

"In contrast, JL's implant did not charge, and photographed and analyzed easily."

The problem with this was the formula, which was now confirmed by two instruments: The object was not just a piece of ordinary glass; it was 99.3 percent silica by weight, more like fused quartz. Ordinary glass is nonconductive, and with this high a silica content, there is no way to see how it should have been possible to examine the object with the SEM without first making the surface electrically conductive.

So it was now strange on three levels: (1) it *wasn't* Bioglass, but it had not been rejected by the body; (2) it was an unusual formula with a very high amorphous silica content and strange surface features; and (3) It was electrically conductive, which should have been impossible.

"In conclusion, the implant *does* exhibit unique surface characteristics that cannot be explained by any assumed biochemical effect arising from extended exposure to a host's body fluids, even after 30 years of *in vivo* exposure. Since there is no known precedence for such a situation as this, we cannot make a reasoned judgment for the anomalous surface topography and general morphology of the shard."

The exact formula for the implant is: silicon, 99.3 percent; potassium, 0.02 percent; calcium, 0.27 percent; and iron, 0.03 percent. The rest of the material (.38 percent) consisted of traces too small to be identified without destructive testing of the object.

I wanted to know if the iron could have made it conductive. The answer was that many glasses contain even larger traces of iron and do not conduct. It would take a much larger proportion of iron in the formula to accomplish this. Dr. Mallow hypothesized that the strange surface structure might be the answer to the conductivity. The effect cannot be caused by a film because the object was cleaned with water, acetone, and alcohol, but it is possible that something exists down in the cracks between the surface cobbles that is providing the conductivity. If so, did this substance come from Jesse's body, or was it applied to the surface as part of a construction? There is at present no definitive answer to this question. But it should be noted that the fact that the object was electrically conductive also made it functional: This could have worked like a radio crystal, receiving its power either from an external source or from the body.

"One interesting observation worth noting is the extreme heat required to generate a glass of 99% silica. Most boro-silicate glasses and flint glasses are processed at under 2500F (1500–2000F), but a glass of 99% silica would require over 3000F to process easily (blow, cast or mold)." Such a glass would have started out as quartz, diatomaceous silica, or pyrogenic silica. In this case, diatomaceous silica was ruled out because there were none of the microscopic anatomical features from the skeletons of the diatoms (tiny sea creatures) that would have been present if this material had been used.

High silica content glass is a substance that is difficult to make and to stabilize but that offers certain significant advantages in terms of things like refractivity and heat conductivity. The manufacture of this glass would have involved an extreme range of heat and a considerable amount of technological expertise. For example, the insulating tiles on the space shuttle, notoriously difficult to produce, are made from pyrogenic silica, an ultrahigh silica content glass.

Is this some kind of a trick, then, something made in a laboratory that would, on examination, appear strange enough to generate the belief that it was an implant?

Possibly, except then how did they create the object's surface, and what was this odd artifact doing in somebody's body? Pictures taken of Jesse as a child show his scar; that same scar is visible in photographs of the removal of the object, with the object being drawn out from under it. And even if the conductivity can be explained, the cobbled surface is still strange, and what such an object might have been doing inside somebody's body is a complete unknown.

Although no known technologies seem associated with the object, it is interesting to note that such a material might have a technological application that we can understand. It could conceivably modulate signals, receiving and possibly transmitting on specific frequencies like a commonplace radio crystal. It might be possible to study the object further in order to determine this, but before that happens, it would be helpful if other such objects could be located and harvested for purposes of comparison.

The report concluded: "The questions outnumber the answers." And that, at the moment, is where the matter stands.

18:

My Implant

After I discovered in 1988 that there were some unknown bright objects in my brain, I was in a terrific quandary. There seemed to be nothing further that I could do to resolve the question of whether these objects meant anything. What worried me was that, because of my books, I had become a person who was looked to for answers. Even if inappropriate, this was inevitable. But what if my mind was somehow being influenced from the outside?

My books were being taken as a sort of message by many people that spiritually evolved aliens were here trying to influence humankind in a positive way. Although I had tried to tell my story as I had experienced it, I thought that what I had also done was raise a series of questions. Yet, when I read the books months after writing them, I could see a disturbing difference between what I had written and what I had intended.

In general, while the books frequently raised and repeated questions through their pages, the descriptive material was so vivid that, as often as they were raised, its impact obscured them. And no matter how often I raised them again publicly, I was generally introduced on radio and television as "alien abductee Whitley Strieber." As I would always point out, I didn't know what had happened to me. Still, I appeared to have become a propagandist for aliens, when what I was trying to do was conduct a public inquiry into whether they even existed.

In the early 1990s, my concern that my public presence was really a form of advocacy for something I thought should remain in question was one thing that caused me to back away from the whole field. I began writing fiction again: *Billy*, *Unholy Fire*, and *The Forbidden Zone*. At the same time, the adventure with the visitors continued to become steadily more intimate and intense.

I set conditions that I thought would be impossible for them to meet if they were figments of my imagination. As I described in *Breakthrough*, they met these conditions with an astounding series of encounters that left me feeling that I had to return to the subject. Still and always, though, I wondered if my mind was really independent of them . . . or some human agency that might be behind them.

Then an event took place that continues to haunt me. I have never recorded it before because it happened after *Breakthrough* was finished and there was no place for it in my book about childhood, *The Secret School*. But I have spoken about it in lectures and have thought a great deal about it.

The night of May 24, 1995, was cool but still at our cabin in upstate New York, and we left our bedroom windows opened. Even through the tumultuous and terrible years that have followed, I have never forgotten those few minutes of extreme terror and wonder that came into my life because we did that.

I had been sleeping lightly but peacefully when, at 3:15, I heard the distinctive sound of car tires crunching on our gravel driveway outside. This brought me instantly to consciousness. There was a locked gate halfway down the drive, well away from the house.

But this car was *here*, right under the bedroom window. We were totally isolated; the only thing that kept us in communication with the outside world was a single telephone line, and that could easily be cut. Then I heard the garage door going up, which couldn't happen without the alarm going off. But it was happening.

As I opened my eyes, I heard a voice behind the house, on the opposite side from the driveway, say, quite clearly in the silence, "Condition red." I thought that I was being invaded by crazy people or perhaps some sort of intelligence community team.

I wanted to do three things: get my gun out of the bedside drawer, turn on all the outside lights, and call the sheriff's office if I could. As I turned to open the drawer, I saw something that terrified me to my very core: Somebody was standing in the hall just outside the bedroom. I couldn't see this person very well. It was dark in the room, which was lit only by the LEDs from the burglar alarm, which still showed itself as armed.

Immediately, two people moved into the room, a young woman in black, featureless clothing, and behind her a man, taller, with a full beard. The woman said something, or generated some sort of a sound, I don't know which, and I was rendered helpless. But my eyes were wide open, and I was totally conscious. I was unable to speak or move, though. I was absolutely beside myself with terror and rage. I'd always feared that some night these sorts of people would show up, and God only knew what was going to happen to me and Anne now.

They came close to the bed. The woman looked perfectly human. She was small, with a grave, rather pretty face. Then, slipping and sliding along behind them, I saw something else. I did not see it well, but it seemed to me by the way it moved—a graceful, almost serpentine motion—that it was one of the nonhuman forms that have become so familiar to me. Then the young woman, who was now right beside the bed, reached down and pushed my eyes closed.

A blast of pure fury went through me. The sensation of helplessness was hideous, the feeling of vulnerability appalling. I was turned halfway on my side and could not tell what might be happening to Anne. I wanted to help her, I wanted to get us out of here. I cursed myself for having continued to live in this isolated place so long.

Then I felt myself lifted up, bending at the waist, with the lower part of my body still on the bed. When I was laid back down again, my head was in somebody's lap. They were sitting on the bed, and I was facing their midriff, meaning that the left side of my face and my left ear were exposed.

Somebody began doing something to my ear, and all the while there was a voice speaking in a sort of singsong. I have never been able to remember what was said. The next thing I knew, I was plunged into the kind of blackness that comes when you are on the operating table and the anesthesia hits. The moment I woke up the next morning, I turned toward Anne. I shook her awake. Even though hours had passed, in my mind it seemed as if the incident had happened just a second ago.

She was fine. As usual, she had not been disturbed during the night. She recalls now that as I described the incident to her, I mentioned that the people had come in a white Jeep Cherokee. I do not know how to account for the fact that I said that, except that there could be components of my experience that I have forgotten. Maybe I got out of bed and looked out the window before I was overcome. If I did this, I would have seen right into the driveway.

My immediate desire was to investigate the incident. Remembering that the garage door had been opened, I threw on some clothes and went downstairs. When I entered the garage, I found that the door behind our car was indeed wide open. But the burglar alarm was still armed and was not indicating this breach of the perimeter in any way. I disarmed the system, anticipating that later I would look at its readout for the night and see if it recorded any entries into the house.

I got into the car with the idea of driving down to the gate and seeing if it was also open. As I backed out, I felt a strange tickling sensation. Then I noticed that there was static everywhere in the car. When I moved my hand off the steering wheel, it made a spark. Touching the back of the passenger seat caused another one. I had just backed the car free when I noticed this. I leaped out, worrying that something might happen to me in that environment.

Although I did not think to examine the driveway for new tracks until that moment, it didn't matter because I hadn't driven over it yet. When I did look for tracks, I couldn't make out anything unusual. We came and went all the time, as did various trucks and so forth, so there was no way to tell much. The shale surface did not, in any case, take deep or detailed tracks.

I went back in the house and tried to settle down. I tried the phone; it was fine. I pulled the last twelve hours of activity on the alarm system, but all it showed was the normal arming and disarming. Whatever had happened had bypassed the system. I shaved and finished dressing, then checked the car. It seemed to have returned to normal inside, so I went down to the gate. It was closed, and it worked perfectly. There were no ruts suggesting that a vehicle might have gone around it and through the woods.

I called the man who had installed the alarm system, and he came out later in the day to check it. Everything worked, including the switch on the garage door. But he explained that a switch like this could be defeated magnetically. If a powerful enough magnet was held near it before the door was opened, it wouldn't trip. But the magnet would have to be very powerful.

Still, that didn't explain why the circuit had never broken. When I'd gone downstairs four hours after the incident, the door was still wide open and the alarm was still on. He replaced the switch and adjusted its placement, but there was nothing really decisive that he could do. I had already been through a terrifying series of incidents where somebody had been calling the system from the outside, disarming it over the phone, then coming in and, in one case stealing a check and leaving a virus on the computer, in others placing firebombs in the basement. The installer had closed off the part of the system that enabled it to answer calls, and I had complained to the New York State Police Criminal Investigation Division about the intrusion. There had been no investigation.

Late that afternoon, my left ear began to hurt. The pinna, or outside, of the ear was sore. Anne looked at it, and it was red. We felt it and found a swelling just behind the crown. The outer part of the swelling seemed hard. On the inside edge of the pinna there was something that felt almost like a coiled wire.

I thought: implant. And immediately I wondered if

I should try to get it operated on. In those days, I was still unaware of Roger Leir's work, so I assumed that the surgery would have to be done by somebody who knew nothing about the possibility. I knew, also, that this would mean that I would not get to keep the materials—if any—that came out. They would go to tissue pathology, be examined for cancerous tissue, and that would be that.

I went to my doctor in New York anyway, though, just to be certain that the swelling wasn't a sign of some disease that was unrelated to the incident. He thought that it was a little strange but essentially innocuous. He counseled me that, if it grew or became irritated again, to come back for a biopsy.

Over the next few months, we were compelled for financial reasons to leave our beloved home forever and began to split our time between small apartments in New York and San Antonio, keeping to a tight budget. In the agony of these days, I wished often that I could return to being a non-controversial fiction writer, but I just could not let this go, not after all that had happened.

The next thing I knew, I had heard of Roger Leir's work, and I immediately thought that I might get my implant removed as well. But then I heard of the warning that had been made to Betty Stewart Dagenais, that she would die if her object was removed. The problem was that our objects were in exactly the same place: on the pinna of the left ear.

So how was I to take this? Was the warning general or specific? Was it even real? All close encounter witnesses deal with a tangled knot of imagination and reality in their memories. Nobody—myself included—can be certain about anything. So I hesitated. Dr. Leir felt the object and commented on the same structures that I could feel. His six patients had not been harmed by their removals. Jesse Long had not been injured.

So, I decided to see if I could find a doctor willing to remove it. I did not go to Dr. Leir because I thought that he would become open to charges that he was the only one discovering these things in people. So I found a general practitioner in San Antonio. For his own peace of mind and because of the weird sequel that involves him, I am not going to name him. However, the procedure was recorded on videotape, and the laboratory analysis of what was removed is a matter of record as well. There is also the scar on my ear.

The surgery was conducted on October 9, 1997, in San Antonio. The diagnosis was a foreign object in the pinna of the left ear that became irritated when I slept on it and interrupted my sleep. The doctor was aware of who I was but conducted the surgery only on the basis of this diagnosis. Prior to surgery, an X ray was taken that did not show a return that would suggest, for example, the presence of a metallic object. But the doctor could palpate the object, which he described as a "hard mass fixed to the pinna of the ear."

The surgery was an in-office procedure with local anesthesia. I was conscious the whole time, and there was little pain. The operation proceeded normally until the surgeon actually uncovered the object. It appeared to be a discrete white oval shape that was to a degree intermixed with the cartilage surrounding it. When the doctor attempted to dissect it out, however, there was an unusual reaction. He commented, "I can't even feel it anymore." Far from being fixed, which he had determined on quite a careful examination of the ear prior to the surgery, the object was proving to be highly mobile.

He opened up the incision a little more to try to

regain the object, but it was no longer present. He tried dissecting away some of the cartilage. He said, "I have the cartilage exposed," but he still could not find the object. He continued, "It's like it moved. I had it marked, and it's like it's lower." He concluded, "The whole idea is that I can see the cartilage, but it's intermixed in the cartilage. And at this point it would take literally excising the cartilage, and we're not going to do that. But it did move down and it did diminish in size, which is even more odd because lidocaine causes things to swell up."

At this point, the surgery was concluded. What we had were two small samples. One was almost certainly ordinary cartilage, but the other might have been a piece of the object. These were taken to Southwest Research, where they were observed under a microscope. The first sample was indeed cartilage. The second appeared to be collagen, possibly of an unusual structure, but this was uncertain because the cutting involved in removing it could have caused its appearance. However, it contained crystals a few microns in size that appeared similar to Jesse Long's much larger object. The crystals were examined under the scanning electron microscope and found to consist of calcium carbonate or possibly calcium phosphate.

As calcium, carbon, and phosphorus are present in the body, the crystals could conceivably have appeared as a result of laboratory procedures. Before being examined, the material was removed from the preservative saline solution, dried in alcohol, then placed under the bright light of the FTIR microscope. It is possible that this caused the crystals to precipitate, but why they would appear as discrete formations rather than in the sort of clumps that normally occur in precipitation was unclear. However, it would be far from a typical finding, as calcereous inclusions are not found in crystalline species in cartilage even given preparation. But with just this rather ambiguous evidence, it would be inappropriate to conclude that anything otherworldly is involved. But it's my ear, and I know when I first noticed the swelling, so I must confess that I am suspicious that the unusual nature of the finding means that we are stumbling around with some kind of technological inclusion that is very far beyond our understanding. But this is hardly a scientific conclusion. What is needed, yet again, is more evidence— more funny lumps in more ears, as it were.

There are two diseases that might cause crystals to appear in tissue. One is gout, but that's ruled out because the crystals would have been formed of uric acid. The second is somewhat more interesting. Pseudogout deposits crystals of calcium pyrophosphate in joints.[1] But it is not a disease of the pinna of the ear, and I have none of its arthritislike symptoms. It is conceivable, though, since it also lodges in cartilage, that this is the explanation for this object. The doctor felt that this should be ruled out because he did not feel that the disease involves the ear.

Over the years since I noticed the object, there have been some instances in which it seems to have become active. The first of these took place during my first meeting with my new literary agent just a few weeks after the object appeared. My left ear became hot, and I began hearing warbling noises. I excused myself and went into the men's room, where I observed the ear to be bright red. I soaked paper towels in cold water, but before I could apply them, the heat and the sound both

[1] *The Merck Manual*, p. 1350.

stopped abruptly. The second incident took place while I was describing this incident to Dr. Mallow, during one of my first meetings with him. He was able to observe the ear turn bright red but could not hear any of the accompanying sounds. This incident also ended abruptly. The third time, I was in a slide program prepared by artist and close encounter witness Steve Neill. Slide after slide of the familiar little aliens with the huge black eyes were flashing on the screen, when suddenly the warbling sound started in my left ear again, and the exterior of my ear became hot. A few moments later, I was called out of the room. Fellow witness Kim Carlsberg, who has published a book about her experiences,[2] was upset. Her left ear had become hot and was glowing bright red exactly like mine. I could not feel anything in the cartilage, but we ended up sitting there and staring at each other in helpless perplexity as our ears slowly returned to normal. Another witness had something similar removed from her forehead, which proved to be filled with microscopic strands of silica.

There was an extremely peculiar sequel to my surgery. It seems that some days before doing the surgery on me, my doctor had scheduled the removal of a lump from his own back after a biopsy that suggested the possible presence of precancerous cells. This lump was excised by his dermatologist on October 27, 1997. It was not precancerous but instead contained what he reported to me was a "small gray inclusion that was unlike anything the dermatologist had ever seen before."

Absolutely nobody involved ever dreamed that this

[2]Kim Carlsberg, *Beyond My Wildest Dreams: Diary of a UFO Abductee*, Denver, Bear & Co., 1995.

would happen. We were not prepared for it, and the inclusion was lost to study. A very frustrating and disappointing outcome for me, I can assure you. The doctor said, when I explained to him the possible importance of objects like this, "Wait a minute. You're telling me that I busted one alien implant, and got another one taken out?"

"If that's what they were, you sure did."

"So what happens to me now?"

I was able to reassure him that nothing untoward has happened to Roger Leir and his colleagues . . . at least, not so far. But if the upsurge in close encounter activity that has been reported by other witnesses who have had their objects removed is any example, it is possible that this doctor—who doesn't remember anything in his life to do with aliens—might be headed for some interesting times.

I could not conclude from my surgery and the analysis of the material removed if it was all natural and explainable or if it was really something unknown. The doctor who did the surgery felt strongly that the movement of the object was quite unusual, because it had so clearly been fixed when he examined it, both initially and just prior to the incision being made.

At the moment, this is where the story ends—almost. As of October 30, 1997, my ear has healed. The object has returned to its former shape and size, including the suggestion of a coiled structure on the inside of the pinna. And last night, while I was out walking the dog with my wife, the ear became very hot, and the tones recurred for about thirty seconds.

I tell this story in such detail because I think that a great many people who have strange objects in their bodies are going to have the experience of getting the objects removed and then being unable to tell for certain what they are. All of the stories will not be as clear as those of Jesse Long and Alice Leavy. A lot of us are going to end up living just as I must live, in a state of question about what might be happening to them.

Although I can say that this has not affected my health in any negative way, it is not an easy thing to live with. I am haunted by implants. What do they do? How might they be affecting my work? Above all, are the objects in my brain and ear even implants? There are credible natural explanations for both of them . . . at least, on the surface.

Anyway, the press always snickers at the idea of implants, so shouldn't we dismiss them as goofy, even paranoid, nonsense? In a society as heavily burdened with secrets as ours is in the late twentieth century, I don't think that would be wise. In this society, anybody who isn't at least somewhat paranoid probably isn't entirely sane.

I would never rule out the possibility of a human connection in the close encounter experience. Many witnesses besides me have seen human beings during their encounters. There is a whole subgroup whose entire abduction experience involves only people, mostly in military uniforms. And given what will emerge in the next chapter, I don't think that any thoughtful American can assume that the intelligence community can be trusted not to engage secretly in mind control research.

I wish that I could report that I couldn't find evidence of any such research, but that is very far from true. In fact, the truth is quite shocking, because not only has there been a great deal of research, the Amer-

ican intelligence community has mounted a shameful
series of attempts to develop outright mind control,
engaging in the process in some of the most horrific
experiments ever undertaken by man.

19:

What Do the Implant Data Mean?

The great strengths of the surgeries performed by Dr. Leir is that all were carefully recorded, that some of the objects were identical, and that none of them should have been in the witnesses. The weaknesses are that there was a time lag between the surgeries and the analysis of the objects, and the objects were not found to be made of unusual materials, although it is hard to see how a T-shaped structured object cored with meteoric iron would have come into somebody's body by accident, or how two totally unrelated people would bear virtually identical objects of the same odd substance.

The Jesse Long case reveals an object that, after two laboratory examinations, remains hard to characterize. It is an unusual substance, fused quartz, with a composition of ninety-nine percent amorphous silica. It has probably been melted and honed, suggesting that it was manufactured. In addition, its cobbled surface is unusual. How it could conduct electricity is not clear, as its surface was cleaned of impurities, and silica is nonconductive. On the other hand, there is no way to confirm that the object actually entered Jesse's leg in 1957 because there are no medical records attesting to this. There could be something else under the childhood scar visible in old photographs of him. Moreover, the seven-year gap between its excision and the analysis means that we cannot be certain that what was analyzed and what was removed are the same thing. In this case, though, the fact that the object is so mysterious outweighs the lack of a clear record of possession.

Beyond these first few cases, there are thousands more. Many more implants can be excised, conditions can be controlled more rigorously, and a very extensive array of studies can be applied both to the objects and their bearers. We can also attempt things like relating the type of encounter to the type of implant, to see if there is some correlation. We can use new techniques to determine from brain biology and function what parts of the witnesses' memories are factual. Before excision of the objects, we can subject implanted witnesses to all sorts of psychological and physical tests, to attempt to determine what the objects do. Afterward, we can search for technology in the objects, then engage in much more thorough materials analysis than has yet been done. In the end, we can probably make educated guesses about the purpose of the objects.

Scientists all over the world are racing to achieve implantable nanotechnologies of all kinds. Already, we implant animals with transponders that emit identifying signals when excited by incoming radio signals on the correct frequency. But they are too short range for tracking, and are used for identification purposes, and only in animals.

Four companies distribute veterinary-grade implants, Destron/IDI, American Veterinary Identification Devices, Identichip, and Infopet Identification Systems. The devices that they manufacture are tiny but not yet small enough to fit comfortably under human skin, which is much thinner than that of most animals. Radio tracking can be accomplished in animal husbandry but only with collars. An implantable tracking device is quite possible, though. Certainly, the miniaturization technology is already available. Hughes Missile Systems manufactures a trackable microchip called the Hughes Position Locating Reporting System for use in vehicles from trucks to missiles. The reason this device cannot be used as an animal implant is that it would require a battery if it did not have a vehicle electrical system as a power source.

Human implantables are already well into the planning stage. Miami surgeon Dr. Daniel Man has patented an implantable chip that could be used to locate lost children or senile patients who have wandered away. A similar project, called KIDSCAN, would bounce a signal off a satellite that would function as a locator.

Advances in piezoelectric technology and decreases in the size and power requirements of circuits of all kinds suggest that it will not be long before tracking devices like these can be implanted in animals and, perhaps soon after, human beings. It is always possible that there are "black" projects that have outstripped what is known and available publicly.

It could be that the conductivity of the Long implant represents a solution to the problem of how to deliver energy to a tiny object without a battery. The Leir objects could offer a magnetic signature without needing any internal energy source at all. How far away this signal might be read would depend on the type of energy pulse applied to it and the sensitivity of the equipment reading the return.

We are making at least as much progress with implantable drug delivery systems as we are with signaling devices. There are systems that encapsulate drugs in nonbiodegradable membranes, such as the Norplant system, and drugs that are delivered via injectable microcapsules. Beyond this, there are sophisticated implants under development that would be injected into the vascular system and would emit their drug loads in a highly controlled manner. Using variants of such technologies, anti-cancer drugs, for example, will be deliverable directly into the interior of tumors.

Depending on the application, such implants might be made either of biodegradable materials or of fibers along the lines of Q-Fiber, an amorphous, high-purity silica fiber manufactured by the Manville Division of Schuller International.

These would appear as fibrous clusters of material with a predetermined void size between the fibers that would carry a biodegradable matrix with one or more drugs dispersed through the matrix. Although such devices are under patent application, they have not yet been manufactured. There is little reason to doubt that they will be, however. And it may be that we already have a prototype.

One of the strangest implants ever found was contributed by Dr. John Mack. Expelled from a witness's nose, it is described as an organic, plasticlike, three-lobed fiber with an internal structure organized into intricate layers in a seemingly irregular manner. The specimen was a "tough," pinkish-colored, one-inch-long, kinky, wirelike object. A pathologist found it to be about twenty to thirty microns in thickness, and it could be stretched out more than three inches. It was reported to have a gelatinous sheath with bumpy outcroppings; it was clearly not a hair. A radiologist found it to be radiolucent, thus not metallic. Neither the pathologist nor the radiologist was able to identify the object, so further tests were done. Using the scanning electron microscope for energy dispersive spectroscopy showed the specimen to consist primarily of carbon and oxygen, with carbon being the dominant element. It was, in short, a carbon fiber filament filled with hollow areas.

Nobody could identify the origin or function of this object, but it is conceivable that it is a carbon-fiber equivalent to the Q-Fiber implant described above that is as yet unpatented and still in the design phase.

As fascinating as this possibility appears, the most urgent issue that close encounter witnesses connect with implants is not tracking or drug delivery. It is mind control. For many of us, this is the bottom line: Do these things mean that somebody is doing something to our minds?

Mind control has been an objective of intelligence services throughout this century. In 1977 it was revealed in a hearing before the Select Committee on Health and Scientific Research of the Committee on Human Resources of the United States Senate that the CIA had spent more than twenty-six million dollars on the notorious MK-ULTRA project, which operated from 1950 until 1971 or later. MK-ULTRA is most famous for the frightful tests of LSD on victims who were not informed that they were being given the drug. This led to the congressional hearings[1] that eventually forced the CIA to release some of its MK-ULTRA files.[2] They told of a massive undertaking that involved

[1] Select Committee on Health and Scientific Research of the Committee on Human Resources, United States Senate, *Project MK-ULTRA, the CIA's Program of Research in Behavioral Modification* (Washington, D.C.: Government Printing Office, 1977).

[2] But not all. In *Central Intelligence Agency et al. v. Sims, et al.* (no. 83–1075; decided April 16, 1986), the Supreme Court held that the CIA could withhold the names of scientists and institutions involved in

186 researchers in the academic community, fifteen foundations, twelve hospitals and clinics, three prisons, and numerous pharmaceutical companies. The envisioned scale of this project was so large, according to the select committee's files, that, at one point in the early 1950s, the CIA ordered a hundred million tabs of LSD (then called EA-1729) from Sandoz Pharmaceuticals. As this was enough LSD to dose half the American population, one wonders what was intended.

MK-ULTRA involved 149 subprojects, and, with 23,000 victims, is the worst known misuse of governmental authority for illegal medical experiments to occur outside of the Nazi death camps, although it is perfectly possible that totalitarian governments have engaged in worse programs that remain unknown.

The disturbing areas of this research, insofar as implants are involved, concern the possibility of using them as receivers for energy that disrupts or alters the mind, or invades it with thought, or as drug delivery systems. It is possible, of course, that the object that was expelled from the nose of Dr. Mack's patient, if it was an implant designed to deliver drugs, represents an illegal use of such a device. There is another instance where this might be a possibility as well, but it does not involve a drug delivery system.

One of the patients that Dr. Leir and his associate assisted was a man with a story very different from those told by the others, all of whom felt that they had been implanted by aliens. This man worked for a defense contractor and had a low-level security clear-

---

MK-ULTRA. The CIA has continued to claim that MK-ULTRA achieved little success, but its willingness to go to the Supreme Court to protect key information suggests that this may not be entirely true.

ance. He developed dental problems and was sent by his employer to a dental surgeon, who operated on his jaw.

Afterward this man began to hear voices that sounded to him like CB radio transmissions. The sudden onset of this symptom was related in his mind to the dental surgery so he returned to the dentist, only to be told that the surgery could not be responsible.

The area was X-rayed on a visit to another dentist, and a triangular object was observed to be embedded in the witness's jaw just below the surgical site. The witness found his way into Dr. Leir's surgery, and a triangular metallic object was subsequently removed from his jaw. However, the voices did not subside, and psychological testing suggested the presence of possible disorder. So it is impossible to tell exactly what happened to this man. Perhaps the object came there by accident during his dental surgery, and the voices were part of a coincidental disease process. Perhaps signals heard consequent to the implantation of the object initiated an abnormal reaction that appears now that the object has been removed as bipolar disorder. Like the story of the Mack implant, though, this one also raises questions about whether the secret government has really abandoned mind control experiments with innocent citizens as the victims.

As the CIA has steadfastly refused to release all of the MK-ULTRA documents, contending that not all of them were relevant to the case that was brought against it, there is no way to tell if it is really out of this business. In addition, there may be substantial additional documentation that has never been placed in the public record. Mind control research was transferred from the Technical Services Staff to the Office of Research and Development in 1962, and no ORD records on the subject have ever been released at all.[3]

United States mind control research probably began during World War II when Colgate University professor George Estabrook suggested to the War Department that there could be military uses for hypnosis. In 1946, Estabrook destroyed his diaries, and no information on his activities has been forthcoming from the government. During his lifetime, he did occasionally suggest that his work had involved the "creation of hypno-programmed couriers and hypnotically-induced split personalities."[4]

After the war, the CIA sought data derived from the death camp experiments of the Nazis, importing alleged Nazi scientists and doctors like Karl Tauboeck, Friedrich Hoffman, Theodor Wagener-Jauregg, Kurt Rarh, and Hans Turnit, who variously engaged in experiments in Germany during World War II with drugs designed to induce paralysis and with lethal gasses.[5] Given that the American intelligence community imported these people and allowed them to continue their research here, it may be conjectured that it has enjoyed the use of scientific discoveries made in the Nazi system, possibly in the death camps.

The Office of Naval Intelligence, allegedly as early as the 1950s, funded the work of neuroscientist Jose Delgado, who specialized in the area of intracerebral implants and electronic brain stimulation. His book *Physical Control of the Mind: Toward a Psychocivil-*

---

[3]John Marks, *The Search for the Manchurian Candidate* (New York: Dell, 1988), pp. 224–29.

[4]Martin Cannon, "Mind Control and the American Government" (Santa Barbara: Prevailing Winds Research, 1994), p. 2.

[5]Linda Hunt, *Secret Agenda* (New York: St. Martin's Press, 1991), pp. 157–75.

ized Society suggests that behavior could be modified by brain implants that would, for example, cause such physical pain when violent behavior was contemplated that the potential criminal would become unable to act as soon as he or she so much as thought of a crime. By extension, of course, it can be seen that all sorts of behaviors could thus be modified, especially given that Delgado achieved much more subtle results. He was able not only to induce extreme moods like passion and exhaustion but also, as he reports, using "radio stimulation of different points in the amygdala and hippocampus," to produce "a variety of effects, including pleasant sensations, elation, deep, thoughtful concentration, odd feelings, super relaxation, colored visions and other responses."[6]

Delgado also figured in an experiment that involved making a cat's ear into a microphone that could pick up conversations the animal was hearing.[7] Obviously, it would also be possible to implant a tiny speaker like a hearing aid that could be a source for voices. Such a device could touch any number of different cranial bones, including the jaw, and still transmit signals that would be low-level hearable.

According to Alan Scheflin and Edward Opton in *The Mind Manipulators*,[8] Joseph A. Meyer of the National Security Agency has allegedly proposed implant-

[6]J. Delgado, *Physical Control of the Mind: Toward a Psychocivilized Society* (New York: Harper & Row, 1969). Also "Intracerebral Radio Stimulation and Recording in Completely Free Patients," in *Psychotechnology*, ed. R.L. and Ralph Schwitzgabel (New York: Holt, Rinehart & Winston, 1973), p. 195.

[7]Cannon, "Mind Control," p. 3.

[8]A. Scheflin and E. Opton, *The Mind Manipulators* (London: Paddington Press, 1978).

ing half of all Americans arrested, whether convicted of a crime or not, so that they could be subjected to continuous monitoring thereafter.

The use of hypnosis in remote control of subjects would be possible given present technologies, conceivably even if the subjects had to be placed in the trance state from a distance. Afterward, a fairly simple device could be effective in triggering a posthypnotic suggestion. This could be something, for example, that would produce beeps such as those that Betty Dagenais claimed to have heard coming from her implant. It could also be that by hypnotic suggestion the victim could be made to remain consciously unaware of the signals. The signals could be used to trigger all sorts of posthypnotic responses.

There has been a rumor that a device invented by Dr. Delgado, which he called the stimoceiver,[9] has been evolved into something that is capable of inducing a hypnotic state via radio transmission. The stimoceiver was developed in the 1950s, and there is a famous film of Dr. Delgado disabling a charging bull in the Madrid bullring by using a radio transmitter that sent signals to a device embedded in the animal's brain. The technology that grew out of the stimoceiver is known as radio hypnotic intracerebral control and electronic dissolution of memory (RHIC-EDOM). Whether RHIC-EDOM programs actually exist is a matter of conjecture.

In 1977, Senator Richard Schweiker (D., Penn.) questioned MK-ULTRA administrator Dr. Sidney Gottlieb regarding these rumors, asking first if MK-ULTRA involved the use of hypnosis.[10] Gottlieb re-

[9]Cannon, "Mind Control," p. 3.

[10]Ibid., p. 7.

plied that it did. The senator then asked if "any of
these projects involve something called radio hypnotic
intracerebral control." Gottlieb replied in the negative,
but when Schweiker pressed him he stated that "there
was a current interest, running interest, all the time in
what affects people standing in the field of radio energy."

One reason that Senator Schweiker was so concerned involved rumors about laboratories where fantastically horrible experiments were being conducted
into the effect of radio transmissions into the human
brain. But it was not until July 28, 1985, that such
experiments received any substantive public exposure.
On that date, David Remnick published an article in
the *Washington Post* titled "The Experiments of Dr.
D. Ewen Cameron," which was subsequently entered
into the Congressional Record.[11] Cameron's laboratory was founded in Montreal at the behest of the CIA,
with funding by private foundations. In its Radio Tele-
metry Laboratory, according to the report, was the
Grid Room in which the subject was strapped into a
chair (being given a dose of paralyzing curare if there
was resistance), then wired to an EEG. Using LSD and
electroshock, the subject was "de-patterned" until his
or her mind was empty. This was enhanced by an
artificial-sleep program that kept subjects in a state of
artificial coma for as long as two months at a time.
Reprogramming was undertaken by the use of end-
lessly repeated messages for sixteen hours a day.

According to the article, Dr. Cameron, who was
president of both the Canadian and American Psychiatric Associations, was assisted by Dr. Walter Free-

[11]David Remnick, "The Experiments of Dr. D. Ewen Cameron," *Washington Post,* August 1, 1985.

man, who during his career performed four thousand frontal lobotomies and was honorary president of the Second International Conference on Psychosurgery in 1970.

According to a paper presented by Harlan E. Girard at the NATO Advanced Research Workshop in the Coherent and Emergent Phenomena on Bio-Molecular Systems at the University of Arizona in January of 1991, research into brain emissions and brain deprogramming has been matched by research into reception methodologies. This paper, "Effects of Gigahertz Radiation on the Human Nervous System: Recent Developments in the Technology of Political Control," describes research into the use of radio activated electrodes implanted deep in the brain to achieve control over subjects.[12]

Unfortunately, most information regarding such research has largely disappeared from public view since the early 1980s, so it is at present impossible even to guess how far this area of intelligence research has progressed. However, the existence of the Girard paper would suggest that it is still ongoing.

At present, many congresspeople maintain what are called "wavie" files of letters from people complaining that they have been negatively affected by radio and microwave interference. It is assumed that these are troubled individuals, and in the case of the man whose object was dissected by Dr. Leir, it was not possible to tell if he was suffering from a naturally occurring

[12]H. E. Girard, "Effects of Gigahertz Radiation on the Human Nervous System: Recent Developments in the Technology of Political Control," presented at the NATO Advanced Research Workshop in the Coherent and Emergent Phenomena on Bio-Molecular Systems, University of Arizona, January 15–19, 1991.

psychological disorder or one caused by his apparent implantation. To my knowledge, as of October 1997, his implant had not been subjected to study.

The degree of sophistication in implant technology that may have been achieved behind the screen of classification is not clear from the available information. Because of the Supreme Court decision rendered in 1986 that held that CIA need not disclose the names of scientists and institutions involved in MK-ULTRA, the CIA has been able to hold back substantial documentation involving mind control experimentation.

In an editorial on May 30, 1997, *The New York Times* stated that "the Central Intelligence Agency has a way of exceeding the worst expectations about its behavior."[13] The CIA has been fighting openness, possibly by destroying documents, and it can be assumed that incriminating records will continue to be destroyed as demands for openness increase. Projects can also be transferred into the hands of defense industry companies and, with destruction of evidentiary records within the agency, become effectively isolated from any oversight.

To have this type of research taking place behind the veil of classification is dangerous to the welfare of our nation and of humankind. Research into mind control should be conducted—if at all—in the most public possible manner. Instead, we have no way to tell if it still goes on, but a certain amount of evidence suggests that it might be taking place, and using unwitting citizens as "volunteers," as happened during the MK-ULTRA years.

I have not dealt with the issue of MK-ULTRA and

[13]"Opening Up CIA History," *The New York Times*, May 30, 1997, p. A16.

children in this book, because there is a paucity of
hard evidence. However, there are a number of people,
many of them terribly disturbed, who claim that they
were the victims of mind control and brainwashing
experiments as children, and numerous close encounter witnesses offer testimony that their encounters began in childhood. A psychologist, Valerie B. Wolf,
gave testimony on March 15, 1995, before the President's Advisory Commitee on Human Radiation Experiments to the effect that a number of her patients
had been telling her that they had, as children, suffered
horrific abuse involving brutal mind control experiments, and that she had discovered, on reading committee testimony, that some of the doctors named in
radiation experiments had also been named by her patients long before their documented activities, such as
injecting uninformed experimental subjects with plu-
tonium, had been disclosed.

Aside from this disturbing fact, little documentation
exists that may support their claims, but one piece of
possible evidence suggesting that the CIA was indeed
interested in children comes in the form of a 1964
memo from Richard Helms, who was then CIA plans
director. He stated, "Cybernetics can be used in mold-
ing of a child's character, the inculcation of knowledge
and techniques, the amassing of experience, the establishment of social behavior patterns . . . all functions
which can be summarized as control of the growth
processes of the individual."[14] The CIA has a special
definition of "cybernetics" all its own. According to a
CIA directive distributed by Mankind Research Unlimited, the "Cybernetic Technique" is "a means by

[14]Walter Browart, *Operation Mind Control* (New York: Dell, 1978),
pp. 261–64.

which information of modest rate can be fed to humans utilizing other senses than sight or hearing."[15]

To allay fears that the CIA has utilized children in mind control experiments or in any other manner, as well as to reassure the public that there is no mind control experimentation now taking place, all of its files on this and subsequent ORD programs in this area should be released.[16]

But even that will not completely solve the problem. The gathering of secret intelligence is useful, even to a republic like ours, and should obviously continue. But the secret agencies do more than that. They are proactive. They evolve and enact policy. In the past, they have engaged in horrific experiments designed to control and disrupt the human mind. During the Cold War, the line between intelligence gathering and the expression of state power became blurred as a result of this irresponsible and inappropriate secret proactivity. And it still is.

Some of our current politicians realize this and have been trying to achieve more openness. This has been marginally successful, but the secret government—the civilian intelligence community and its military counterparts—has proved that it will do anything it can, even violate the law if necessary, to keep its secrets. A memo from the inspector general of the CIA to the director dated October 20, 1975, states, "A number of documents concerning the destruction of MK-

[15]A.J. Weberman, "Mind Control: The Story of Mankind Research Unlimited, Inc.," *Covert Action Information Bulletin* 9 (June 1980): 20.

[16]John Marks, author of *The Search for the Manchurian Candidate*, has claimed that ORD has 130 boxes of unreleased documents covering this area. As many of these documents may refer to others also altogether hidden, the actual number could be much larger, especially when the military and other intelligence agencies are included.

ULTRA drug records are attached at Tab A. In general, they show that the records were destroyed on the instruction of Dr. Sidney Gottlieb, then Chief, TSD, on 31 January, 1973. Both Branch files and records retrieved from Archives were destroyed." In addition, it states, "The destruction of MK-ULTRA drug files was ordered by Mr. Helms."

This practice of losing and destroying records does not end with the CIA and has survived into modern times. Recent events surrounding the "Gulf War Syndrome" controversy make a case in point. On January 28, 1997, "the Pentagon claimed that all full copies of the chemical-warfare logs maintained by the military during the 1991 Persian Gulf war had disappeared, even though copies on paper and on computer disks had been stored after the war in locked safes at two locations in the United States."[17] To its credit, Congress has fought back against this outrage. "After a 20-month investigation, the panel that has led the chief Congressional inquiry into the illnesses of Persian Gulf war veterans will ask that the Defense Department and the Department of Veterans Affairs be stripped of their authority over the issue."[18]

This process of "lying by losing" may well have also saved the Air Force from having to admit that anything unusual happened at Roswell, New Mexico, in July of 1947, the date of a famous alleged UFO crash. In the General Accounting Office report on this matter, initiated by Congressman Stuart Schiff (R., New Mexico), it was stated that all of the outgoing records

[17]Philip Shenon, "Pentagon Reveals It Lost Most Logs on Chemical Arms," *The New York Times,* January 28, 1997, p. 1A.

[18]Philip Shenon, "House Committee Assails Pentagon on Gulf War Ills," *The New York Times,* October 26, 1997, p. 1A.

from the Roswell army air field from 1945 through 1949 had been improperly "destroyed," which effectively ended the investigation.[19] Nevertheless, on March 18, 1997, the accountant who was stationed at the Roswell air base publicly stated that he remembered paying the bills for the equipment used during the cleanup.[20] On March 19, 1997, the *Newark Star Ledger* reported that a series of apparent arson fires set over a two week period at the Iron Mountain storage facility in South Brunswick had destroyed in excess of a million records. Whether these records were pertinent probably will never be known. In addition to classified documents, this Iron Mountain facility stored many corporate records, so there could have been other motives for this arson.

Unfortunately, because UFOs represent rejected knowledge, no serious press institution, *The New York Times* included, has bothered to investigate this deficiency in the GAO report. Instead, the absurd stories promulgated by the air force in the summer of 1997 to explain Roswell were treated as essentially factual in the serious press, the *Times* included.

It does not appear that the kind of large-scale reform needed to change the overall situation will be taken anytime soon, but until the black budget is ended and pertinent records are revealed, we will never learn the true history of our country's secret activities in the latter half of the twentieth century. Thus we will not know the degree to which, if any, the intelligence community and the defense industry are re-

---

[19] General Accounting Office, "Results of a Search for Records Concerning the 1947 Crash near Roswell, New Mexico," GAO/NSIAD-95-187, July, 1995, p.4.

[20] *Strange Universe* television program, March 18, 1997.

sponsible for the implantation of the objects that have recently been removed or the many others that remain in people's bodies.

The Congress may be uneasy, but the Senate is firmly on the side of secrecy. For all of its posturing about greater openness, the fact remains that on June 19, 1997, the Senate passed the latest black budget by a vote of ninety-eight to one.

20:

"A New World, If You Can Take It"

Of course there exists a possibility that aspects of the close encounter phenomenon have been induced as a side effect of illegal mind control experiments. But unless a substantial part of humankind has moved far ahead of the rest of us technologically and somehow managed to keep this secret, the massive scale of the overall phenomenon would seem to preclude this. Although there has been no study of the number of witnesses reporting implants, when the Communion Foundation attempted to start its study in 1996, in just twenty-four hours it received more than a hundred responses from people who had both close encounter memories and visible surface signs of implants. This suggests that the number could be very large.

So a human factor is unlikely to be the entire explanation for close encounter, and it is hard to see how any human agency could be responsible for the breathtaking hardware that has been put on display in our skies for at least the past fifty years. Of course, if there are aliens here and they have co-opted our own military and intelligence infrastructure, then there could be the very combination of human and apparent alien activities that are being reported.

Hypnosis and mind control experiments of the type discussed in the previous chapter could easily have advanced to the operational level by now, and this could offer an explanation for some implants and even some, UFO claims. But witnesses have been reporting these things since long before the knowledge appears to have been available to organizations like the CIA, and there is a smattering of historical evidence that suggests that encounters have been taking place on a smaller scale almost forever.

One thing is clear: Given the data, the answers to the questions posed in this book are certain to be extremely bizarre. But we don't need to answer the more difficult origins questions before we can usefully address the issue of the significance of the phenomenon to human life and the human future. Even though it might be a long time before we make a definitive determination about origins, there is much that can be learned about effects, because they are unfolding in our skies and happening in our minds and bodies.

The first thing that is clear is that the phenomenon is putting humankind under great pressure. No matter its origins and the motives of whoever is creating it, whether this pressure is destructive or evolutionary depends on how we respond to it. There are two kinds of people in the close encounter experience: those who are being destroyed by the pressure, and those who are surviving and growing because of it. As the experience continues to spread and grow in complexity even after fifty years, it is important to make the choice to use it however we can, regardless of the motives behind it.

If the visitors ever come crashing into every life in the same way that they burst into the lives of witnesses, a tremendous amount of strength is going to be needed for us to face this. Careful science is going to have to be done beforehand if we are to expect rational, considered, and mature behavior on the part of the individual and society. To live with this complex experience and make use of it, we are going to have to face the fact that we, also, are complex, and we live in an ethical and moral world that is like the ethical context of the phenomenon, full of ambiguities, a place in which plain good and plain evil are rare.

There is a very individualistic, laissez-faire quality to close encounter. It is between the individual and the visitors. It tries to bypass official institutions, and I suspect that it has been effective in doing this, because if certain knowledge of an alien presence had reached Congress and the White House, it would surely have leaked. That it may be known by intelligence or military officers who have illegally used our secrecy system to conceal their activities from their own superiors or isolated themselves from accountability within defense industry companies I would not doubt. Our enormous system of secrecy is a holdover from the Cold War era, and you could hide something the size of a small country inside its arcane byways. If there is ever aggressive reform of the system or radical budget cutting, such activities, if they exist, will come to light, as long as the records concerning them are not destroyed first.

Only if the government has been threatened into silence by a powerful alien force bent on carrying out its policies without interference could it be that the secret may be more widely known. If so, then it is understandable that even politicians could keep it, given the extraordinary nature of the threat.

On July 4, 1997, Anne and I met Colonel Philip Corso, the author of *The Day After Roswell*. Colonel Corso, a brilliant and fascinating man of eighty-two, told a remarkable story of an attempt he and his superior officers had made to bleed technological information gleaned from recovered UFO debris into the defense industry. He had no obvious motive to write this book. He received an insignificant payment for it and has no pressing financial needs that I was able to discover. What he was doing was breaking an oath that he had kept throughout a sterling career, and his true motive for doing that must have been quite powerful.

Colonel Corso entered military intelligence during World War II and so he would have signed a draconian secrecy agreement that made the release of any classified material at all an act of treason. I asked him if he had violated such an agreement to write his book, and he replied that he had waited until his commanding officer had died, out of loyalty to him.

It was an indirect reply and suggested to me either that he did not violate his oath because the book isn't true, or that he was released from it to write the book and was not able to reveal that.

Although I have no way of determining how accurate his book is in detail, I do feel that it is in general a true account. This is because he was telling his version of the same story that so many other military men, among them Colonel Jesse Marcel and General Arthur Exon, have told. To my knowledge, I was the first person outside of the military to whom General Exon talked. I was introduced to him by my uncle, Colonel Edward Strieber, who had been his lifelong friend and a member of his command.

These two officers did not offer me the rich treasury of detail that I wanted, but I would be extremely surprised if they were lying. Among the things that Exon was very specific about was that everybody "from Truman on down" had known about the Roswell incident from the day it happened, and that it was known to be an alien spacecraft "almost as soon as we got on the scene."

One thing that Exon said is relevant in terms of Corso's book. When I asked him if any technology had been recovered, he replied that a lot of it had stayed with the Army, except for the airframe. The reason it would have happened this way is that the crash took place just as the Air Force was being split off from the Army and made into a separate service. So parts that did not seem relevant to flight might well have been left with the Army. They would have gone to Army Research and Development, and that is where Corso was employed, under Lieutenant General Arthur G. Trudeau, in the 1960s, when he claims that he was ordered to feed them into the defense industry in order to increase the speed of technological development.

In private conversation, Corso appeared to me to possess a knowledge of the visitors that went beyond what he had recorded in his book. So I was fascinated when he told me that they had communicated to the military that they were offering something to humankind, which was "a new world, if you can take it."

This statement fits the situation that we are living with right now. Under the scenario that it suggests, the visitors are not going to give us anything. But what we can take, we can keep. The reason would be that there is such a great knowledge gap between us and them that they fear—or know—that our culture would be disempowered if we were exposed to theirs.

In "Searching for Extraterrestrial Civilization," T. B. H. Kuiper and M. Morris theorize that "complete contact with a superior civilization (in which their store of knowledge is made available to us) would abort further development through a 'culture shock' effect. If we were contacted before we reached this threshold, instead of enriching the galactic store of knowledge we would merely absorb it." Given that the insights of new minds might be the only thing in the universe that such a species might desire, "by intervening in our natural progress now, members of an extraterrestrial society could easily extinguish the only resource on this planet that could be of any value to them."[1]

This suggests a positive motive both for the visitors' reticence and the government's parallel policy of secrecy. It also suggests that they will fight us and resist us at every turn—not to destroy us but to prevent the very thing that has ruined practically every indigenous culture on this planet that has come up against our own Western technological civilization: the descent of the less technologically potent culture into nonmeaning.

If this is a true picture of the situation, we need to get a lot more aggressive. Either we are going to close the gap between us or we are not. They will not act any more than they must to help us, and everything they do diminishes our future value not only to them but also to ourselves. To wrest knowledge from them, we need to be tough and smart and courageous, not passive and secretive and scared. Science needs to admit that the whole phenomenon represents knowledge that should not have been rejected and start exploiting that knowledge.

The vast majority of the American people believe that the government is covering up something about UFOs. There is an assumption that it is concealing immense knowledge. But if this was true, then it must

[1] T. B. H. Kuiper and M. Morris, "Searching for Extraterrestrial Civilization," *Science* 196 (1977): 620.

have obtained a substantial amount of that knowledge from the pool of close encounter witnesses, and that it has not done. It wouldn't have been a matter of questioning one or two of them but of sampling thousands, if only because the experience is so complex and varied.

We have not only received letters from more than two hundred thousand witnesses, we have spoken personally to thousands of them as well. Surely, given all this dialogue, if there had been any extensive effort of this kind made, we would have learned at least a little bit about it. Rather than concealing knowledge, what the government may be hiding is the fact that it has been told by the visitors that either we make the progress we need to make on our own, or we do not get to join the cosmos. Any decent human being would put up with practically anything to keep such a secret. The government would be in precisely the position of doing what Corso says it has done. Under this scenario, all the leaks and the gradual acclimatization of humankind that have been occurring would involve the government trying to fudge the rules as much as it dared by slipping what technology it could into private hands.

But if we are to make any progress with this, the first step is probably to quit looking to the government for the big answers. For whatever reason, given the evidence at hand, the government has been unable to act. One area where it could possibly be of help involves validation: If it is able, it should admit at least that it is aware that UFOs may be intelligently guided objects. Then we could finally get past the denial that pervades our society and start harvesting the valuable knowledge that is currently being thrown away.

It is not a matter of examining the evidence that is

now available, which is diminished as a source of really clear answers by the fact that it has generally been gathered by amateurs and investigated by people like me who, while sincere, have limited resources. What is needed is a group of well-conceived and organized scientific programs that will methodically obtain fresh evidence at a professional level of recovery, then analyze it as deeply as possible—and that will not be sponsored exclusively by groups and individuals who start out with such a heavy bias against the rejected idea that UFOs may be real and close encounters actual experience that they simply create another level of confusion.

The rewards of doing this objectively could be very great. As there is already enough UFO evidence to suggest that they are genuine anomalies, a really good-quality record of these objects might very well lead to insights into their power engineering that would help us provide for ourselves a new means of transport that would get us out into the solar system on a large scale and maybe even beyond. Perhaps, if the visitors are aliens, we will even be able to trace them back to their point of origin and answer that question as well.

In the process, I expect that we can colonize this solar system and see a billion healthy and prosperous human beings living off-planet by the end of the next century. If we can gain this new means of transport, we can guarantee the future health of the growth economy that now sustains us, which at present is limited by the ability of Earth to meet its needs.

By properly questioning and examining the close encounter witnesses, perhaps using the PET scanning technique referred to earlier, we can also uncover the reality that triggers the wild encounter memories and provide a baseline in fact to support the use of hypnosis to learn more. With patience and careful effort, we can, in all likelihood, build a true picture of what happens during missing time by piecing together fragments of memory from many different people.

I hope this book will not cause a rush to judgment, with skeptics trying to prove that evidence so far retrieved is worthless while UFO believers conclude that it is proof. Both approaches are a waste of time, because the conclusive evidence has not yet been gathered.

What can be said now is that these questions are worth scientific time and effort. We need a program to recover implants under controlled conditions, such as the one I originally proposed to the Mind-Science Foundation, which would involve first examining the witnesses, then extracting objects and analyzing them immediately thereafter.

Obviously, the presence of evidence of things like implants also could mean that we are in a lot of trouble. But before we become certain of that, we might examine some of the compelling reasons for another species to exploit us that might not be evil.

Here is one example. Let's turn the table for a moment. It's, say, five hundred years in the future. Humanity now fills the solar system with a teeming, fabulous civilization, wondrous beyond compare. But something is terribly wrong. For whatever reason, we are in need of something from some other species. And this something is vital to us: Without it we will go extinct.

This donor species, whom we have found living on a planet of a distant star, isn't nearly as advanced as we are. In fact, they're primitive, although not so primitive that they couldn't conceivably organize themselves to resist us if they were inspired to do so.

Even though there is a gap between us, we see that they are very bright, and they might just possibly respond positively. We send a task force, which takes generations to arrive, but when it finally does, it begins by making an attempt to contact their official world. From their standpoint, they see vast numbers of UFOs, as happened here over the ten years between 1947 and 1957. We show ourselves to their scientists and military personnel, as happened with Dr. Hill and Chief Newhouse, among others. We show ourselves to their government, as happened during the massive sightings over Washington in July of 1952.

But they do not react well. Because of paranoia induced by conflicts internal to their species, they fear that we might be a danger to them. Having just endured a long period of territorial conflict, they are obsessed by the idea that they must control their own space. As a result, they shoot before they talk. We find that we can't communicate with them at all. Worse, we don't see how we can overcome their fears. When we do make any direct contact, they tend to integrate us into their religious mythology, identifying us with their version of demons. Worse, because they don't understand the way that the process of contact artificially threatens the personality with a false sense of ego-annihilation, they can't overcome their fears.

They are completely unable to cope with us, so we can't ask them for what we need, and even if we could, they couldn't understand the request.

As we get to know them, it becomes an additional concern to us that any sudden introduction of our technology will destroy their own initiative and devalue their culture. We know this because of what happened here on Earth between 1550 and 1950. As technological civilization spread, the native cultures that weren't subjugated and destroyed succumbed to irrelevance and died.

Our exoanthropologists warn that this could happen to this entire planet if we were to put in an appearance before they are able to communicate with us meaningfully and absorb the shock of our presence. They would become scientific and technological beggars, soon declining into a pallid shadow of our own civilization. So what are we to do—sit back and go extinct because they are too primitive to understand that what they are giving up will save us?

We know that we could overcome their resistance by a slow process of acclimatization and education. But we'll have to be extremely careful. If we're too friendly, they are going to start looking for technological handouts. Worse, they might not want to give us what we need. So we decide to keep our presence secret for two reasons. The first is to enable us to exploit them without their resisting. The second is to enable them to maintain their self-empowerment by inducing them to take from us what they need for their own growth, rather than destroying them by giving it to them.

Our ethical situation seems clear: We take what we need to survive while at the same time carrying out the acclimatization attempt. At the same time that we finish exploiting them, we hope that they will have made enough progress to close the gap between us and join us as a cosmic species.

We will have taken some part of their heart from them while giving them the chance to take a new world from us. As a result of our actions, both species may be saved from extinction.

If something like this is happening here, it would explain why some witnesses have awful experiences and others are given what is essentially an education, and some end up in both situations. It might also explain why the close encounter aspect of the phenomenon is so extremely clandestine while the air show that's been going on for the past fifty years could hardly be more public. It explains why many people are taken to an evolutionary edge by their experiences.

From where I sit, having come to know so many people who are in contact, having heard them speak of their struggles and their triumphs, their terrible fears and private agonies, I do not see humankind as being fundamentally helpless before this. The helplessness that we have displayed so far has been induced by ignorance, and the ignorance has been caused by secrecy on the part of the visitors—and, perhaps, official secrecy as well.

Humanity is not a frightened infant but more a giant in bondage, and the chains that bear us down are fashioned from these secrets.

From all I have seen, I believe that the greatest of the secrets is that we are well capable of understanding every mystery that the phenomenon has presented to us. The science of the visitors that appears so magical is accessible to the human intellect. If our minds and the institutions we have founded, especially our scientific institutions, were able to deal meaningfully with this, bringing the immense resources of the human community to bear, we would quickly wrest control of our destiny back from whoever has taken it.

A new world awaits, one that offers access not only to such things as the breathtaking propulsion system used by the visitors but also to age-old secrets such as whether a soul exists and, if so, then the potential to enter its world in a scientifically meaningful way. I suspect that we stand ready, most of us, to offer everything we possess to this effort. We are soldiers, it would seem, drafted into a war. Ours is the cause of a human future in the stars, and it is a struggle that we must not lose, for if we do lose it, then the glory that is the human mind will never be expressed fully and properly into the universe, and the goal for which we were doubtless created will not be fulfilled.

What is contact and who are the visitors?

For whatever reason, if it knows or if it does not, the government cannot tell us. No authority can lead us—none except the authority of the individual will, fully informed and correctly educated, and so made free. Behind all the secrecy and confusion that shadow this situation stand the visitors and the truth about what they are and what they are doing. It is on their heads that the greatest blame for the negative effects of any policy of concealment must rest. But it is also true that the gulf between us is obviously vast, and it could turn out that they are already doing all they can on our behalf without risking our disempowerment.

In the end, it is to one another that we must turn to regain our freedoms and overthrow the culture of denial and the policy of secrecy that together have so diminished and hindered us; but above all, it is upon our scientific institutions and the foundations that support them that the greatest responsibility rests.

The visitors may be at once tempting us with their theater in the sky and forcing us into action by the outrageous invasion of our bodies represented by close encounter. Whatever they are doing, it seems clear that they are not preparing for some great event where they finally put in an overwhelming appearance. Anybody who has a close encounter ends up feeling that something big is about to happen. The sense of incipience is part of the experience, part of what drives us forward, what lures us to do battle with the impossible. But the reality may be very different: If we are to get anything out of this, I suspect that we are going to have to take it.

In all the past fifty years, there has been no instance of the visitors directly adding resources. Nobody gets the plans to a starship. Nobody gets a map back to the home world. What we get instead are fear, confusion, cryptic messages, and a feeling of being pushed around—and the sense of something beyond price, lying just out of reach.

In short, we get a prescription tailor-made to drive us so crazy with questions and terror and outraged pride that we are finally going to stand up for ourselves. I think, in other words, that the visitors are looking for a fight—but it is a strange one, because if we don't win, they also will lose.

A new world is on offer—if we can take it. If we can tear the raw truth out of their hands, and if we can bear it when we get it, then we are going to get off this little planet where we are so clearly beginning to suffocate. Otherwise, we are probably going to die here, if not from the environmental effects of overpopulation, then because of some natural catastrophe or other, just like the dinosaurs and all the others.

Getting out into space in large numbers means becoming an immortal species, and that is what I want for us, because I see a huge genetic content that has not yet been expressed, billions and trillions of lives yet unlived, and on the reaches of future time, I see the pure light of children who will not be born if we do not escape this place.

If this new world is anything like what the close encounter experience suggests, it is going to mean that humankind will gain scientific tools that reveal final truths. If there is a soul, we are going to find it and find out what it means. If there is none, then we are going to face the fact that we are fabulous little lights, soon gone. But does that not make us, in a way, even more precious? Does it not mean that we have an overwhelming obligation to fill each expiring moment with wonder?

There is a gap between us and the visitors, and they cannot close it without destroying our ability to innovate on our own. But if we embrace the question now, there can be a spark, and then everything will change. That spark will occur when science suddenly realizes the value of the discoveries that lie in this direction and rushes to take advantage of what fear and confusion have been making it shun for fifty years.

Suddenly, we will begin to capitalize on the phenomenon instead of rejecting it. And when science and society acknowledge it, the visitors will respond—but I doubt that it will be with the catharsis that by then every human heart will be longing for. Rather than satisfying us, they are likely to tempt us further and further—with outrages, with dazzling displays, with promises—with whatever it takes. And then, when we are finally traversing space on our own, I wouldn't be at all surprised to find that they disappear. When we meet the visitors, it will be because we have gone to their place of origin and done it on our own.

The knowledge that will lead us there is all around us, in the skies, in our bodies, in our minds. All we need to take it is the courage.

Appendix

An interview with Monsignor Corrado Balducci of the Congregation for the Evangelization of Peoples and Propagation of the Faith, The Vatican

by Michael Hesemann
Editor, Magazin 2000

Translated by Matthias Schubnell, Ph.D.

UNIVERSITY OF THE INCARNATE WORD

EXTRATERRESTRIALS AND CHRISTIANITY

THIS INTERVIEW WAS CONDUCTED BY MICHAEL HESEMANN, EDITOR-IN-CHIEF OF *MAGAZIN 2000*

Monsignor Balducci, in August 1996, NASA announced the discovery of traces of extraterrestrial life on a meteorite stemming from Mars. How did the Catholic Church react?

The Catholic Church did not react at all because it accepts all truly scientific discoveries. Science—true science—originates with God. God has revealed his secrets in nature, and science discovers them when it explores nature.

God has spoken to us, has told us what truth is. There can be no contradiction between God's revelation in scripture and in his creation, and thus there is no contradiction between true science and the true proof of God's existence. The Catholic Church welcomes scientific progress, for it is necessary to reveal God's miracles. The Church uses science as a tool to prove a miracle, for only scientific research can provide evidence whether an occurence is the result of natural, divine, or demonic forces.

Is there a conflict between the belief in extraterrestrial life and the Christian faith? Or is it acceptable for a Catholic to believe in extraterrestrials?

There is no conflict, not at all! It is reasonable to believe and to affirm that extraterrestrials exist. Their existence can no longer be denied, for there is too much evidence for the existence of extraterrestrials and flying saucers as documented by UFO research. To assert categorically that they are illusions and hallucinations, or that eyewitness accounts are not credible, is wrong. This would mean to question the value of such testimony per se, and this would have serious consequences for religion itself, since religion is founded on an historical incidence, on the birth of a human being, Jesus Christ, who was not only man, but also God, and of whom we have knowledge through testimony, the gospels. Religion is based on the testimony of human beings who had become witnesses to God's revelation. When human reason attempts to prove that this is impossible, that such testimony is unreliable, then faith will collapse, and humans would become ignorant. It is right to have faith, but it is sensible when human reason can explain everything.

How would Rome, how would the Church react if contact with extraterrestrials were made?

If such a contact were to occur, it would confirm the truth that extraterrestrials exist. The question is whether these extraterrestials are inferior or superior to us, and both possibilities are quite feasible; however, such an occurence would not call into question the teachings of Christianity.

There is a passage in Holy Scripture, in the New Testament, in which St. Paul refers to Jesus Christ as the King of the universe, not just the King of the world. This then means that everything in the universe, including extraterrestrials, UFOs, etc., are reconcilable with God, because He is the King of the universe.

For science, such contact with extraterrestrials will prove once and for all the existence of extraterrestrial

life, and the Church and science will unify this knowledge with the other truths of which we are aware.

*Jesus taught: Venture out and teach the gospel to all
peoples. Would the Church teach the gospel to extraterrestrials?*

This question leads us far into the future and is, of
course, hypothetical. If I made contact with extraterrestrials, I would first of all ask them what their opinion is of a higher being, what their concept of God is.
It might be that they are much more religious then we
are. This question is still highly speculative. It is, however, not a speculation, not a fantasy that UFOs exist,
but it is a speculative question about this modality, for
it is possible that we must help them to believe more
deeply, and conversely, that they are superior to us in
their faith.

Once this question is answered, when these contacts
are no longer limited to exceptional occurences, we shall
know what we need to do. As I pointed out, it is very important to lend credence to the eyewitness accounts, but
we must be very careful to be sure that they are authentic. I have also heard of people who claimed to have had
contacts, but who unfortunately were not mentally
sound. We must not exclude everything, yet we should
not reach too far with our curiosity.

Certain is that the Christian religion, that theology,
does not rule out the existence of extraterrestrials. We
know with certainty of the existence of God, of the
angels, and of us. We need not discuss our existence,
for we can see and feel each other. Science allows us
to think about the existence of other inhabited worlds.
There are also clues which seem to confirm this, such
as the existence of flying saucers, which also indicate

that extraterrestrials are further evolved than we are, for UFOs are machines that we, too, might build one day, but only in the distant future.

If we compare our nature with that of angels, we note a difference: angels have only one spiritual side, while humans have a spiritual and material side. The spiritual aspect of humans is strongly conditioned by their material aspect; in fact, it is subordinated to it. Our spiritual nature cannot exist without our material nature, while it is extremely rare that the spiritual side dominates the material side, and these exceptions lead us into the realm of parapsychology. Our spiritual side cannot be active without our material side. This is the argument of relation. There can also be a form of existence which is exclusively spiritual, that of the angels. The angels are nearly perfect, but our soul is not, otherwise the deceased would reach perfection the very moment their soul is separated from their body. Yet they are not perfect, for their soul remains, even after the separation from the body, conditioned by their material side, and thus imperfect. The soul of angels is pure, while that of humans is not. Thomas Aquinas discusses this argument of relation. It is possible that beings exist whose soul is a little more independent from this instrument, the body, and thus the grandiose possibilities of the spirit manifest themselves more clearly. Possibly, and this is strictly hypothetical, there is a kind of "lighter matter," matter that is more spiritual than material. Let us be mindful that extraterrestrials are able to traverse outer space and travel through time and space. Where does our soul travel when it is separated from the body? To the moon? Of course not—it exists beyond time and space. Space and time are simply categories in our thought. If we consider now experience with extraterrestrials, which is documented by the UFO research, we find clear indications that these are beings whose soul is more independent from the body, from the material. While they do have a body, their body, the material aspect of it, is no longer so dominant. The body should only be an instrument of the spirit, it should follow the soul, not condition it. When we see what these flying saucers are capable of, how fast and nearly weightlessly they can move, indeed faster than the laws of gravity allow, as UFO research has shown, we cannot help but acknowledge that extraterrestrials are superior to us.

If we now assume logically that extraterrestrials also have a spiritual and a material side, we must ask ourselves which side is dominant, what value, what influence the material side has for them. Perhaps extraterrestrials are beings whose material side only follows the spiritual side. This is, of course, only speculation.

When we speak of flying saucers and extraterrestrials, we always assume that these beings are our superiors. It is, of course, also possible that they are like us or that they are spiritually even inferior to us, even though they are scientifically more advanced.

When we talk about other inhabited worlds, we are thinking, of course, first of our solar system, our tiny part in this huge space with its billions and billions of suns and milky ways, with its distances of billions of light years which are so large that when the light of a star reaches us, it is possible that this star no longer exists. How can we deny that other inhabited worlds exist in ·this enormous universe? God did not tell us everything, but St. Paul refers to Christ as the King of the universe. This is so because he is one with God, the creator of all life, of plant life, animal life, human life, and the elevated life, since before he created humans, he created angels. As many theologians and church teachers, but especially St. Paul, have said: Everything originates in Christ. For we believe that Christ is God's son, but at the same time also God himself. This is the secret of the Holy Trinity. And that is a fact, not speculation. For, as I said in the beginning, we can prove this man's existence as well as his divinity, and in addition God's word, for God can not lie, and there is nothing He does not know. What He reveals to us pertains to the way we need to live in order to join Him one day, and that is the most important thing that should concern us. However, God has told us nothing about the inhabitability of other worlds, because he thought it unnecessary. He has left it up to us to explore this possibility, just as he has left it up to us to discover ourselves.

Christianity's fundamental teaching concerning the condito humana *asserts that man has fallen through original sin and has been saved through Christ's sacrificial death. Do you think it is possible that other extraterrestrial beings have not fallen through original sin and thus perhaps still exist in an edenic state of harmony with God's laws?*

Only in the future will we be able to answer this question, when open contact has taken place. It may also be that on other inhabited worlds beings exist that are subject to original sin. The creation of humans belongs to our world. Naturally, it is also possible that God has created humans and animals and plants in other worlds, but the creation story we know relates to our world.

In our world, the fall of man occurred through our ancestors. Only our ancestors are responsible, and they have not traveled to other worlds or colonized other planets. For this reason I would assume that original sin pertains only to us humans. Perhaps extraterrestrials have also been subjected to a test, the same, a similar or a different test, to find out how they would behave—but this test was ours, not that of other beings who are not the successors of Adam and Eve.

Is it possible that other humans are closer to God because they have never distanced themselves from Him?

Not necessarily. The angels live in the immediate proximity of God, and still a separation has occurred; the fall of a group of angels has come to pass. The angels have seen God, have lived with Him, and have been subject to a test that we do not know anything about. Not God, but they have subjected themselves to this test; we must not think in our categories here. But of what nature was this test? It was a sin of hubris, but what caused it? In the gospels we find no clear indication of the nature of this test. These beings have been created with incredible potentialities, potentialities which are unthinkable for us, because we belong to a different category. The Holy Father has recently addressed this question.

These beings had such great potentialities that some of them said: Why do we need God when we have such an enormous potential ourselves? Others perhaps said: Well, perhaps we do not need God anymore, but we should be grateful to God that He had created us and given us these possibilities. Let us worship Him, let us adore Him, for He is infinitely perfect, infinitely good. The fall of the angels resulted from the sin of autosufficiency, the fallacy that one could exist without God, that one need not thank God for one's existence.

The situation of these fallen angels, that of the Devil, will always remain the same into eternity, according to the New Testament. The angels who have committed this sin will remain evil spirits forever. Now one might ask: Why does God, who is so good, not absolve them of their sins? The answer is that they have never asked for His forgiveness. If each of these angels were to say, "Lord, forgive me," they would be immediately forgiven.

Do you think it possible that some of the angels might be extraterrestrials from planets located closer to God?

The angels, God's messengers, have always concerned themselves with humanity. They have helped humans to live according to God's will. And it is certain that they are still doing this today. The existence of guardian angels is not established as an absolute truth of faith, but it is quite certain. Each human being has his or her own angel that follows him or her everywhere. Thus, the angels help humans to better themselves. That is the Church's doctrine. But you asked whether the extraterrestrials are angels.

Well, if you ask whether the angels can assume a body to reveal themselves, I would have to say yes— that is possible, but it would be an exceptional case. Normally, they affect us through inspiration; both good and demonic influence originate from them. Then there are visible appearances of angels. We know of appearances of the Virgin Mary—not all of them are authentic, and often we need science to answer this question. I would not assume that angels use flying saucers. But of course they can utilize them to show us something.

As you know, in March 1983 I gave a presentation at the "Croce" bookstore in Rome on Giorgio Dibitonto's book, *Angels in Starships*. I was told on that

occasion that it was the first time a theologian and
priest had made a presentation on a book about UFOs;
I had read and very much liked the book. In the end,
I praise it as a book that shows us the infinite love of
God, the Virgin Mary, and the angels for us. It is a
book that awakens in us a desire for an exchange of
our love with God. But I did not want to imply, neither then nor now, that angels really come to us in
flying saucers. Such a claim requires scientific proof.
Let science prove that angels travel in flying saucers! I
shall neither rule this out nor affirm it.

What is your position on the UFO phenomenon?

My position concerning the UFO phenomenon? UFOs
exist, there's no question about that; nobody can deny
it anymore. Some may say, to be on the safe side, that
much originates in the human psyche, is derived from
human complexes and dysfunctions, that they are hallucinations, etc. This may be true in some cases, but
not in all. One thing is certain: the UFO phenomenon
exists; the wealth of evidence is obvious and cannot
be denied.

We cannot trace everything back to "psychic problems" because if we do we would question human testimony per se. And that is very dangerous. The human
testimony is a very important element that helps us in
our social life. If we question it, we may soon reach
the point where we question the testimony of Christ's
existence.

*How do you interpret the UFO phenomenon in the
theological context?*

I would prefer to speak of a human interpretation and
not of the theology because it is not necessary to be

Christian in order to determine that something is real.
It is entirely sufficient to be rational.

I could try to interpret it theologically, even though
it is actually a philosophical question. Philosophy
teaches us that we should not ignore human testimo-
nies. However, if we want to talk about a theological
representation, as Dibitonto has done, then I would
say that these extraterrestrials—if that is what they
really are, rather than angels—and the Virgin Mary
are very good beings who aim to bring us nearer to
God. But here we are in the realm of speculation, you
see.

*What influence will the discoveries of the UFO re-
search and the discovery of extraterrestrial life have
on the theology of the third millennium?*

They will certainly influence the theology of the third
millennium. I wish that theologians would orient
themselves more with the help of scientific discoveries
and accept parapsychology.

Parapsychology is a difficult science; it has a small
scientific foundation, but is based on two facts:

1. It employs a scientific method, as does the UFO
research.

2. The parapsychological phenomena originate in
nature, a realm we do not yet know completely. We
should seek the explanations in our world and look at
these phenomena separately—phenomena such as telepathy, telekinesis, psychometrics, etc. What is not for
certain yet is the modality, how these phenomena are
to be categorized and explained. There are many hypotheses, but they are very controversial.

The same is true of the UFO research. First: The
UFO research is already quite advanced as far as its

methodology is concerned; that is undeniable. Like parapsychology, it deals with phenomena that have existed since the beginning of humankind.

Second: The explanations of the UFO research should be sought in this world or, to put it more succinctly, in science and not in the world of angels or the Virgin Mary or the demons. The phenomena should be explained from within themselves. That is why scientific progress is very important. Each individual event should be thoroughly examined, not as a miracle, but as something supernatural; not as a divine or demonic incident, but as physical reality, as part of nature. Over time, scientific progress will come to the aid of parapsychology and UFO research.

Thank you, Monsignor.

Monsignor Corrado Balducci is a member of the Curia of the Roman Catholic Church, a prelate of the Congregation for the Evangelization of Peoples and Propagation of the Faith, a noted theologian and expert on demonology. He has been an exorcist for the Archdiocese of Rome and is the author of two books on the subject, *La possessione diabolica* (Rome, 1973) and *Il diavolo* (Monferrato, 1990).

Michael Hesemann is a cultural anthropologist and historian. He is the editor-in-chief of *Magazin 2000*, published in German and Czech, and the author of *UFOs: A Secret History* (Marlowe & Co.), *Beyond Roswell* (Marlowe & Co.), and *Cosmic Connections* (Gateway Ltd.).

Afterword

The Communion Foundation solicits contributions for its work in UFO studies. It exists to foster understanding of the UFO and close encounter phenomena. Among its planned activities are a study of implants, a sky search, and research into the biology of memory. It also seeks close encounter narratives for its files.

Contributions may be made in any amount and are tax deductible. Please send contributions and narratives to:

The Communion Foundation
5928 Broadway
San Antonio, TX 78209

News of the foundation's activities will be posted on its Web page: http://www.strieber.com

Because of the volume of mail, Whitley Strieber cannot reply personally to letters or E-mail, but every narrative is read and evaluated.

Many of the videos and books mentioned in this volume are available from their publishers. Further ordering information can be found on the Web page.

Further Reading

There are many good books on UFOs, the close encounter experience, and related subjects. There are as many, or perhaps even more, bad ones. This is a very short list of books that rank among the classics in the field.

Timothy Good, *Above Top Secret: The Worldwide UFO Cover-up*, Morrow, New York, NY, 1989. Exhaustively researched, highly accurate, thorough, and altogether amazing.

Paul R. Hill, *Unconventional Flying Objects: A Scientific Analysis*, Hampton Roads Publishing Company, Inc., Charlottesville, VA, 1995. The best book about UFOs ever written.

Richard Haines, ed., *UFO Phenomena and the Behavioral Scientist*, Scarecrow Press, Metuchen, NJ, 1979. Where any behavioral scientist should begin.

Budd Hopkins, *Missing Time*, Marek, New York, NY, 1981. Established alien abduction as a phenomenon worth attention.

J. Allen Hynek, *The UFO Experience*, Regnery, Washington, D.C., 1972. The classic casebook, by one of the great originators of the field.

Carl G. Jung, *Flying Saucers*, Princeton University Press, Princeton, NJ, 1978. Still among the most thoughtful and useful books ever written about the phenomenon.

John E. Mack, M.D., *Abduction: Human Encounters With Aliens*, Random House, New York, NY, 1994. The book that establishes abduction as a legitimate unknown. Mack is a Pulitzer Prize–winning psychiatrist on the faculty at Harvard.

Prevailing Winds Research: *The Mind Control*

Reader, Prevailing Winds, Santa Barbara, CA, 1994. A solidly researched compendium, carefully annotated: the beginning of any journey into intelligence community abuse of the public.

Carl Sagan & Thornton Page, ed., *UFOs: A Scientific Debate*, W.W. Norton, New York, NY, 1974. Twenty-three years old, but it still identifies the outlines of the controversy with decisive clarity.

The Internet

There is a vast amount of information on the internet about UFOs and related subjects, and most of it is bunk. However, there are some really excellent resources out there, also. These are among the best.

CNI NEWS
www.cninews.com
News about contact with nonhuman intelligence. Edited with rigor and precision by Michael Lindemann, this site offers well-filtered news of UFOs, close encounters, and all sorts of unusual events.

THE NATIONAL UFO REPORTING CENTER
www.nwlink.com/~ufocntr
Peter Davenport runs this outstanding operation, where he and his colleagues assemble and organize sighting reports from all over the world. Can be counted on for reliability.

THE ART BELL WEBSITE
www.artbell.com
A huge site, full of fun, passion, wildness, and sur-

prises. Art Bell runs a late night radio program that will—and does—entertain practically any possibility and any claim. Art is the best in the world at what he does. He presents, you decide.

SCIENCE, LOGIC, AND THE UFO DEBATE
www.primenet.com/~bdzeiler/index.html
This site is constructed around debate, with a bias—stated—toward the hypothesis that aliens are responsible for UFOs. But the debate offered is very real. Intelligence abounds here.

SCIENCE FRONTIERS
www.knowledge.co.uk/frontiers
The site of William Corliss, who for three decades has been assembling reports of anomalies gathered from the scientific press. Fascinating unanswered questions of science are revealed here.

JOURNAL AND SOCIETY OF SCIENTIFIC EXPLORATION
www.jse.com
The Society of Scientific Exploration explores the extreme edge of the possible, but with a solid scientific approach. Breathtaking ideas abound.

Whitley Strieber is widely known for his bestselling account of his own close encounter, *Communion: A True Story*, and has produced a television special based on *Confirmation* for NBC in association with Wolper Productions. He is engaged in the most advanced research being conducted into the physical evidence of close encounters.

Index

abduction, 98
· continuing experiences,
   136, 147
 psychological aftereffects,
   108, 171–72
 See also aliens
 See also close encounters
*Abduction: Human
   Encounters with Aliens*
   (Mack), 205
Adjective Check List (ACL),
   159
Adobe Photoshop 4.0, 30
aerial photography, 81
aeronautical engineering 33,
   73, 83
Air Force Intelligence, 79
aircraft spotters, 79
Alcabierre, Miguel, 87
Alexander, John, 209
Alice Springs, Aus., 66
"alien autopsy" (film), 37
aliens, 2–3
   attempts to disrupt U.S.
     space program, 69
   benevolent intentions of,
     70–71, 142, 282

body-sharing, 191–93
co-optation of military and
   intelligence
   infrastructure, 277
death visitations, 111, 127,
   129–30
desert environments of, 149
difficulties of
   communication with, 58
directions for research
   on, 3
evidence of intelligent
   planning by, 19–20, 95
evidences of presence on
   earth, 5, 19–20, 74
faces of, 40, 100, 108–9,
   219
interrogation of, at
   Roswell, 64–65
migratory mating and
   reproduction theory, 59
motives and expectations
   of, 170, 281–82
passenger theory of, 59
physical appearance of, 37,
   40–41, 100, 108–11,
   113, 115, 116

possible military action against, 67–72

sadness of, 89

secrecy of. *See* secrecy

sexual and genetic approaches of, 103–5, 226

transportation through solids, 110

videos of, 9, 10–16, 29–30, 37–38, 61–65, 95

violent approaches of, 113

See also close abduction; close encounters; witnesses

Aliens and the Scalpel, The (Leir), 211

allergies, as response to visitors, 193

American Psychiatric Association, 166, 269

American Psychological Association, 228

amnesia. *See also* missing time

anecdotal evidence, science and, 168

Apollo Command Module, 64

Area 51, 57, 61, 66

Arizona, University of, 3

Arreguin, Guillermo, 13–14

astronomers, 16

atmospheric science, 3, 16, 50

Australia, 60, 66

autopsy, of an alien, 37

Avid Illusion software, 32

AVRO Flying Platform, 83

Aztec calendar, predictions of 10

Balducci, Corrado (Monsignor), 3
interview with, 293–305

Bauhaus Media (San Antonio), 32

behavioral sciences, 3, 100, 267

Bender Gestalt Test, 159

Billy (Strieber), 246

Bioglass, 238, 240

blimp, 24–25, 80

Bosques de las Lomas, Mex., 26

brain
bright objects in, 177–81, 183, 187–88, 257
hippocampus, 166, 267
imaging, 166–67
implants in, 177–85
inflammation of, 28
research into, 3, 269–70

Breakthrough, 246

Breton, Efrain, 14–15

Buchanan, Leonard, 55

Camarillo, CA., 213–15

Cameron, Dr. D. Ewen, 269

Canadian Psychiatric Association, 269

carbon fiber filament, 263

Carlotto, Mark J., 61–65

Carlsberg, Kim (witness), 255, 255n

Carlson, Jack and Ruth, 205

CAT scans, 178, 185, 188
Central Intelligence Agency.
  See also CIA
chemical warfare, 274
Chicago Tribune, 101–2
children
  changes in intelligence,
    138–40
  education by aliens, 142–
    44
  encounter experiences of,
    19–145, 219–20, 224–
    27
  encounters across
    generations, 136, 194
  flying lessons, 135
  and mind-control
    experiments, 271–73
  sibling contacts, 193–95,
    219–20
  terror of aliens, 136–37
CIA (Central Intelligence
    Agency), 4–5, 66, 269
  destruction of records, 274
  MK-ULTRA Project, 263–
    64, 265, 268, 271–72
  refusal to reveal
    documents, 265, 271
"CIA Papers Detail UFO
    Surveillance" (NY
    Times), 4
classified information, 4–5,
    82, 270–71
Clemens, Bert, 205
close encounters
  amount of testimony, 9,
    96
  assault on sense of being,
    108–9

author's own experience,
    98, 159–61, 171–72,
    195–97, 233–58
  explanations as fantasy,
    1–2
  search for scientific
    evidence, 1–2
  significance of
    phenomenon, 278–80
  truth or falsehood of, 4,
    155–57, 173
  See also abduction; aliens
CNES (French space agency),
    3
Cold War, 82, 91, 273, 279
  arms race, 69
Communion Foundation,
    234, 277
Communion Letter, 182
Communion (Strieber), 96,
    105
computer simulation, 20
Constable, Trevor James, 49,
    49n.
Cooke, Catherine, 223, 233
Corso, Col. Philip, 68–69,
    279–83
"Cosmic Pulse of Life, The"
    (James), 49, 49n.
cover-ups, 73, 76, 282–83
crop circles, 89
cryptographic materials, 67
cults, 97
cultural anthropology, 3
cybernetics, 272–73

Dagenais, Betty (witness),
    197–99, 202, 220, 223,
    250–52

Day After Roswell, The (Corso), 68–70, 279
death threats, 251
defense system technology, 66–71
  for shooting down alien spacecraft, 64–71
Delgado, Jose, 266
  stimoceiver, 268
demonology, 3
demyelinization, 181
denial, official policies of, 2
Diaz, Carlos (witness), 43–45
Dilettoso, Jim, 29–31, 52
disappearing pregnancy, 185
Discovery space shuttle, 60–71, 80
Dowell, Colette (witness), 185–89, 202
  pituitary abnormalities, 185–89
downdraft, 32
Doyle, Sir Arthur Conan, 50
dreams, 101, 114
Dresden Codex, 10
Duane, Maryellen, 159
duplication of species, 90

ear, implant in, 197–98
eclipse (July 1991), 10–11, 17
Edwards, Tim, 21, 51, 53
"Effects of Gigahertz Radiation on the Human Nervous System: Recent Developments in the Technology of Political Control" (Girard), 270

Einstein, Albert, 87–88
Elders, Britt, 16, 29
Elders, Lee, 16, 29
electrical conductivity, 243, 259, 261
Electromagnetic pulses (EMP), 69
electron microscope, 235
electronic brain stimulation, 266
encounter memories, stress response to, 168–70, 190–91, 228
Encounters, 185
energies, positive and negative, 144
environmental welfare, 169
Escamilla, Jose, 47–51
Escamilla, Karen, 47–51
Estabrook, George, 266
Evans, Mike, 205
evolution, force of, 105
Exon, Gen. Arthur, 280

false memories, 102, 160–69, 228–30
  See also hypnosis; trauma-search therapy
False Memory Syndrome Foundation, 160
fantasy, filtering out, 165–66
fantasy-prone individuals, 158
faster-than-light movement, 87–88
Feria, Demetrio, 18, 21, 54
ferromagnetism, 210
field-effect engine, 84–85, 87
flaps. *See* UFOs

Flores, Jeronimo, 49
Flores Arroyo, Juan, 21
Forbidden Zone (Strieber), 246
force-field effects, 84–87
Ford, L., 87n, 88
Forward, Dr. Robert, 35
Freeman, Dr. Walter, 269–70
freeze frame, 54
frontal lobotomies, 270
Fuentes, Mr., 13, 14
Fuller, Buckminster, 144
future of humankind, 134, 283–85

galaxies, gravity of, 86
Galileo, 74
general theory of relativity (Einstein), 87–88
Girard, Harlan E., 270
Gonzalez, Felipe, 20
Gottlieb, Sidney, 268
gravity, 85–86
Green, Dr. Joseph, 228
Gulf of Mexico, 25
Gulf War Syndrome, 274
gyroscope, 31

Hampton Roads, VA., 77, 80
handheld camera, 29–30, 32
Harder, James, 76
headaches, cluster, 177–78
healers, 169
Helms, Richard, 272
High Altitude Observatory, 3
High Energy Laser Systems Test Facility (White Sands, N.M.), 67
Hill, Julie M., 73

Hill, Paul R., 33, 73, 76–85, 92, 202, 214
  sightings, 77–81
hoaxes, 16–17, 24, 32–33, 44, 98–99, 155
holographic projection, 23
Holzer, Thomas, 3
Hopkins, Budd, 227–28
"Horror of the Heights, The" (Conan Doyle), 50
House-Tree-Person Test, 159
Hughes Position Locating Reporting System, 261
Hughes Research Laboratory, 35
Human Figure Drawings Test, 159
humans, working with aliens, 126, 133, 247, 257–58
Hynek, Allen, 76
hypnosis, 97, 102, 212, 228–29
  military uses for 266
  post-hypnotic suggestion, 268
hypotheses of alien motivation, 285–91

"ice particles" theory, 63–65
implants, alien, 4, 9, 140, 220–24, 233–44, 263
  brain, 178–85, 256–57
  cantaloupe seed shape, 207, 208
  in ear, 198, 217, 248, 250
  encased in membrane, 207, 208
  excision, after-effects of, 207, 214–17

excision of, 9, 23, 201–16
lab tests, 208–10, 233–44
liability issues, 234
mineral composition, 209–10, 236
nasal, 177–78, 192–95
pituitary, 185–89
plan of study, 260
possible tools of communication, 190–91
shin, 199, 225
T-shaped, 203, 207, 209, 210, 259
warbling noises, 254, 256
X-ray images of, 202–7, 238, 240–41
implants, human, 260–62
drug delivery systems, 261–62, 265
identification systems, 260
intracerebral, 266
scientific development of, 260–63
implants, natural, 203–4
Independence Day (film), 70
inertia, 86–87
infrared film, 49
injuries
burns, 28, 83–84
normal pressure hydrocephalus (NPH), 28
instantaneous communications, 89
international UFO panelists, 2–3
Internet, 58–59, 59n.
interstellar travel, 87, 282–91
mathematics of, 88–90

Intruders (Hopkins), 227
ion sheath, 84
Iron Mountain storage facility (South Brunswick, NJ), 275

Javier, Francisco, 23
Jokipii, Randy, 3
Journal of American Psychology, 101
Journal of Psychiatry, 164
Juarez, Mex., 23

Kasher, Jack, 61, 64
King, Tom, 51, 53
Krasnodar, Russia, 52
Kress, Martin P., 61–62, 61n.
Kuhn, Thomas S., 73–76

Langley Research Center, VA., 67, 77
Lawrence Livermore National Laboratory, 62
Leal, Alejandro, 19
Leavy, Alice (witness), 205, 210, 228
Lee, Dr. T. D., 34–35
Leir, Roger, 201–13, 216, 220, 251, 256, 259, 264, 270
LEM/Satum V third stage, 64
levitation, 169
Lewis Research Center (Cleveland), 34
lights
balls of, 111, 125
pulsating, 53
lip compression, 55–56

Loftus, Elizabeth, 102, 162
Long, Jesse (witness), 199–
201, 219–32
and babies, 227, 229
implant, 220–24, 227–31,
232–44, 259–60
Long, John (witness), 219–
20, 227
Louange, Francois, 3
LSD, 263–64
"lying by losing," 274–75
Lynn, Dr. Steven J., 228

Mack, John, 202, 205, 262
magnetic fields, 85–86
Mallow, Dr. William, 224,
235, 242, 255
Man, Dr. Daniel, 261
Marcel, Col. Jesse, 280
Mars, 148
mass suicide, 97
materials analysis, 3
matter, exotic properties of,
88
Maussan, Jaime, 11, 16, 18,
26, 29, 39, 41
Mayan calendar, 10
McDonald, James E., 76
Melosh, Jay, 3
memories, natural, 97, 100–
102, 220–22, 225
memories, recovered. *See*
hypnosis
memories, false. *See* false
memories
mental ten-scale, for
evaluation of testimony,
222
Messina, Denise, 205

metallic cylinder, 12
meteorologists, 16
meteors, 25, 210
Metepec, Mex., 17, 39–41
Mexico, 9–25
Mexico City, Mex., 9–14, 15–
16, 21, 25–26
Meyer, Joseph A., 267
Miami, Fla., 24
microphone implants, 267–
68
microwaves, 28
Middletown Record, 160
Mid-Infrared Advanced
Chemical Laser
(MIRACL), 68
Midway, New Mexico, 47
Military Airlift Command
(U.S.), 67
mind control, 262–73
Mind Manipulators, The
(Scheflin and Opton),
267
Mind-Science Foundation,
224, 233, 235, 285
miniaturization technology,
260
Minnesota Multiphasic
Personality Inventory
(MMPI), 159
missing time, 96, 105–6,
108, 109, 112, 115–16,
118, 121, 123–24, 134,
141, 147, 193
Monterrey, Mex., 49
MRI scans, 178–89, 192–96,
201, 223
imaging artifacts in, 182–
84

multiple sclerosis, 181
multiple-witness contacts, 101, 109–11, 116, 132–33, 147, 155, 158, 193–95
Munoz, Daniel, 16
Mutual UFO Network, 201
Mutual UFO Network (Seguin, Tex.), 103
Myth of Repressed Memory, The (Loftus), 162–63
mythologies, Mexican, 11

NASA, 60, 70, 77, 222
  explanations of *Discovery* videotape, 61–64
National Advisory Committee on Aeronautics (NACA), 77, 79–81
National Air and Space Agency. *See* NASA
National Independence Day parades (Mex.), sightings at, 18–19
National Institute of Discovery Sciences (NIDS), 209
National Reconnaissance Office, U.S., 66, 67
National Security Agency, 67, 267
Naval Intelligence, U.S. Office of, 266–67
Nazi death camps, scientific experiments in, 266
near-space
  extraction of energy from, 34–35

near-space
  military action in, 70
  weapons system in, 60
Neill, Steve (witness), 220, 255
neuroradiology, 186–87
neuroscience, 266
Never A Straight Answer (nickname for NASA), 70
New Mexico, 3, 37, 67
New Scientist, The, 87
New York Times, The, 4, 69, 271
Newhouse, Delbert, 81–82, 86, 91
Newport News Daily Press, 79
Nobel Prize, 34–35
normal pressure hydrocephalus (NPH), 27–28
nose, implants in, 177–78, 179, 192–95
Nova (TV program), 1

O'Brian, Brian, 90
"old hag" attack, 231
Opton, Edward, 267
orange-peel effect, 240
Orbital Maneuvering System/ Reaction Control System (RCS), 62
oscillating movement, 21, 31
out-of-body experiences, 169

Pandora's box, 136
Papike, James, 3
parallel lives, 191
paralysis, 101, 231

paranormal themed media, 12–13, 16
Parnell, Julie, 159
Particle Physics and Introduction to Field Theory (Lee), 35
Pentagon, 67
perception, derangement of, 170
peripheral vision disturbance, 181, 187
persecution, 223
PET scanner, 166
Pfennig, M., 87n, 88
photo analysis, 61, 214
Physical Control of the Mind: Toward a Psychocivilized Society (Delgado), 266–67
Pine Gap, Aus., 66–67
planetary travel, 153–54
plasma, 43–46, 84, 214
Popocatepetl, Mt., 17
post-traumatic stress disorder (PTSD), 160, 164–65, 167
press, American, attitudes towards UFO phenomena, 4–6
Project Blue Book, 76, 90
Project-Y, 83
    AVRO Flying Platform, 83
proof *vs.* evidence, 9
propulsion technologies, 3, 34
    Breakthrough Propulsion Physics Workshop (NASA), 34–35
psychological tests, 159

Psychological Trauma (van der Kolk), 165
psychosurgery, 269–70
Puebla, Mex., 14–17

Q-fiber, 263
quantum theory, 89, 152

radar contacts, 40–42
radiation exposure, 28, 129
radio control, 31, 35, 270
radio hypnotic intracerebral control and electronic dissolution of memory (RHIC-EDOM), 268
radioactive waste disposal, 34
RAND study, 83
Ratch, David, 60
Redondo Beach, CA., 67
regression. *See* hypnosis
Reitz, Guenther, 3
religious community, response to UFO evidence, 3
Remembering Satan (Wright), 162
Remnick, David, 269
repression, psychological, 162
repulsive-force field, 85
Research and Development, U.S. Office of, 265
Richmond Filter Center, 79
Rodolfo Lara, Luis, 15
"rods," 47–52, 56
Rogersville, TN, 219
Rorschach Test, 159

Roswell incident (New Mexico), 49
  cover-up, 274–75

Sagan, Carl, 90, 155
  on physical evidence, 1, 233
Sakharov, Andrei, 86–87
Salida, Colo., 21, 51
Sanchez Guerrero, Vincente, 18
satellite intelligence-gathering facilities, 67
Saunders, David, 76
Schacter, Daniel, 166–67
Scheflin, Alan, 267
Schweiker, Sen. Richard, 268
science, controversial theories in, 73–77
scoop marks, 198, 212–13
SEALITE Beam Director, 68
"Searching for Extraterrestrial Civilization" (Kuiper and Morris), 281
secrecy, 70–72, 91–92, 95, 156–57, 239, 279, 281, 288–89
  government, 70, 264, 273, 274
Secret School, The (Strieber), 246
segmented shapes, 54–58
Select Committee on Health and Scientific Research, 263
sexual abuse, 166, 227
shape-shifting, 191–92
shimmering air, 16

sightings, 9–25, 39, 47, 52, 213–15
  physical injuries from, 26, 84
silica, pyrogenic, 242–43
Sims, Derrel, 201–2, 205–7, 220
six-fingered hands, 37
16 Personality Factors Test (16PF), 159
skyborne life forms, 50, 53–59
sleepwalking, 133, 138–39, 168
Slick, Tom, 223
Smith, Yvonne, 228–29
solar system
  colonizing of, 34, 284
  incineration of radioactive waste into, 34
  See also Interstellar travel
soul, existence of, 119–31, 138
Southwest Research Institute (SRI), 224, 253
space, bending of, 87
Spanos study, 158, 159
sperm extraction, 229
Stanford University (Cal.), 3
static-energy fields, 85–86
Stone, Dr. William H., 233–34
"Strange Universe" (TV program), 38
Strategic Defense Initiative (Star Wars), 61–62
stress responses to encounter memories, 169, 190–91, 228

Strieber, Anne, 248
Strieber, Col. Edward, 280
Strieber, Whitley, 29
  close-encounter
    experiences, 98, 159–60,
    245–58
  implant experience, 248,
    251–57
  post-encounter side effects,
    171–73, 195–97, 224
string theory, 88
*Structure of Scientific
  Revolutions, The* (Kuhn)
  73–75
STS-48, See *Discovery* space
  shuttle
Sturrock, Peter, 3
Stuttgart, Ger., 23, 45
sulfur, 239
Sumerian art, 100
sunburn, 28
Super Channel 3 (Puebla
  TV), 17
superposition, 171
superstitions, 3

TASC, 61
telepathy, 115, 134, 144
telescopic targeting system,
  68
Televisa, 13
Tepeji Del Rio, Mex., 15
Thematic Apperception Test,
  159
"third eye," 169, 185
thrusters, firing of, 62
tilt-to-control devices, 33–34,
  83

time, missing. *See* missing
  time
time travel, 147–52
tissue rejection, 236–42
Toluca, Mex., 39, 41
"toning," 197–98
tools, scientific, 2
trampled fields, 41
transformation of
  appendages, 56–57
transmitters, 199, 244
trauma, 118, 165
  and injury to
    hippocampus, 166
  and truth of witness
    testimony, 167–70
trauma-search therapy, 161–
  63
Tremonton, Utah, 81
Trudeau, Gen. Arthur, 281
Truman, Harry, 280
TRW Space Systems, 67
Turner, Stansfield, 5

UFOs (Unidentified Flying
  Objects)
  connection with U.S.
    military intelligence, 279–
    82
  diameter of, 15, 26, 29
  doubling, 22–23
  genuineness of, 1–2, 31,
    33–36, 82, 155–57
  motion of (flight
    characteristics) 12–14,
    20, 72
  NASA clearinghouse, 81,
    91
  origin of, 92

Project-Y objective, 83
propulsion system of, 83
relative location of, 12
scientific acceptance of, 1–
2, 74–75
shapes of, 19–20, 22, 26–
27, 78
sightings, 9–25, 39, 66,
155–57, 213–15
speeds of, 14, 81
"target" object, 60–66
ultraviolet, exposure to from
UFOs, 29
*Unconventional Flying
Objects* (Hill), 73, 91
understanding, as form of
control, 172–73
undiscovered life forms, 57–
59
Unholy Fire (Strieber), 246
Unidentified Flying Object.
See UFO
United States
defense system
technology, 64–71
mind control research, 266
secrecy system, 71–72
University of California at
San Diego, 166
Uribe, Rosi, 23–24

vacuum, engineering of
energy from, 34–35, 87–
88
van der Kolk, Bessel, 165,
167
Vatican, 3
Velasco, Jean-Jacques, 2
Venus (planet), 11, 15–17

Veyret, Bernard, 3
videos
amateur, 9, 11–13
analysis of, 29–30
fake, 95
method of taping into
sunglow, 50–53, 55
Mexican, 10–16, 18–27
of rod-like airborne forms,
47–50
of Venus, 11, 16
Village Labs (Tempe, Ariz.),
29, 52
violet haze, 29, 34, 55, 56
Von Neumann, John, 90,
170–71
Von Neumann Machine, 90

Walker, John, 58
Warnick, Janet, 205
warp drive, 87, 90
Washington Post, 269
"wavie" files, 270
Wechsler Adult Intelligence
Scale Revised, 159
What is Your Opinion?
(TV), 11
White Sands, N.M., 67
Wilkie, John, 51, 53, 57
witnesses
alien implants in. *See*
implants, alien
blurring of self, 101, 108,
169
children's experiences. *See*
children
deepened awareness of,
121
disturbances of
reproductive system, 185

feelings of being "called,"
43

a grandmother's story, 114–
15

as medium of
communication, 96

normality of, 101–2

panic and fear of, 123

persecution of, 223, 224

post-encounter trauma,
118, 128–30, 156, 162–
70

preference for anonymity,
103

psychological analyses of,
159, 164–70, 190

recurrent experiences of,
124

relationships with the
dead, 169

resistance to alien
encounter, 119–20

taking control of the
encounter experience,
117–73

testimony of, 2, 15–16, 28–
30, 40

worlds, interior and exterior,
105

wormhole, 88

Wortman, Donald, 5

Wright, Lawrence, 162

"X," Doctor, 22

X-ray examinations, 4, 240

Yale University School of
Medicine, 166

Yturria, Santiago, 49

Yucatan, 25